De Religione

De Religione

Telling the Seventeenth-Century Jesuit Story in Huron to the Iroquois

Edited and Translated by
John Steckley

University of Oklahoma Press : Norman

Also by John L. Steckley

Beyond Their Lives: Five Native Women's Lives (Toronto, 1999)

(with Bryan Cummins) *Full Circle: Canada's Native People* (Toronto, 2000)

(with Bryan Cummins) *Native Policing: A Canadian Perspective* (Toronto, 2001)

Library of Congress Cataloging-in-Publication Data

De religione: telling the Seventeenth-century Jesuit story in Huron to the
 Iroquois / edited and translated by John L. Steckley.
    p.   cm.
 Includes bibliographical references and index.
 ISBN 978-0-8061-3617-2 (hardcover)
 ISBN 978-0-8061-6881-4 (paper)

 1. Wyandot Indians—Religion.   2. Wyandot Indians—Missions.
 3. Jesuits—Missions—Canada—History.   4. Wyandot language—Texts.
 5. Wyandot language—Transliteration into English.   I. Steckley, John, 1949–

E99.H9D47 2004
277.13'07'0899755—dc22

                                                          2003067234

To Ojibwa Elder Fred Wheatley,
who first taught me that my writing and thinking
were incomplete without words from
Native American languages.

Contents

Acknowledgments

First, I must acknowledge the vision of the people at the University of Oklahoma Press. Jo Ann Reece, in particular, saw its potential, was patient with its difference (and mine) from the usual, and was helpful every step of the way. The outside readers chosen by the Press helped me improve an idea that needed a lot of work. Thanks especially to copyeditor Jane Kepp and managing editor Alice Stanton for seeing me and my project through the critical last stages.

Nearer to home I have to thank the people who have supported my Wendat language work over the years. Charles Garrad, Linda Sioui, Janeth and Darren English (my adoptive mother and brother) come immediately to mind. Herman Suligoj, my colleague at Humber College, came to my aid when my Latin knowledge failed me.

As always I must acknowledge the understanding of my wife, Angelika, and the constant, helpful distractions of our dogs: Egwene and Cosmo.

Introduction

De Religione is a seventeenth-century document written by a Jesuit missionary in North America, very likely the Belgian Father Philippe Pierson. The French-speaking Jesuit wrote the document in Wendat, the language once spoken by the Huron people of what is now southern Ontario, even though it was addressed to the then five nations of the Iroquois: the Mohawk, Oneida, Onondaga, Cayuga, and Seneca.[1] In the document, the writer explained the nature of Christianity, primarily by putting forward the reasons the Jesuits did missionary work and telling the Iroquois why they should become Christians. He used Wendat rather than one of the languages of the Iroquois because the Jesuits had already established missions among the Huron and had learned the Huron language, which Iroquois listeners were able to understand.

At fifty-three pages, *De Religione* is, to the best of my knowledge, the longest text ever written in the Wendat language. The document's existence takes on special significance because Wendat is no longer spoken; the last native speaker died in Oklahoma in the mid-twentieth century.

The text of *De Religione* can be seen to be divided among the following subjects:

The nature of God, plants, animals, humans, and spirits (pp. 629–34)
The body-soul division in humans (pp. 635–38)
Heaven and hell (pp. 638–45)
The rejoining of body and spirit after death (pp. 645–47)
The end of the world and the resurrection (pp. 647–57)
The nature of the devil (pp. 657–58)
The resurrection of the body (pp. 658–60)
The Jesuits and the Iroquois mission (pp. 660–68)
Baptism (pp. 668–80)
Creation (pp. 680–82)

Unfortunately, no known documents tell us how this text was used. I assume that new missionaries wrote it out as part of their lessons in learning Iroquoian languages and that sections were used as homilies or sermons or for one-on-one religious instruction.

Although it was written much earlier, *De Religione* was first published in 1920, as pages 629–82 in the *Fifteenth Report of the Bureau of Archives for the Province of Ontario*. This publication consisted of a collection of material written in and about the Wendat language, originally compiled in the mid-1700s by the Jesuit Father Pierre Potier, a Belgian, then missionary to the Wyandot in the Detroit area. Along with *De Religione*, the collection includes other religious works in a section entitled "Extraits de L'Evangele" (1747; Potier 1920:457–688), an extensive Wendat grammar, "Elementa Grammaticae Huronicae" (1745; Potier 1920:1–157), and a detailed Wendat-French dictionary, "Radices Huronicae" (1745; Potier 1920: 159–455). The entire collection was printed as a facsimile of Potier's handwritten documents.

With minor exceptions, Potier did not write the pieces in the collection but copied them from what had been written before him, a typical and often effective Jesuit strategy for learning languages. Potier's contribution to the texts usually took the form of superscript additions of Wendat dialect differences, notably a *k* over a *t* before an *i*, representing the dialect feature *ky* as opposed to *ty*, a difference also shared by dialects of Mohawk. He sometimes added the Latin short form "non aud," meaning that he had never heard the word he was writing, and he sometimes inserted an alternative word that he had heard into the line above the original entry.

As published in 1920, *De Religione* is undated, but it contains historical references that enable us to assign it a date. The earliest such reference is to an event in which Ondesonk ('hawk')—the Huron name for Father Isaac Jogues—had his fingers cut off while he was a captive in *ιannien[n]ιe* ('[the country of] the Mohawk'; Potier 1920: 660, line 15). This took place in 1642–43, when the Mohawk first captured Jogues.

Next, the author writes of Jesuits going to *ιannienta* in *onnontaιe* (660:16),[2] referring to a community in Onondaga country. Fathers Pierre Chaumonot and Claude Dablon made such a trip in 1655, although the initiative was proposed and pushed by Jogues in 1646—possibly the reason it is mentioned at this point.

On the next page (661:1–3), the writer refers to the death of Arontoιennen, or Father Antoine Daniel, in 1648, and to the deaths of Hechon, or Father Jean de Brébeuf,[3] Atironta, or Father Gabriel Lalemant, and ȣracha, or Father Charles Garnier in 1649, all at the hands of Iroquois.

This is followed on the next page (662:16) by a report of the Iroquois-driven devastation that hit the countries of the ȣendake (the

Wendat, or Huron), *etionnontate* (the Petun), and *ɪeraɪenrek* (the Neutral) in the early 1650s and of the mysterious Trakwae (see Steckley 1985 for a potential identification), who, in the Jesuit Relation of 1652 (JR37:105, 111) are said to have had their community destroyed by the Iroquois. Mentioned right afterwards are the Rie (Erie), who would disappear later that century, and the *askik8annhe* (Nipissing) and *ehonke* (Algonquin), both of whom would survive this period. The historical references end with mention of the attack by French forces on the Mohawk communities in the fall of 1666 (663:14–17).

Judging from the material presented on pages 660–63, *De Religione* was written at a time when the Iroquois mission was just being established and had as yet experienced no real success. A Jesuit author would certainly have mentioned such success if it had been won. Beginning in 1667 and continuing well into the 1670s, the Jesuits made a big effort to missionize the Iroquois, establishing what was to become the town of Kahnawake near Montreal and setting up shop in the home territory of the Iroquois as well. I believe it was during this time that *De Religione* was composed.

The Jesuit missionaries' practice of copying the works of their predecessors in the Huron-Wyandot mission, a religious project that by Potier's time had lasted well over a century, can make it difficult to determine who the original author of a piece might have been. Such is the case with *De Religione*.

Potier placed the name of Father Daniel Richer underneath the title. Richer, missionary to the Huron of Lorette, or Wendake, from 1715 to 1760, was adept in the language and had been Potier's first teacher of Wendat. It must have been Richer's copy that Potier used as a model for his recopying. We can rule Richer out, however, as the author of *De Religione* on the basis of two elements of the text. First, the messages of *De Religione* were directed toward the Iroquois, who were not the targets of a major Jesuit missionary drive during Richer's time. Second, the historical events referred to in *De Religione* all occurred long before Richer worked with the Huron.

The prime candidate, instead, is Father Philippe Pierson. The timing is right. Father Pierson was born in Belgium on January 4, 1642. He entered the Jesuit order in October 1660 and arrived in New France on September 25, 1667, about a year after the last historical reference made in *De Religione*. Because Pierson was not ordained until 1669, he did not get involved with missionary work immediately upon his arrival in New France. For a year he taught grammar at a college in Quebec, and then for two years more he studied theology. Once ordained, he worked at the "domestic missions" at Sillery and, significantly, at the Christian Iroquois community that is now Kahnawake.

In 1673, Pierson ventured west to the Wyandot mission of St. Ignace at Michilimackinac, where Lake Huron meets Lake Michigan. In the Jesuit Relation of 1675, the father superior of the Jesuit order in New France spoke highly of Pierson, praising him for his "zeal and skill in instructing" (JR59:219; see also JR58:71). In a letter Pierson wrote in April 1676, we learn that his work was progressing well but that he was worried about the possible hidden agenda of a Seneca emissary who had recently come to ask the Wyandot to help the Seneca fight the Sioux (JR60:209–11). Pierson left the Wyandot in 1683 to go farther west to work with the Sioux, with whom he stayed until 1688. He died that year at Lorette.

Pierson probably put *De Religione* together, then—with help from the writings and teachings of his Jesuit and Christian Huron and Iroquois mentors—sometime between 1669 and 1673, after he began working with the Huron and Iroquois and before he left for St. Ignace.

We have solid evidence that Pierson was likely to have composed a religious work in the Huron language. Potier attributed to Pierson several shorter works found in the same collection (see Potier 1920:539, 542, 556, 570). No other individual, other than the incorrectly attributed Richer, is presented as being the author of any of the other works in the compilation. Accordingly, I refer to Pierson in the following pages as having been the author of *De Religione*.

THE SIGNIFICANCE OF *DE RELIGIONE*

De Religione is important for two primary reasons: it offers an alternative to the Jesuit Relations and it adds to the literature on Iroquoian languages. As a complement to the Jesuit Relations, *De Religione* helps to reveal the differences between what the Jesuits reported they communicated to Aboriginal people and what they actually said.

Much of what scholars know about Jesuit missions in North America and about Jesuit interactions with North American Aboriginal peoples in the seventeenth century comes from the Jesuit Relations, seventy-two volumes consisting mainly of annual reports compiled and edited by the superior of the order in New France. Reliable research with these documents entails two basic types of filtering. One involves sifting through the biases of the Jesuits as observers of Aboriginal culture.[4] The other entails sorting out the effects of the documents' highly political nature. The reports were written with a particular audience in mind. Not only did the Jesuit superior in Rome read them, but so did others in positions of ecclesiastical, political, and financial power who could affect the fate of the Jesuit missions in North America.

De Religione had no such a doctrinally critical audience. As a written document, it would have been read only by those engaged in the mission, who were aware of the demands of the field and of the religious compromises or innovations that sometimes had to be made. It probably also was a spoken piece, intended for the Iroquois, who would not have recognized deviation from Catholic orthodoxy. *De Religione* is a unique primary document, one not available in other Jesuit works in the languages of the Iroquois or, to the best of my knowledge, the languages of the many other Aboriginal peoples with whom the Jesuits did missionary work.

Although it carries the religious views of the Jesuit who wrote it, *De Religione* also bears the verbal soul of the Wendat language. In its religious images and concepts we see a unique synthesis of the ideas of Iroquoian and European Christian cultures, a synthesis not reported in the Jesuit Relations. Elements of this synthesis traveled with both Jesuits and Iroquoians as they journeyed and spoke to people of other cultures across the Great Lakes and farther west and south, affecting the future of Aboriginal beliefs across the continuum from Christian to traditional.

De Religione is also in a unique position to add a meaningful element to researchers' understandings of Iroquoian languages. Insights into the history of the Iroquoian languages, especially the effects of contact on them, can be garnered by enabling Wendat language material to assume a larger role in the literature. This is especially true because *De Religione* was written in the seventeenth century, whereas texts analyzed in related languages come from much later times, after Native speakers had experienced centuries of contact and some assimilation.

Two examples illustrate this point. First, in a paper on Wendat kinship terms (Steckley 1993), I noted that although seventeenth-century Wendat contained separate terms for paternal and maternal grandparents and grandchildren,[5] as well as separate terms for cross-sex siblings and same-sex siblings, such distinctions were absent from writings on nineteenth- and twentieth-century Wyandot and other Northern Iroquoian languages. I suggested that this loss was due to contact with speakers of European languages in which no such distinctions were made (Steckley 1993:52). We would not know that these terms had existed at all if it were not for the early Wendat material.

Second, and more germane to the content of *De Religione,* we can see that the origin of Christian terminology in the languages of the Iroquois lay in terms first developed in the Huron mission. This can be seen in the following short comparative list of terms in Wendat and Oneida. Keep in mind that Oneida has an *l* where Wendat has an *r,* that the Oneida *k* corresponds to the Jesuit Wendat *ι,* and that the Jesuits' *8* represents a *w* or *u.* The initial *l* in two of the Oneida words presented below corresponds to a masculine pronominal form in Wendat that is usually represented by an *h* but sometimes by an *r.* (See also the note on the Jesuits' writing conventions on page 45.)

Oneida	Translation	Wendat	Translation
lolihwiyostú:ne?	he was Christian	horih8iostinnen[6]	he made the matter great
onéshu?	hell	ondechon[7]	inside the earth, hell
kaluhyá:ke	in the sky, heaven	ιaronhiaιe[8]	in the sky, heaven
lotiilihwanélu?	they (m.) have sinned, are sinning	hotirih8anderaιi[9]	they (m.) made mistakes, sinned

Generally, then, the significance of *De Religione* lies in its offering an alternative view, differing from the standard materials such as the Jesuit Relations and later Iroquoian language works on which scholars have relied in the past.

THE HISTORICAL AND CULTURAL CONTEXT OF *DE RELIGIONE*

The Huron whom the Jesuits encountered in the first half of the seventeenth century were an alliance of at least four and possibly five member nations. The Hatinniawenten ('they [masculine] are of bear country'), or Bear, was the largest.[10] My dialect research (see Steckley 1997), together with a reading of the Jesuit Relations, suggests to me that the Bear were made up of two "ethnic" groups, the Northern Bear and the Southern Bear. The Bear and the Hatingeennonniahak ('they [masculine] used to make cord', i.e., for fishing), or Cord, moved north to the Georgian Bay area sometime between A.D. 1300 and 1420. The two nations formed a nucleus around which would gather the other three—the Arendaieronon ('people at the rock'), or Rock, the Atahontaenrat ('two white ears'), or Deer, and the Ataronchronnon ('people in the swamp, mud, or clay'), or Bog— during the latter half of the sixteenth century and the early seventeenth century (Steckley 1997).[11]

The Huron established a successful trade relationship with their Algonquian-speaking neighbors to the north and east (e.g., the Ojibwa), with the closely related Etionnontateronnon ('people at the mountain'), or Petun, to the immediate west, and with the Neutral (so named because of their presumed neutrality in the battles between the Iroquois and the Huron) to the southwest.[12] The French were eager to take advantage of this already existing trade network, so they formed an alliance with the Huron.

Battles between Huron and Iroquois, not a serious danger in earlier years, accelerated after the formation of the Huron-French alliance. By the end of the 1640s, Iroquois war parties had driven the Huron out of their homeland. The Bog nation disappeared. Three other member nations joined with various members of the Confederacy of the Iroquois. The Deer joined the Seneca, first in a mostly independent community near the southern shore of Lake Ontario. In 1657, the Rock people left the diminished Huron alliance to join the Onondaga. At the same time, the Bear migrated to the country of the Mohawk, leaving the Cord to form the nucleus of the remaining Huron community that would eventually settle on the outskirts of the city of Québec in 1697, at Lorette, or Wendake, where they have remained to this day. Some of the Huron would link their fate with that of the Petun to become the Wyandot, a people whose history would take them into Michigan, Ohio, Kansas, and Oklahoma. In the last two states, strong communities still exist.

The Jesuits and Their Linguistic Work

The Jesuit order, whose missionaries set out to convert the Native people of North American in the early 1600s, was founded in 1540 by a Basque nobleman, Ignatius of Loyola, along with a handful of his followers. Early in their history, the Jesuits began to display their distinctiveness. They soon took their place among the foremost educators in the Western world. Within their first one hundred years they set up twenty-four universities and one hundred colleges, and from the late sixteenth to the eighteenth century they helped mold some of the most influential minds in Europe, including those of Descartes and Voltaire. They themselves numbered among the most skilled and knowledgeable scholars of languages, philosophy, and the classics of Greek and Latin literature. Throughout much of their history, especially during the sixteenth and seventeenth centuries, the Jesuits employed their considerable and well-honed intellectual abilities in the doctrinal debates that were challenging Christian Europe. They exerted a powerful intellectual influence on the Counter Reformation, the fight by the Catholic Church to combat the expansion of Protestantism throughout Europe.

It was not long before the Jesuits' distinctiveness took on controversial aspects that earned them not a few Christian critics. Among other things, theirs was a comparatively "democratic" view of Christianity. Unlike some of their detractors (e.g., the Jansenists),[13] they were unsympathetic to the idea of the existence of an immutable religious elite, predestined from birth to be among God's chosen few. They believed that salvation was available to everyone through a conscious act of free will on the part of the individual. This made them ideally suited for missionary work, which, along with teaching, formed the bulk of early Jesuit activity.

It was in this mission work that the Jesuits drew the most vehement opposition. Probably their most controversial characteristic was their capacity and propensity to accept, adapt, and employ the languages and cultures of their mission charges in their effort to convert them. This propensity was evident in the Jesuits' missionary work during the sixteenth and seventeenth centuries in China and India, where they adopted the dietary, sartorial, and broader social customs of the elite and condoned, or at least did not actively oppose, various "pagan" practices such as caste taboos, ancestor worship, and the honoring of Confucius.[14] They even became locally recognized experts in the languages and philosophical traditions of their host countries.

Such behavior led in the early eighteenth century to papal condemnation of the so-called Chinese rites—Christian rites with a distinct Chinese flavor—and was one of the main reasons the Pope temporarily dissolved the Jesuit order in 1773.

Jesuit work in New France began when Fathers Pierre Biard and Ennémond Massé landed in what is now Nova Scotia on May 22, 1611. Although Jesuits accumulated some limited experience with Huron people in French settlements, they did not begin working with the Huron alliance in earnest until 1626, when Father Jean de Brébeuf went to live with the Huron in their own country in the land surrounding the southern shores of Georgian Bay, the northeastern lobe of the lake named after them—Lake Huron. The Jesuits were eager to do missionary work among the Huron because they were corn-growing agriculturalists who lived in sedentary communities, as well as major trading partners of the French in the fur trade. Brébeuf knew something of the Wendat language, courtesy of another Catholic order, that of the Recollects, members of which had spent short periods of time in Huron villages. One Recollect in particular, Brother Gabriel Sagard, had stayed in Huronia from 1623 to 1624 and had composed, from his own work and the uncited efforts of others, a French-Wendat phrasebook.[15]

Brébeuf stayed with the Huron from 1626 to 1628. Early on, he threw his considerable energy and intellect into studying the Wendat language. By some time shortly after 1628, he had composed a catechism in Wendat. It was a translation of Father Diego Ledesma's influential "Doctrina christiana," which by the end of the sixteenth century had already been translated from Latin into such languages as Spanish, Polish, and Lithuanian. Brébeuf's translation was an impressive, fifteen-page effort, and it presents a good example of the way Brébeuf thought. One can see his initial caution in features such as his using the word *atonesta*, meaning 'one gives recognition, thanks by such a means', for *Eucharist* (Steckley 1978:

113). The Wendat word derives from the verb root -atones- 'to thank, give thanks' (Potier 1920:199), and choosing it was likely Brébeuf's effort to avoid being seen as promoting the Huron practice of ritual cannibalism of captured enemies (a custom shared with the Iroquois) by a literal reference to eating the body of Christ.[16]

One also sees in Brébeuf's early work the noun bias of a European language speaker. Comparatively, Indo-European languages (a language family that comprises almost all European languages) contain many nouns, and nouns make up a relatively large percentage of words spoken and written. Like many other Aboriginal North American languages (my experience is primarily with Iroquoian and Algonquian languages), Wendat is dominated instead by verbs. Most Wendat nouns are incorporated into verbs, rarely standing on their own, whereas verbs are often used with no incorporated noun. In his catechism, Brébeuf created more than thirty new nouns to express Christian concepts. Almost all of them were ungrammatical in Wendat, violating both morphological rules and the verb dominance of the language. In the end, his Wendat language creations would not reappear in the literature, but they are worth looking at briefly as precursors of later Jesuit usages.

Some examples of ungrammatical nouns that Brébeuf developed for use in the Ledesma catechism are *orrihoüaienstecha* 'la doctrine [the doctrine]' (Brébeuf 1830:1); *endionrhencha* 'la remission [the remission (of sins)]' (Brébeuf 1830:4); *ottirihoüanderacha* 'des pechez [of sins]' (Brébeuf 1830:4); *hontonnhontaionacha* 'sa . . . passion' [his (Jesus') passion] (Brébeuf 1830:5);[17] and *Achincacha* 'Trinité [Trinity]' (Brébeuf 1830:4). These words are ungrammatical for several reasons.

First, Wendat noun stems are made only from simple verb roots. The first four examples here have noun roots plus verb roots as their bases, disqualifying them grammatically from being well-formed Wendat noun stems. The word *orrihoüaienstecha* is composed of the noun root -rihꙍ- 'affair, matter, news' (Potier 1920:453), the verb root -ien- 'to have ability, skill' (Potier 1920:266), and the causative-instrumental suffix -st-. *Endionrhencha* is formed from the noun root -ndiꙍnr- 'mind, thought' (Potier 1920:449) plus the verb root -en- 'to fall' (Potier 1920:375). *Ottirihoüanderacha* is composed of the noun root -rihꙍ- plus the verb root -nderaɩ- 'to be mistaken, to make mistakes' (Potier 1920:284). *Hontonnhontaionacha* is formed from the noun root -onnh- 'life' (Potier 1920:455) plus the verb root -ont- 'to attach, be attached' (Potier 1920:418).

The fifth example, Achincacha, is ungrammatical because it takes the particle achink 'three' and makes it into a noun. By definition, a particle in Wendat is a word that takes on the structure of neither a verb nor a noun.

Brébeuf used not only the nominalizer but also the instrumental to create what he undoubtedly believed were nouns. Typically, the instrumental verb root suffix, which the Jesuits represented as -k8-, adds to the verb a meaning such as 'by such a means' or 'at such a place or time', sometimes simply adding the notion of causation. Examples are the following:

Wendat Word	Brébeuf's Translation	English Translation
Ainstacoüa[18]	leçon [lesson]	one teaches by means of it
Ondatonnhõtacoüa[19]	la resurrection [resurrection]	they are made alive by means of it
Ottichorrecoua[20]	peines [pains; i.e., of hell]	they feel pain by means of it
Andaeratikoüa[21]	l'experance [hope]	she/it copies something for some reason
Ichihoncoüa[22]	oraison [prayer]	you say it for some reason, by some means

Like Brébeuf's other Wendat language creations of this time, these words would not reappear in the literature. Eventually, Brébeuf and the Jesuit linguists who followed him would learn that the Wendat language was much more verb-based than European languages, and they would express most of these same concepts with well-formed Wendat words. In De Religione, for example, Pierson employed 445 different verb roots but only 136 noun roots (in addition to 15 noun stems formed from verb roots).[23] The terms he used for sin, Christian, God, and the three personages of the Trinity all take the form of verbs rather than nouns.

Owing to a brief takeover of the St. Lawrence River by the English, the Jesuit mission in Huronia was interrupted after Brébeuf's stay until 1634, when the Jesuits returned. One of the main tasks to which they set themselves was to become fluent in Wendat. Their position as humble students of the language was early laid out by Brébeuf in this often-quoted instruction to those who would join him in the mission: "The Huron language will be your Saint Thomas and your Aristotle; and clever man as you are, and speaking glibly among learned and capable persons, you must make up your mind to be for a long time mute among the Barbarians. You will have accomplished much, if, at the end of a considerable time, you begin to stammer a little" (JR10:91).

In 1639 the Jesuits established the mission community of Sainte-Marie-Among-the-Hurons in the center of Huron country, near the shores of Georgian Bay. It was the base from which they extended missions to the member nations of the Huron alliance and their immediate neighbors. This elaborate mission edifice came crashing down in 1649, when the Iroquois triumphed militarily over the Huron, and the Jesuits were forced to burn Sainte-Marie and flee from Huron country.

The mission continued in the Québec area, as did Jesuit linguistic work. The earliest surviving Jesuit Wendat dictionary known is a French-Wendat dictionary that contains some Onondaga entries in a right-hand column (hereafter I refer to this dictionary as FHO). It appears to be a field manual dictionary employed by Fathers Pierre Chaumonot and Claude Dablon when they stayed with the Onondaga in 1655–56 (Steckley 1982, 1991). One indication of its early date is the remnants it contains of the Jesuits' use of the Northern Bear dialect, something that was gradually phased out during the writing of the Jesuit Relations of the 1640s (see Steckley 1997).

Probably written shortly afterwards was the French-Wendat section (FH62) of a dictionary that, like FHO, shows forms from the Northern Bear dialect not found in the more extensive Wendat-French portion of the dictionary (HF62), which probably dates from around the time of *De Religione*.

Father Etienne de Carheil compiled a list of Wendat verb and noun roots between 1666 and 1700 (Potier 1920:xvii). It probably was this compilation that formed the basis for three seventeenth-century Wendat-French dictionaries (HF59, HF62, HF65) as well as Potier's copy, in which a few Wyandot forms were added. There are three surviving French-Wendat dictionaries that may be of a later date. Two can be dated to roughly 1693 and 1697 (FH1693 and FH1697, respectively). The third (FH67) has not yet been dated.

The Iroquois and the French

The Iroquois, or Five Nations, who defeated the Huron alliance and then absorbed many of its survivors, are a third group important to the cultural context of De Religione—especially in their relationship to the French. To understand who the Iroquois were (and are), one must understand their concept "the Great Law" (lit., the Great Good). The Great Law is centuries old, long predating the people's contact with Europeans.[24] It is both a story and a series of teachings concerning the establishment of what is termed in English the League or Confederacy of the Iroquois. The people did not call themselves Iroquois.[25] Their name, Haudenosaunee (Monture-Angus 1995:249), usually pronounced something like "hoh-deh-no-sho-neh," means 'they are of the extended house' or 'they build a house', signifying that all the five (later six) peoples are together under one political roof.[26]

The story begins with a woman and her daughter going to live on their own.[27] They were worried about the warfare that surrounded them. The daughter gave birth to a boy, who would come to be known as the Peacemaker. As a child, he had a vision in which he saw a way for warring peoples to have peace. When he became a man, he decided to share his vision of peace with the then-warring five Iroquoian nations (from west to east, Seneca, Cayuga, Onondaga, Oneida, and Mohawk) living in what is now New York State. The heart of the message was that these linguistically and culturally related neighbors had more to gain from mutual peace than from the destructive warfare that had figured so prominently in their past relationships.

As the "eastern door" of the confederacy "house," the Mohawk were the first to experience warfare with the French. In 1609, the "Father of New France," Samuel de Champlain, decided to strengthen the French government's connection with its Native allies, the Montagnais, Algonquin, and Huron, by attacking the common enemy of all three—the Mohawk. Prior to Champlain's decision, the Mohawk had experienced no significant contact with the French. It would be easy to think of Champlain as a warmonger in this instance, but that is perhaps unfair, judging him more by the effects of his decision than by his reasoning. There was a logic to the move that made sense in terms of the politics at the time. These Native nations had helped the French, and military assistance was what they requested in return.

In July 1609, Champlain approached the southern end of the large lake that now bears his name. He was deep in Mohawk country. Accompanied by two well-armed compatriots and sixty Montagnais, Algonquin, and Huron, Champlain attacked a Mohawk war party. The French guns determined the victory. The Mohawk had not been in a fight against such weapons before. Fifty warriors, including two chiefs, were killed. Ten to twelve were taken prisoner. The next year, along the Richelieu River, which connects Lake Champlain with the St. Lawrence, one hundred Mohawk warriors were similarly attacked and beaten in their own country. Fifteen were captured, the rest killed.

The Mohawk would feel another effect of being the member of the confederacy nearest to the French: the presence of black-robed missionaries in their midst. Father Isaac Jogues was the first. He had a somewhat limited impact, because he was a prisoner while he lived with the Mohawk from 1642 to 1644. In 1646, he was killed by members of one faction of that nation.

The early 1640s were rough times for the Mohawk. It has been estimated that by then they had lost up to 75 percent of their number to European diseases (Richter 1992:59, 312–13 n. 18). The Jesuits suffered, too. In the late 1640s, when the Iroquois were driving the Huron, Petun, and Neutral from their Ontario homelands, they killed a number of Jesuits, including those mentioned in De Religione: Father Daniel in 1648 and Fathers Brébeuf, Lalemant, and Garnier in 1649.

The Jesuits made another attempt to do missionary work among the Iroquois in 1655, when Fathers Chaumonot and Dablon went to Onondaga country. In 1657, as earlier mentioned, two Huron nations joined the Mohawk and the Onondaga, respectively. The Jesuits hoped that this might lead to a missionary opportunity with the host Iroquois nations.

Instead, the next such opportunity was created militarily. In the fall of 1666, Alexandre de Prouville de Tracy led an invasion force of more than a thousand men, made up for the most part of the crack troops of the Carignan-Salieres regiment. They directed their offensive at the very heart of Mohawk country. De Tracy was attempting to crush the Mohawk's capacity to send raiding parties into territory the French claimed as theirs. This was the third attempt at such an offensive that year; the first two had failed. Luckily for the Mohawk, when the French army approached this time, the three hundred to four hundred Mohawk warriors, along with more numerous women and children, easily eluded their attackers. Unfortunately for the Mohawk, the French torched their villages, fields, and much of their crucial winter supply of food, mostly corn.

After De Tracy's punishing expedition, the Mohawk were forced to accept Jesuit missionaries as part of a peace treaty in 1667. Fathers Jacques Fremin and Jean Pierron went to the Mohawk community of Tionnontoguen ('between the hills'). There they set up the mission of Sainte-Marie-Among-the-Iroquois at Agnie (Kanyenke). Father Jacques Bruyas, who had traveled with them, set up his mission among the Oneida to the west. The Tionnontoguen mission seems to have fared reasonably well. By 1669, Fathers Fremin and Pierron claimed a baptism head count of 251, followed by at least 53 the next year and 80 the next.

By at least 1670, Father Fremin was traveling every week to villages close to Tionnontoguen. In the Jesuit Relation of 1673 we get the first reference in that series of mission records to the "Mission of Gandaouague," or Saint Pierre in the Country of Agnie (JR57:89).[28]

The Jesuits were also setting up an Iroquois community in French territory, partly to serve as a buffer between the Iroquois and the French. In 1667, Father Pierre Raffeix, feeling that the French had pacified the Mohawk, believed that an Iroquois mission could be established in the Montreal area. He encouraged half a dozen Oneida who had been visiting to winter on the south shore of the St. Lawrence River. The mission, named St. François-Xavier, would early become a success, at the cost of a significant depopulation of Mohawk communities. In 1677, the village moved upriver to the Lachine Rapids and became known as Kahnawake ('at the rapids'), both after the location and after the name of the eventually abandoned Mohawk community (Gandaouague) in more traditional territory from which it drew its population.

The history of relations among the Huron, Jesuits, Iroquois, and French explains why—strange as it might seem at first glance—*De Religione* was written in Huron even though it was addressed to the Iroquois. Because of France's trade alliance with the Huron, the

Jesuits were able to establish missions among them early and to learn their language. They did not gain safe and consistent access to the Iroquois nations until later, after French forces had defeated the Mohawk militarily.

Consequently, during the seventeenth and eighteenth centuries, when Jesuits trained for the Iroquois mission, they did so by first learning the related language Huron. A well-developed Jesuit linguistic and religious literature in Huron existed by the mid-1600s, which was not the case for any of the Iroquois languages at the time. Father Thierry Beschefer wrote in 1666, "I studied the language of the Huron, in order to go next year, as I hope, on a mission to the upper Iroquois" (JR50:171).

In the seventeenth century, Jesuit missionaries often used Huron as a liturgical language when they worked among the Iroquois, at least until they became fluent in the language of the Iroquois nation with which they were working. Father Etienne de Carheil began his missionary work with the Cayuga in November 1668. In the Jesuit Relation of 1669, we read that "the Father used at first in his instructions only the Huron language, which the Iroquois all understand, when it is well spoken. He has since composed a discourse on Baptism in the Oiogouen [Cayuga] language, using in its composition only simple roots and the study of the Iroquois tongue that he had made during his journey" (JR52:179).

It was reported in the Jesuit Relations that from the 1660s to at least 1735, the Mohawk and other Iroquois at the Kahnawake mission near Montreal used Huron for Christian prayers (JR63:149 and 68:279).

TRANSLATING *DE RELIGIONE*

No one today speaks the Wendat language as a native tongue. No elders exist who might have explained to me the more obscure senses of words or the metaphors that I understood only literally. Much is lost this way. My sources for translating *De Religione* are quite good nonetheless, much better than might have been expected for a "dead language." Despite facing linguistic and cultural differences on a large scale, seventeenth-century Jesuit linguists were among the best in the world at learning and transcribing languages. They put great effort into learning all they could about Wendat, for they believed that the fate of the Huron's very souls depended on that learning. The dictionaries they wrote (I have eight) offer a wealth of historical linguistic information, including multiple entries and metaphors, for which no parallel exists in any other North American Native language. These dictionaries rival any contemporary dictionary. Certainly they were far superior to anything that existed about the English language in their day.

In the twentieth century, other pioneering linguists conducted ground-breaking research on Iroquoian languages. Foremost among these scholars in terms of the impact their work has had on my own are Floyd Lounsbury, in his epic study of Oneida (1953), and Wallace Chafe, in his works on Seneca (1961, 1963, 1967) and Onondaga (1970).

Translating *De Religione* was an enormous challenge for an English-speaking, non-Aboriginal Canadian attempting, in the twenty-first century, to translate material written in the language of a seventeenth-century Aboriginal group as it was used by people of that time but of a very different language and culture. The process might be likened to a conversation among three strangers who share no native language in common but who need to communicate. Compromises to everyone's linguistic and cultural purity—the Huron's, the Jesuits', and mine—were inevitable.

One of my aims in translation was to favor, whenever possible, the culture of the Huron over that of the Jesuits. That is, I wanted, as much as possible, for the document to have a "Huron read"—to be understood in the way a Huron might have understood it—rather than to convey the Jesuits' intent. Of course with the Jesuits as my major source, this was a difficult undertaking. It entailed, for example, attempting to see what the Jesuits did not see, as well as trying to uncover their strategies of avoidance. The Jesuits considered certain potential Huron interpretations too dangerous—for example, the implied cannibalism of a literal translation of *Eucharist*. Such interpretations could lead to practices or beliefs counter to the Jesuits' mission purposes.

Translating Concepts across Cultures

Much of the message of Christianity is embedded in the culture of Europe and the Mediterranean. All one has to do is think of images of pastoralism, sheep, shepherds, camels, and horses to recognize the truth of this statement. Jesuits who wanted to convey the culturally loaded concepts of Christianity to speakers of Aboriginal languages in North America struggled to find ways to express themselves in terms the Natives would find meaningful, just as I have struggled to find adequate ways to translate Wendat terms into English.

One good example of the way cultural differences impeded the Jesuits' and Iroquois's understanding of each other lies in European concepts of rich and poor. The Bible is replete with images of wealth and poverty and of their significance, perhaps the best known being that "it is easier for a camel to go through the eye of a needle than for a rich man to enter the kingdom of God" (Matthew 19:24). Such notions of material wealth and poverty did not translate readily into Iroquoian languages. In seventeenth-century Europe, "rich" and "poor" were easily measured through disparities in the number and kinds of material possessions people had. Such disparities did not exist in Iroquoian culture at that time. What options did that leave the missionary linguists?

To describe in Wendat someone's being rich, the Jesuits employed a word that referred specifically to the greatness of an individual's spirit connections. They used the verb root -aki- 'to be a spirit' (which I say more about later) with the augmentative suffix -ι8annen-, which adds to a noun or verb the meaning of 'large, augmented' (see De Religione 638:14, 671:5, 675:2, 680:2). This combination has the literal meaning 'to be an augmented, large spirit.' What did it refer to in traditional Huron culture? This is difficult to determine. Sagard translated it as 'to be rich' in his 1623–24 phrasebook (Sagard 1866:126), in which he spelled ihoüen what I have transcribed as ι8annen:

Ie suis riche. [I am rich.]
Oukihoüen.
Tu es riche. [You are rich.]
Sakihoüen.
Il est riche. [He is rich.]
[H]Oukihoüen.
Les ames de N. sont riches. [The souls of N. are rich.]
[H]Okihouey [h]atisken N.

The term was likewise used in an apparent European sense in a prayer composed by the early Huron convert Joseph Chihoaten-hwa (JR21:256–57) and published in the Jesuit Relation of 1641.

Only one reference in a Wendat dictionary gives any clue to the original meaning of the term *aki8annen*. It comes in FHO, the earliest surviving French-Wendat dictionary (ca. 1655–56), which makes a contrast between two terms that other, later dictionaries replicate, though the others lack reference to any specific meaning:

Riche
Aki8anne estre riche . . . p[ro]prie riche en Bled [to be rich . . .
    properly, particularly, rich in corn]
ιAannra'k8anne riche en robes, porcelaine, meubles . . . [to be
    rich in robes, porcelain, furniture] (FHO)

It is not difficult to see that someone in a horticultural society who is blessed with good crops might be considered to be augmented in spirit.

Unraveling one mystery seems to create another tangle. Why did the Jesuits not use the second term in the quoted dictionary entry, which has more the sense they might have wanted to express, to talk about being "rich in possessions"? It certainly was not because the term wasn't well known to them; a number of dictionaries contain entries in which the term has the meaning of being rich in robes and porcelain (i.e., in wampum beads and necklaces). For example:

Riche   Aki8anne / v Aki8annen . . . devenir riche . . . etre
riche en Robes, porcel[aine], meubl[es] [to become rich . . . to
be rich in robes/clothing, porcelain, furniture] ιannrak8anne
(FH1697:184)

Riche aki8annen . . . ιaannrak8anne etre rich en robe, meuble
[to be rich in robes/clothing, furniture] (FH67:173)

The only explanation I can offer entails a possible connection with shamanism, something the Jesuits might not have wanted to express. The verb root involved in the word is -ιannra- 'to look at'

(Potier 1920:235). With the addition of the augmentative, one gets a meaning something like 'to look at in an augmented way'. A verb that has a similar meaning, -uat- 'to look at' (Potier 1920:240), has a direct connection with the acts of a "juggler" (jongleur),[29] or shaman:

> Akat . . . Se tourner de q[uelque] coté, y porter les yeux, la vue, l'y tenir tournée . . . regarder un malade comme font les jongleurs, pour dire la cause de son mal; et tous les evenemen[t]s [To turn to some side and bring one's eyes there, view, to hold the turning there . . . to look at a sick person as the jongleurs do, to say the cause of their malady, and all the developments, events]

> Hakaθa / v saιoθa. C'est un jongleur, un regardeur de malade [he is a jongleur, a 'looker' of the sick].

> atiaꝛenre d'aniontatakat. La jonglerie est defendue ["jongling" is forbidden]. (Potier 1920:240)

That there might have been some link between shamanism and the verb root -uannra- is also suggested in Bruyas's seventeenth-century dictionary of Mohawk (Bruyas 1970:44), in which, under the entry for this verb, appears a reference to dream visions:

> Kagannere, voir . . .
> Kaganneron vel Kaganneraon, . . . voir en songe [to see in a dream]

European and Huron cultures differed not only in their notions of being rich, in the sense of having material possessions, but also in their ideas about being poor. That is why I have translated the verb root -esa-, which the Jesuits used when they intended to depict material poverty, as the more general (and culturally appropriate) 'to be in a poor state' (see De Religione 638:11, 639:4, 640:10, 652:22, 660:7, 671:14, 672:2, 673:11, 675:15). I believe this verb root signified a state of physical, emotional, and/or spiritual deprivation more than a relative lack of possessions, as can be seen in the following examples (all from Potier 1920:231):

ιaesandi . . . in fieri et in actu experientia presentis tomber en
un etat de pauvreté, d'affliction & . . . [to become and to be
actually experiencing presently falling into a state of poverty,
of affliction]

etre tombé en pauvre etat, en pitoyable etat, en etat d'afflica-
tion, de pauvreté et de misere, dans un etat de dependance ou
l'on depend pour son soulagement des autres qui souvent se
rient et se moquent du besoin qu'on a d'eux; dans un etat ou
l'on est sujet a etre meprisé et maltraité (item etre de deuil,
porter le deuil p) . . . [to have fallen into a poor state, into a
pitiable state, into a state of affliction, of poverty and of misery,
into a state of dependence where one depends for one's relief
on others who often laugh at and mock the need that one has
on them; into a state in which one is subject to contempt and
maltreatment (also to be in mourning, to bear mourning]

ιandatsaesaha n'onι8annenoa notre chaudiere est hors de
service, hors d'usage devenue inutile, toute gatée, perdue [our
pot is out of service, out of usage, has become useless, totally
ruined, lost]

ιaataesandi uxores non posse habere prolem . . . (item ne trouver
pas ceux dont on a besoin p) [wives unable to bear children
(also, unable to find those whom one has need of)]

echiataesaha non habebis prolem et hau uxore, et vieillit [you
are unable to have offspring and are not a wife, and you are
aging]

Along with disparities between rich and poor in the Jesuits'
European society came a much more hierarchical structure than
anything the Iroquois knew—another cultural difference that had
to be accounted for in translating *De Religione*. In European society,
certain people were masters who gave orders that others had to
obey. I have translated the Wendat word that the Jesuits intended
to mean 'to obey' with the literal 'to be with or follow someone's
word' (see *De Religione* 633:15, 17, 634:20, 638:9, 663:10, 666:23, 676:
10). My goal is to give it a meaning that would have had greater

resonance with political reality in Iroquoian society, in which a greater degree of personal choice was available in response to leaders than was the case in seventeenth-century Europe.

Similarly, I have translated the word the Jesuits used for *God* with the literal 'he is great in voice', or 'Great Voice', rather than with the 'Master' that uniformly appears in the Jesuit Relations and other Jesuit literature of the seventeenth century in translations of this term. It is difficult to know how Huron used the combination of the noun root -ꞗend- 'word, voice' (Potier 1920:452) and the verb root -io- 'to be great, large' (Potier 1920:396), prior to European contact. Sagard (1866:78; see Steckley 1987:22) recorded the following usages of this combination:

> Ie suis le maistre du lac, il est a moy. [I am the master of the lake; it is mine.]
> Ni auhoindiou gontara. [I am great in voice (concerning) the lake.]

> N. est le maistre de la riuiere, du chemin. [N. is the master of the river, of the path.]
> N. anhoindiou angoyon. [N. is great in voice where he goes.]

What this appears to be is a reference to those who had ownership or were in authority concerning trade routes, a less authoritarian position than that of the *maistre* that Sagard and the Jesuits used to translate the term.

TRANSLATING CHRISTIAN CONCEPTS

Obviously, the spiritual worlds of the Jesuits and the Iroquoians were quite different. It is instructive to look at the Wendat words into which the Jesuits chose to infuse Christian meaning. It is also important to know the traditional meanings of the terms as an aid to understanding the impact on the Iroquoians of the Christian message as presented in the Wendat language. In *De Religione*, I have biased my translation in favor of the traditional meanings.

A good first example is the concept of the Trinity, in which we witness Brébeuf's struggle, described earlier, to express with verbs what he normally expected to express with nouns. Kinship terms such as "the father" and "the son" were formed from verb roots and required Wendat pronominal prefixes, which denoted the two parties of the kin relationship. The elder of the two parties had to be mentioned first as the subject, as can be seen in the example *sand8en*, which is derived from the verb root *-nd8en-* and translates literally as 'she to you is mother'—that is, 'your mother'. Brébeuf made errors of gender in his pronominal references. For example, he had seen the word *-ona-* in the Northern Bear dialect and believed it meant 'our', but with kinship terms it actually meant 'she to us'. He used it in the Lord's Prayer in his translation of the Ledesma catechism (Brébeuf 1830:6) in attempting to say 'our father': *Onaistan* (lit., 'she to us is father').

Brébeuf was concerned early on about the doctrinal correctness of his attempts to place pronominal prefixes on Wendat words representing the Trinity. He discussed the matter at length in the Jesuit Relation of 1636:

A relative noun with them includes the meaning of one of the three persons of the possessive pronoun, so that they cannot say simply, Father, Son, Master, Valet, but are obliged to say one of the three, my father, thy father, his father. However, I have translated above in a Prayer one of their nouns by the word Father for greater clearness.[30] On this account, we find ourselves hindered from getting them to say properly in their Language, *In the name of the Father, and of the Son, and of the holy Ghost.* Would you judge it fitting, while waiting a better expression, to substitute instead, *In the name of our Father, and of his Son, and of their holy Ghost*? Certainly it seems that the three Persons of the most holy Trinity would be sufficiently expressed in this way, the third being in truth the holy Spirit of the first and of the second; the second being Son of the first; of the first our Father [*sic*], in the terms of the Apostle, who applies to him those fitting words in Ephesians 3. It may be added that our Lord has given example of this by speaking, not only in the Lord's Prayer, as we call it from respect to him, but by way of commandment to Mary Magdalen in Saint John 20 to bear from him these beautiful words to his Brethren or Disciples, *I ascend to my Father and to yours.* Would we venture to employ it thus until the Huron language shall be enriched,

or the mind of the Huron opened to other languages? We will
do nothing without advice. (JR10:119)

The pronominal policy had been abandoned by the time *De Religione* was written. In that document, the names for the three persons
of the Trinity take the following forms, the first two employing the
same verb, -*ɩen*- 'to have as child' (Potier 1920:219). The Father is
sa,[e]n 'he has them (indefinite) as children'; the Son is *honaen* 'they
(masculine plural) have him as child'; and the Holy Ghost is *hoki
daat hoatatoɩeti* 'he is a spirit, the very, he is a true one'.

To take another central Christian concept, the Wendat term that
the Jesuits chose to represent the notion of sin involved the noun
root -*rih8*- 'matter, affair, news' (Potier 1920:453) and the verb root
-*ndera*- 'to make mistakes, to be mistaken' (Potier 1920:284). Note
that in the following entries from Potier's dictionary (Potier 1920:
284), only the word for 'sin', in the last entry, conveys any sense
that the mistake involves deliberate wrongdoing:

ɩanderaɩi . . . se tromper, se meprendre par inadvertance, ou
sans reflexion . . . ou avec assez de connoissance, et meme par
mal . . . [to be wrong, to be mistaken inadvertently, or without
reflection, or with some cognition, the same for bad]

ɩandatanderaɩi [with -*ndat*- 'village', Potier 1920:449] prendre
un village pour l'autre [to (mis)take one village for another]

ɩachiendanderaɩi [with -*chien*- 'name', Potier 1920:446] prendre un nom pour l'autre [to (mis)take one name for another]

ɩannonchianderaɩi [with -nnonchi- 'house', Potier 1920:449]
prendre un cabane pour l'autre sans y penser, entrer dans un
cabane voulant entrer dans un autre . . . [to (mis)take a house
for another without thinking, entering into a house wishing to
enter another]

ɩarih8anderaɩi pecher, faire une faute avec assez de connoissance, ou meme avec malice [to sin, make a mistake with some
cognition, or the same with malice]

I have chosen to translate this term as 'to be mistaken in some matter'. For me, such a translation maintains in the message the sense of confusion and frustration that Huron and Iroquois people must have felt upon being told that "mistakes" could be deadly and that priests were the only ones who could determine for sure which mistakes were lethal to one's eternal life and which were harmless.

A third important spiritual concept that the Jesuits needed to communicate in their missionary work was that of holiness. Except in Brébeuf's Ledesma catechism, the term the Jesuits used was a verb root, -toie(n)-, plus the causative root suffix -'t-, which I have translated as 'to be certain, true.' They used the -toie't- combination in the following ways:

1 With -at- 'body' (Potier 1920:446) to refer to the Holy Ghost (De Religione 629:2, 4, 7), the saints (Potier 1920:177), guardian angels (634:1), and those who live a "good Christian life" on earth and thus go to heaven (639:4, 645:9, 646:10, 651:5–6, 652:16, 653:4, 7, 654:21–22, 657:8, 677:13)
2 With -ndek8- 'water' (Potier 1920:449) to refer to the holy water of baptism (669:23)
3 With -nnonchi- 'house' (Potier 1920:451) to mean 'church' (676:13)
4 With -h8atsir- 'matrilineage' (Potier 1920:447) to refer to the holy family of Mary (see Steckley 1992a:496–97; FH1697:74; FH1693:141)
5 With -ientiok8- 'clan' (Potier 1920:455) to refer to the family into which Jesus would adopt those who became Christians (653:8)
6 With -ent- 'day' (Potier 1920:454) to refer to Sunday (JR15:93; Potier 1920:367)
7 With -endich- 'platform, bench' to refer to the altar (Steckley 1987:26; FH1697:13)[31]
8 With -8hist-, which traditionally referred to fish scales and the hard skin of flint corn and came to refer to metal or glass (see De Religione, note 6), to refer to a holy medal (FH1697:117) or to the bell that rang to announce prayers
9 With -hiatonchr- 'marking, writing' (Potier 1920:447) to mean 'holy writing' (Potier 1920:326)
10 With -hach- 'flame' (Potier 1920:447), sometimes a traditional metaphor for 'meeting', to mean 'mass' (Potier 1920:327)

11 With -asont- 'night' (Potier 1920:445) to refer to Christmas night
    (Potier 1920:195)
12 with -ndats- 'pot' (Potier 1920:449) to refer to the sacred chalice
    (Potier 1920:401)

This form eventually came also to be used in other Northern Iroquoian languages to signify the Holy Ghost (for Mohawk, and Tuscarora, see Hewitt 1928:609 and Rudes 1987:289, respectively), the
Bible (for Cayuga, Mohawk, and Tuscarora, see Kick et al. 1988:45,
Michelson 1973:109, and Rudes 1987:289, respectively) and Sunday
(for Mohawk, Seneca, and Cayuga, see Michelson 1973:46, Chafe
1963:38, and Kick et al. 1988:18, respectively).

To try to get some understanding of its meaning in Wendat speech,
let us again look in depth at an entry from Potier's dictionary for
explanation and examples. The entry begins as follows, with the
verb root taken without the causative root suffix but with the she/it
pronominal prefix and stative aspect added:[32] "ɩatoɩen . . . etre vrai,
assuré, certain; prout opponitur falso [to be true, assured, certain, as
opposed to false]" (Potier 1920:366). Examples of this meaning are
abundant in *De Religione* (634:3, 8, 641:7, 643:12, 647:12, 654:19,
655:3, 6, passim). Pierson seemed eager to emphasize that what he
was saying was true.

The next section of Potier's dictionary entry adds the inchoative
suffix, which typically adds a sense of coming into being:

> ɩatoɩendi . . . devenir certain, assuré, se verifier, se trouver veri-
> table, se reconnoitre veritable, s'assurer, concevoir, comprendre
> [to become certain, assured, to verify, to find true, to recognize
> as true, to assure oneself, to conceive, to comprehend] . . . etre
> certain, assuré, l'etre devenu, etre verifié . . . [to be certain,
> assured, having become so, to have verified] (Potier 1920:366)

Again, numerous examples appear in *De Religione*, all related to the
noun root -ndiɩonr- 'mind, spirit of thoughts' (634:18, 641:7, 644:7, 9,
654:19, 20, passim).

After examples presented with other suffixes, Potier presents the
verb root again with a slightly different nuance to its meaning:

> ɩatoɩen . . . certain prout opponitur communi et universali:
> idemq: signat qd: particular, special [certain, as opposed to

common and universal, also signifying particular, special] . . .
certain prout opponitur vago et indeterminato, idemq: signat
qd: determiné, designé, marqué, destiné [certain, as opposed
to vague and indeterminate, also signifying determined, designated, marked, destined] (Potier 1920:367)

All examples of this nuanced meaning that appear in the Jesuit
writings pertain to their missionizing, so it is not known exactly
how the Huron might have used the verb traditionally. In *De Religione*, Pierson did not use this sense of the verb root by itself. It
was, however, to this sense that he used the verb root plus causative to mean "holy" springs. The following indicates how this combination is translated:

ιatoιeti . . . active determiner q[uelque] c[hose], la specifier,
designer, marquer en particulier [active, to determine something, to specify it, designate it, mark it in particular] . . . passive q.c. etre determinée, specifiée, marqué, designé pour q.
action, pour q. travail [passive, something to be determined,
specified, marked, designated for some action, some work]
(Potier 1920:367)

In the dictionary entry, examples that do not relate to the spiritual
are separated by the following, which relates to the Jesuit words
designating the Holy Ghost, the angels, and those who live "good
Christian" lives. It seems that the parenthetical translation, supplied by Potier, the copyist or writer of this version of the dictionary, is the more traditional Wendat, whereas the French translation
not enclosed in parentheses is more Jesuit influenced (my translation of both is in brackets):

ιaatatoιeti . . . (une personne dans un etat de consistance, etre
un vrai honnete homme p[otier]) . . . etre une personne
choisie, elue et predestinée, une person: sainte [(a person in a
state of consistency, to be a real, honest man, Potier) . . . to be a
chosen person, a chosen or blessed one, a predestined one, a
holy, sanctified person] (Potier 1920:367)

We should also look at another entry that gives the simple form
of the verb:

ιatoιen . . . etre ferme, stable, permanent, constant, reglé, reg-
ulier, etre toujours la meme, etre uniforme, egal [to be firm,
stable, permanent, constant, settled, to be always the same, to
be uniform, the same] (Potier 1920:368)

As an example, Potier used this verb in composition with the noun
root -niend-, meaning 'manner (of doing things)':

te haniendatoιen il n'est pas constant, egal, uniforme dans la
maniere d'agir [he is not constant, the same, uniform in his
manner of acting] (Potier 1920:368)

There is a sense that this verb refers to what should be, and that
somehow this is because a spiritual hand has influenced the situation. The latter is subtly alluded to in the writer's careful use of fortuna and providentia in the following passage:

ɣtoιeti v/ otoιeti: usurpatur ad gratulandum . . . active sumpti,
quae refertur ad providentiam seu fortunam, signat q: eam
recte facille, quasi dicas: fortuna et providentia direxit qd
accidit, qd factum est . . . vbi passive sumpti: quasi dicas: recte
factum qd accidit, cum directione factum: [it is used with giving thanks . . . assuming the active, it refers to providence or
fortune. It also signifies, you could almost say, taken in the
passive voice, that whatever happens does so rightly, justly,
that it is done with direction, purpose] (Potier 1920:369)

We can see this form used with the sense of giving thanks in Sagard's
writing: "Grand mercy. Ho, ho, ho, atougetti" (Sagard 1866:66).
     French translation for examples using this word appear as "c'est
à propos [it is appropriate]," "cela est ajusté au tem[p]s [that is
suited to the situation, to the times]" and, with the optative prefix
and combined stative and punctual suffix,[33] "c'eut eté justement
que . . . [it would have been justly so that . . .]" (Potier 1920:369).
     What we have, then, is a verb that relates to something or some-
one being true, certain. The entity being referred to is a particular,
special one that is constant and firm, and this state may have something to do with the rightful, directing role of providence (i.e., the
spirit world).

The Soul

One of the most difficult intellectual tasks the Jesuits faced in developing a Christian vocabulary in Wendat was to select a term for "the soul" of Christian belief. To a large extent this was because the Huron belief system allowed for a broad range of entities or concepts along the lines of the soul, each of which overlapped somewhat with the more limited (in being essentially singular) Christian concept. Brébeuf articulated both knowledge of Aboriginal culture and an appreciation of the linguistic challenge ahead of him in a chapter in the Jesuit Relation of 1636 titled "The Ideas of the Hurons Regarding the Nature and Condition of the Soul, Both in This Life and After Death." On the first page of the chapter he wrote:

They give it [the soul] different names according to its different conditions or different operations. In so far as it merely animates the body and gives it life, they call it *khiondhecwi*; in so far as it is possessed of reason, *oki andaérandi*, "like a demon, counterfeiting a demon"; in so far as it thinks and deliberates on anything, they call it *endionrra*; and *gonennon-cwal*, in so far as it bears affection to any object; whence it happens that they often say *ondayee ihaton onennoncwat*, "That is what my heart says to me, that is what my appetite desires." Then if it is separated from the body they call it *esken*, and even the bones of the dead, *atisken*. . . . they think of the soul as divisible, and you would have all the difficulty in the world to make them believe that our soul is entire in all parts of the body. (JR10:141)

Let me begin a discussion of the Christian term *soul* and its Wendat translation by considering the last term in the preceding passage, *atisken*, first, because it was the verb that Brébeuf first employed in trying to express *soul*. A good translation or explanation of the traditional meaning of the verb root -*sken*- in Wendat is 'to be a manifestation of humans after death, particularly, but not exclusively, bones.' I believe the Huron used -*sken*- to refer to the manifestations of the dead only in the plural. This plurality is especially reflective of the bones buried in the Feast of the Dead, a ceremony in which the bones of those who had died over the last eight to twelve years were buried together as a group.

One reason for my belief in the plurality of the reference of this term is that every time a Huron practice, name, or belief is mentioned using this verb in the early French documents, it is always in the plural. In Sagard's journal (1939:172), we learn that the Huron called the Milky Way "Atiskein andahatey [i.e., *hatisken hondahate*]," 'they (masculine) are manifestations of the dead, it is their path'.[34] In his phrasebook, the verb always takes the plural reference, once as the indefinite form *-e-*, but all others as the masculine plural *-hati-* (often imperfectly recorded by the Jesuits without the *h*).[35] In all the Jesuit dictionaries, the verb appears only with the masculine plural prefix *-hati-* (Potier 1920:350; FHO; HF59:148; HF62: 120; FH67:13; HF65:175).

In the Ledesma catechism, although Brébeuf himself used *Attisken* and *Ottisken* to refer to *ames* (Brébeuf 1830:7, 8, respectively), he also attempted, with no lasting effect on the Wendat language or the mission literature, to singularize this verb in two ways. One involved referring to a Christian's *Ange Gardien* ('guardian angel') in an ungrammatical way:

Esken de ihaacarratat . . . mon Ange Gardien [they are the dead, who, he takes care of me] (Brébeuf 1830:7)

Chiesken . . . vostre Ange Gardian. [You are the dead] (Brébeuf 1830:7)

Aesken de iskiacarratas . . . Ange . . . commis pour me garder [Angel commissioned to guard me] [I am the dead, who, you take care of me] (Brébeuf 1830:7)

This appears to be another example of Brébeuf's creating verb forms (and concepts) that did not exist previously in the Wendat language. He was expressing a singularity that exists nowhere else in the literature. One can only speculate what the effects of this might have been on the Huron. Imagine having a stranger, whom you suspect of possessing shamanistic powers, say to you, "You are the dead," or "I am the dead." It probably did not take Brébeuf long to discover the inappropriateness of such an expression.

As we will see, the Jesuits would later use another verb, -aki-, to refer to guardian spirits. They would replace Brébeuf's esken 'to be dead' (Brébeuf 1830:2–5), in reference to the Holy Ghost, with the verb root -aki- as well.

Jesuit use of -sken- was restricted later on. It appears only once in De Religione, in the sentence, "Do you think that the spirits of the dead of the enemies you mistreated have forgotten?" (663:4). This reflects not Christian use but Pierson's appropriation of a traditional Iroquoian concept and expression referring to the spirits of the dead wishing vengeance on their killers, a justification for a raid.

As can readily be seen in De Religione, the term the Jesuits eventually decided upon to refer to the soul was based on the verb root -(e)nnonk8at- 'to be medicine' (Potier 1920:454). In Sagard's phrasebook, we see this verb root having a meaning that both relates to medicine as English speakers tend to think of it (the first two examples presented below) and connotes something with spiritual connections (the third example):

La medicine, cette herbe, ne guerist de rien, ne les guerira point. [The medicine, this herb, cures nothing, will not cure.]
Danstan túhatetsense énonquate. [It does not cure; it is a medicine.] (Sagard 1866:67)

Onguent, toutes choses medicinales. [Ointment, unguent, all things medicinal]
Ennonquate. [It is medicine.] (Sagard 1866:141)

Il a songé qu'il luy falloit vne medicine, ou quelque drogue pour estre guery. [He has dreamed that he needed a medicine or some drug to be cured.]
Athrasqua, ou Aesthrasqua atetsan énonquate. [He dreams it, it cures, it is a medicine.]

The phrase given by Brébeuf in the previously quoted passage from the Jesuit Relation of 1636 (JR10:141) relates to a meaning for "medicine" that existed in Huron but was new to Brébeuf and his colleagues. The phrase, written in Northern Bear,[36] and its translation are as follows:

ondayee ihaton onennoncwat
[He or she/it, he says, it is our medicine]
It is what our medicine says.

This statement related to the all-important communication
between the spirit world and an individual that was well described
by Father Francesco Gioseppe Bressani in 1653, when he wrote about
the religion of the Huron. He began the heart of his discussion with
an often-quoted remark about the Huron's distinguishing among
three kinds of diseases: those with natural causes, those brought on
by the desires of the soul, and those caused by sorcery. The second
of these was vital to his discussion and to ours. He stated that such
diseases could be cured "by satisfying the desires of the soul"
(JR39:17). He added that

> for the second, it must be recognized that, besides the free—
> or, at least, voluntary—desires that we usually have, the Hurons
> thought that our souls had other desires, in a manner natural
> and hidden, both in the depth of the soul,—not in the way of
> conscious knowledge, but through a certain migration of the
> soul into some object proportioned to itself. . . .
> The Hurons, then, persuaded themselves that the soul
> revealed the first desires by means of dreams, which are its
> own voice; and if these dreams . . . are fulfilled, it remains
> content; otherwise, it is vexed, and not only no longer seeks
> good and happiness through the body, but, revolting against
> it, causes it various infirmities, and often death. (JR39:19)

The Huron believed in the existence of two souls. Bressani spoke
of this when he talked about the means through which soul desires
were expressed:

> In a dream, then, when one thinks of some distant thing, they
> believed that the soul went forth from the body, in order to
> become present in the thing dreamed of,—not the perceptive
> soul, which (they said) never abandoned the body, but the
> rational one which in its operation does not depend on the
> body. For this reason, they diligently observed dreams, in order
> to know the desires of the soul, that they might not irritate it;

and they often obeyed it at the cost of blood,—causing their very [fingers] to be cut off, with extreme pain, if the dream so commanded. (JR39:19)[37]

This "rational" soul is the one Brébeuf referred to in his 1636 chapter when he wrote that "in so far as it thinks and deliberates on anything, they call it [the soul] *endionrra*."[38] The Jesuits spoke of it with respect to the Onondaga, but with equal application to the Huron, in the Relation of 1656: "These people believe that sadness, anger, and all violent passions expel the rational soul from the body, which, meanwhile, is animated only by the sensitive soul which we have in common with animals. That is why, on such occasions, they usually make a present to restore the rational soul to the seat of reason" (JR42:51).

The communication of these "desires of the soul," expressed as dreams and visions, was "our medicine" in the sense that it brought cures and prevented illness. It was a metaphor of medicine, not an entity such as *endionrra*. Perhaps this made it, in the Jesuits' eyes, a safer term to use.

The Jesuits seemed very much inclined to meet the Huron and other Iroquoians halfway in discussing what the soul was like. We can see this in *De Religione* in the way Pierson said that "our medicine" can perform the following function: "Whenever we are sick, it makes for us a medicine with which to cure" (636:21). Further, he wrote that "our medicine" is a soul that is also possessed by animals and plants, which he described in the following comparison between those souls, spirits, and the souls possessed by humans:

It is a medicine of a particular nature, that which provides life for a tree. It is another way, that which provides life for an animal. They are different, too, those who provide life for humans and spirits; the medicine is different. The life-provider of a human is a very valuable medicine. The life-provider of an animal or a tree is hardly a valuable medicine. A tree's medicine makes it grow and lengthens its treetops. It is impossible for the tree to make itself go far away. Who would see a tree withdraw from where it was standing, fleeing far when it sees the ax when you go to cut it? When would a tree cry out as you cut down its body? A tree does not walk, nor cry out when it is cut; however, an animal walks, flees when it is chased, and cries out when wounded. . . . An animal's life-provider is a medicine of at least a little value, because it causes it to leave. One knows by means of it all that which tastes and smells good and, equally, that which tastes and smells bad. The life-provider of humans is valuable, as, equally, are those of spirits. It is extremely valuable, the life-provider of spirits, more valuable than the lives of humans. (630:11–16, 631:1–3)

Despite the extensive use of the term *our medicine* in Jesuit writing, it seems never to have become a major term used by the Huron, Wyandot, or other Iroquoians in their more traditional stories and ceremonies. It never appears in Barbeau's extensive Wyandot mythology, recorded early in the twentieth century, and is likewise absent in twentieth-century writings in the languages of the Iroquois. Perhaps J. N. B. Hewitt, a Tuscarora anthropologist who worked for the Bureau of American Ethnology, best captured the fate of this term in an 1895 article about the soul concept among the Iroquois: "The word, on-non'-kwa't, in the modern acception of the term, signifies 'medicine', whether it be something used on account of inherent value, or it be something used according to the arts of sorcery. In archaic usage it is found to be a name of the soul" (Hewitt 1895:113).

Another of the terms for the soul that Brébeuf mentioned was *khiondhecwi*, which was used "in so far as it merely animates the body and gives it life" (JR10:141). This term, *tionnhek8i* in the dialect in which *De Religione* was written (see Steckley 1997), means 'it is that which is instrumental to our living, that which provides us with life' and is often translated in related languages as 'our life-provider' or 'our sustenance'. In traditional Iroquoian culture, the word has an intimate connection with the food grown by these horticultural people. It is the name given to the spirits of the "Three Sisters"—corn, beans, and squash (Chafe 1961:8; Fenton 1968:47; Foster 1974:67). According to Wallace Chafe's eloquent interpretation of traditional beliefs, the Seneca believed that the function of the *tionnhek8i*, or Three Sisters, was "to contribute to people's contentment and to strengthen people's breath, breath being thought of as a basic manifestation of life" (Chafe 1961:8).

Brébeuf was initially hesitant to use this term in the expression of Christian concepts, but the Jesuits later incorporated it in a way that showed a degree of cultural resonance between Jesuits and the Huron. Both of these points can be illustrated in the Jesuits' evolving translation of the part of the Lord's Prayer that goes, "Give us this day our daily bread." Brébeuf, in the Ledesma catechism, initially used a literal translation: *onendatara* 'our bread'. In a version of the prayer said to have been written in the 1670s by Father Chaumonot, the Hechon of that time, we see the usage of the two Huron spiritual concepts "our medicine" and "our life-provider" (the pronominal prefix is the first person exclusive instead of the usual inclusive; the English translation is mine):

ta[ı]8annont	asken	edentate	ondaie	d'
[give us	let it is	this day	it	that which]

ora8enstak8i	n'	on[ı]8ennonk8at	ta[ı]8annont
[it is an instrument of goodness[39]	that which	it is our medicines	give us]

iθondi	d'	ate8entaıe	d'	aionnhek8i.
[also	that which	every day	that which	we live by means of it]

[Give us this day that which puts our medicine in a good state. Give us also, every day, that which makes us live.] (Wilson 1884:102)

In *De Religione*, we find that *life-provider* is used virtually interchangeably with *medicine*, as can be seen in the passage from pages 630 and 631 quoted earlier.

Spirit

As Algonquian languages have the term *manitou*, so Iroquoian languages have their near equivalent in the verb root that appears in Wendat as *-aki-* 'to be a spirit'. Potier's dictionary includes an extensive entry on this verb root. It is again worthwhile quoting the dictionary entry at length, first for the meaning given to the word and then for illustrations, because it is exhaustive in its citation of the uses to which Huron put the term. Of significance here is that it refers to both "good" and "bad" spiritual forces:

aki . . . etre un esprit, un ange, un demon, avoir un pouvoir au dessus de toute la nature corporesse . . . avoir q. bonne ou mauvaise qualité, talent, pouvoir, merite, extraordinaire, avoir des biens du corps, de l'esprit, de la fortune au dessus des autres [to be a spirit, an angel, a demon, to have a power over all corporal nature . . . to have some extraordinary good or bad quality, talent, power, or merit, to have qualities of the body, of the spirit, or fortune over those of others] . . . un principe, un cause secrette et inconnu qui produit q. effet merveilleux, rare, miraculeux, prodigieux, soit pour faire du bien ou du mal, q. qualité, maligne ou bienfaisante, comme venins, poissons [sic], sortileges & [a principle, a secret and unknown cause that produces some effect that is marvelous, rare, miraculous, prodigious, whether for doing good or bad, some quality, malignant or benevolent, such as venom, poison, spells, etc.] (Potier 1920:167)

It is evident that early on the French had a good sense of the breadth of meaning of the -aki- concept (see Champlain 1929: 143–44; Sagard 1939:117, 141, 170–71, 193, 201; Steckley 1978:97). Witness the following meanings of the word that appear in Champlain's text and observe how similar they are to what appears in Potier's dictionary:

They have indeed some regard for the Devil, or a similar name, although this is a matter of doubt because in the word they use are included different meanings and it embraces in itself several things; so that it cannot easily be known and determined whether they mean the Devil or something else, but what makes one rather believe that it is the Devil whom they mean, is that when they see a man doing something extra-ordinary, or cleverer than usual, or indeed a valiant warrior, or else infuriated as if out of his mind and beside himself, they call him Oqui [Oki], as we should say, a great well-informed mind or a great Devil. (Champlain 1929:143)

The first type of use specified in the Potier dictionary entry involves pronominal prefixes that refer to the one being talked about, as can be seen in the following set of examples. The first of my translations is from the Wendat, and the second is from the French; the asterisks are reproduced as in Potier's original text:

Hoki *c'est un hom[me] d'un rare merite
[he is a spirit]
[he is a man of rare merit]

saki eιenk *tu es un hom[me] de coeur, un heros
[you will be a spirit]
[you are a man of courage, a hero] (Potier 1920:167)

It is relatively rare that a human is referred to as "being" (rather than "having") a spirit in this way, just as it is rare that any pronoun other than the form for "he" or "she, it" is used. I believe this is because the spirit is apart from the individual, as a guardian spirit. The Huron made extensive use of metaphor, as we have seen concerning "our medicine." I believe that calling something a spirit is just such a metaphor, one I have yet to encounter in any of the Jesuits' religious works concerning any Christian person.

The second type of example is much more common. The human is referred to separately; the pronominal prefixes relating to the human appear in the other verbs in the sentence, not in -aki-, because the spirit and the human are separate. Again, translation from the Wendat precedes translation from the French:

Oki isaton *tu es devenu extraordinaire
[it is a spirit, you have become something]
[you have become extraordinary]

okiιe haon chieraθa *tu te serts de sortileges
[from a spirit, you make it with something]
[you make use of spells]

oki hatechiaθa /v saιochiaθa *C'est un sorcier q[u]i tue le
   monde par ses sortileges

[it is a spirit, he terminates by means of it, he terminates them
    by means of it]
[it is a sorcerer who kills people by spells] (Potier 1920:167)

The relationship between this spirit and a human is perhaps best
described in the phrase *oki andaérandi,* which the Jesuits used to
refer to a person's "familiar demon" (see, for example, JR10:167,
33:193, 39:21). The phrase first appears in the previously quoted
passage from Brébeuf's chapter in the Jesuit Relation of 1636, in
which he listed terms for the soul: "in so far as it is possessed of
reason, [it is called] *oki andaérandi,* 'like a demon, counterfeiting a
demon'" (JR10:141). Brébeuf was attempting to say something that
was later recorded in Jesuit dictionaries in entries such as the following (my translation from the Wendat again precedes my translation from the French):

oki handaterandi   il a un demon familier qu'il imite
[it is a spirit, he imitates, copies it]
[it is a familiar demon that he imitates] (HF65:102; cf. HF62)

The phrase appears again, but in a slightly different form, in the
Jesuit Relation of 1639, in which Father Jerome Lalemant wrote
about dream desires, stating: "And, in fact, if you ask, from him
who desires in this manner, what is the cause of the desire, he
makes no answer except, '*ondays ihatonc oki haendaerandic,*' 'the
thing under the form of which my familiar Demon appeared to me,
gave me this advice'" (JR17:155). Lalemant was attempting to write
a phrase that in the dictionaries would have appeared as *ondaie ihatonk oki hatendaerandik,* meaning 'this is what he says, the spirit who
imitates me'. Having the spirit imitate the human perhaps suggests
the notion of "spiritual double" that Barbeau referred to for the
Wyandot concept in the early twentieth century.
    To get a better sense of the relationship between the spirit and
human beings that is being described here, it is useful to learn more
about the verb root *-ndater-.* Although it can be literally translated as
'to copy, to imitate', as I have done in translating *De Religione* (643:18,
655:5, 660:17, 667:18), there is more to the meaning than that. We can
see this in the dictionary entry given for the verb root when it takes
the semireflexive prefix *-e-* and the causative suffix *-a't-:*

se faire une regle de q.c., prendre q actuellement pour regle, pour principe de sa conduit, pour 1er mobile des ses actions, s'en rapporter a lui, le prendre pour chef, capitaine, maitre . . . item attendre q, attendre les ordres, la vanue, la presence pour agir . . . prendre q.c. pour regle . . . avoir q.c. pour regle [to make it a rule to do something, to take someone presently for a model, for a principle of one's conduct, for the prime mover of one's actions, to rely on, put one's faith in someone, to take him for chief, captain, master . . . also, to wait for someone, to await the orders, the coming, the presence of someone in order to act . . . to take something for a model, to have something as a model] (Potier 1920:274)

Whereas most examples of this combination refer to political leaders, perhaps a preoccupation or bias of the hierarchically minded Jesuits, the following sentences, taken from the same entry, tell us that the meaning goes beyond the merely political. That which is designated by the verb form -enda ιera't- is shown in italics:

asχ8aθas onι8endaιerati de 8endat d'onn'aonχichien
un tems de soleil de pluie *est un presage ordinaire* à nous autres Huron que nous bientot etre tues. [A time of sun and rain together *is a common omen* to our other Huron that some of us have just been killed.]

Taoten chiendaιeraθa d'ichiatonk achietek eιa8asθa?
quelle *regle as tu* pour dire qu'il fera demain beau tems. [What is *the principle you use* to say that tomorrow the weather will be good?] (Potier 1920:275)

The spirits send signs, particularly in dreams, which humans are waiting to see and to act out or "copy" exactly. Interestingly, in *De Religione* Pierson has God telling the Iroquois not to copy spirits in this way (643:18), whereas he states that the Jesuits want the Iroquois to copy them in such a fashion (655:5).

As Champlain's reference to the devil in the previously quoted passage (Champlain 1929:143) suggests, early missionaries faced a dilemma concerning the use of the verb -*aki*-. With its combined "good" and "bad" spheres of reference, should it be used only to refer to the devil and his demons, linking them with traditional Huron spirituality, or could it also be used to refer to "good" Christian spirit entities? Both Sagard and Brébeuf appear to have struggled with this dilemma.

Although Sagard conceded that the verb could be used when speaking of a "great angel" (Sagard 1939:170), in his phrasebook he used it solely in referring to the devil:

> Le Diable en a peur, a peur de cela. [The devil is in fear, has fear of that.]
> Oki atandique. [It is a spirit, it fears something.]
> Le Diable ne craint point les Huron. [The devil does not fear the Huron.]
> Oki téatandique d'hoüandate. [It is a spirit, it does not fear it, the Wendats.]
> Les François ne craignent point le Diable. [The French do not fear the devil.]
> Téhoätanique otignonhaque oki. [They do not fear, they are French, it is a spirit.]
> La demeure du Diable est sous la terre, dans la terre. [The living place of the devil is under the earth, inside the earth.]
> Oki ondaon ondechon. [It is a spirit, it has a place, inside the country, earth.] (Sagard 1866:143)

Similarly, Brébeuf wrote in 1635 concerning the way the verb was potentially useful in communicating about God. He began by talking about the Huron's reaction to French technology:

> It would be impossible to describe the astonishment of these good people, and how much they admire the intelligence of the French. But they have said all when they have said they are *ondaki* ['they (feminine) are spirits'],[40] that is, Demons; and indeed we make profitable use of this word when we talk to them: "Now, my brothers, you have seen that and admired it, and you think you are right, when you see something extraordinary, in saying *ondaki*, to declare that those who make so many marvels must be Demons. And what is there so wonderful as the beauty of the Sky and the Sun? What is there so

wonderful as to see every year the trees almost dead during the Winter, all bare and disfigured, resume without fail, every Spring, a new life and a new dress? The corn that you plant rots, and from its decay spring up such beautiful stalks and better ears. And yet you do not say, 'He who made so many beauties, and who every year displays before our eyes so many marvels, must be some beneficent *oki*, and some super-eminent intelligence.'" (JR8:111)

But in the Ledesma catechism and in the prayer he presented in the 1636 Relation, Brébeuf, like Sagard, focused on the devil-demon side. In the former, he used the phrase *ondaki ondatoatacoüa* to refer to the "tentations du diable." This Wendat phrase translates as 'they are spirits, they penetrate bodies'. The noun and verb combination in the second word involves *at* 'body' and *oıat* 'to penetrate' (Potier 1920:404). In Potier's representation of this verb, sexual acts are highlighted, but I believe that what Brébeuf was more concerned about here was demon possession. In his 1636 prayer, he translated the combination as follows (JR10:70):

le demon	noun prouoque
[the demon]	[provokes us]
oki	esoniatoata
[it is a spirit]	[it will penetrate us][41]

Although he freely used -*aki*- to refer to such negative spirits, Brébeuf was initially reluctant to extend his use of the term to the Christian notions of guardian spirits and the Holy Ghost. He misused the verb root -*sken*- 'to be a manifestation of humans after death, particularly, but not exclusively, bones' to serve that purpose. Perhaps one reason for this misuse was his hesitancy to use -*aki*-.

In *De Religione* we find that Brébeuf's reluctance no longer applied. Pierson used -*aki*-, with the addition of the noun-verb combination -*at*- 'body' plus -*toıe(n)*- 'to be certain, true', in referring to the Holy Ghost: *hoki daat hoatatoıeti* (629:2, 3) 'he is a spirit, the very, he is a true, certain body'. Likewise, with some form of *ıaronhi-aıeronnon* 'it is a person of the sky', -*aki*- is used to refer to guardian angels (634:5). The negative reference to demons is maintained, for he used *ondechonronnon* 'it is a person of inside the earth' with *-aki-* to refer to the demons whose tempting words are intended to counter those of the guardian angels (634:7).

The Mohawk cognate of *oki* is *otkon*. References to the term in the ethnohistorical literature show that it had a meaning very similar to that of *oki* (Bruyas 1970:36, 38, 94, 98, 120, 122; Chafe 1961:8; Fenton 1968:27; Michelson 1973:34). In the following passage from Hewitt, we see that in terms of its Christian use, the Mohawk cognate followed the same path as that of its Wendat equivalent. In his discussion of the meaning of *otkon*, Hewitt wrote the following:

> The term has found a peculiar use in a translation of the Gospels by one Joseph Onasakenrat into the Iroquois [i.e., Mohawk] tongue[42] . . . where it is employed to translate Spirit and Holy Spirit; this is done also in a Mohawk Catechism by the Abbe F. Piquet. . . . In both it is made the equivalent of the English 'spirit' and in both Holy Spirit or Holy Ghost is rendered *Rotkon* [cognate of the Wendat *hoki*], 'he, a human being, is an *otkon*', modified by *Roiatatokenti* [cognate of the Wendat *hoiatatoιe'ti*], or by *Ronikonratokenti* [cognate of the Wendat *hondiιonratoιe'ti*], 'his mind is holy'. (Hewitt 1928:609)

It is also important to note that the traditional use of *-aki-* among the Huron had not changed much for the Wyandot elders whom Marius Barbeau interviewed early in the twentieth century, as can be seen in his description of the Wyandot's use of *uki,* their dialect version of *oki.*

> The uki are essentially supernatural beings endowed with "powers" either harmful or useful to man. A magnified personal "double," it is believed, exists at the head of almost every species of animals and plants, the main external features of which it retains. Rivers, rocks, and other natural objects, moreover, possess similar personal souls or spirits. Held in reverence or dreaded on account of their "powers," they are not all considered as enjoying the same standing. Most of the uki dwelling in rivers, plants, and rocks are considered as benevolent or harmless; and they are only occasionally propitiated or given offerings. The animal uki and the monsters are

either the friends or the enemies of the Wyandot. . . . The friendly uki are, as a rule, the supernatural guardians of individuals, clans, and societies . . . The uki whose function it is to appear to individuals during the puberty seclusion are classified by some informants into approximately the following hierarchy: the Eagle, the Raven, the Otter, the Buzzard . . . and others down to the wild fowl. These . . . supernatural helpers extended their good offices usually to their protégés individually or, in some cases, to a group of people who thereby became a new clan or a society. (Barbeau 1915:9)

We can see, then, that despite the Jesuits' ambivalence concerning the *aki* concept, it showed a resilience that persisted beyond the mission period. The guardian spirit of Wendat speakers remained connected with the word itself in the thinking of the people even into the twentieth century.

A NOTE ON THE JESUITS' WRITING CONVENTIONS

In the Jesuits' written transcriptions of Iroquoian languages, as reproduced in this book, the superscript ' represents pre-aspiration (rather like the *h* in "hat") when it appears before a consonant. The Greek letter theta, θ, represents *t* plus post-aspiration (again like an *h*, but this time following the consonant). The character 8 represents a sound like the *u* in "lute" when it precedes a consonant and a *w* sound when it precedes a vowel. The digraph *ch* represents the sound normally spelled *sh* in English, and the Greek χ, chi, represents a *kh* combination. The ι, or Greek letter iota, signifies a *y* sound, as does *j*. An *n* after a vowel indicates a nasal vowel.

De Religione

THE NATURE OF GOD, PLANTS, ANIMALS, HUMANS, AND SPIRITS

Page 629

1   aierih8iost ichien aiaɩenrhon s'aatat ha8endio st'aɩionnhe di8 haatsi._

2   oten de di8 haatataɩe achink ihennon skat ichien ondaie de saɩ[e]n oten de skat honaen d'achink atonθa hoki daat hoatatoɩeti aat._

3   stan achink te hennon d'ha8endio ti tionnhe skat ichien ha8endio atiaondi._

4   ondaie ha8endio ti tionnhe de saɩoen, ha8endio iθondi honaen ha8endio iθondi d'[h]oki daat hoatatoɩeti[1]

5   ondaie io'ti st' es[']aatat, de skat hennonhe'k8i, shotindiɩonrat iɩen ehendas ichien, ehotindiɩonras, ehatindaɩ8ras a8[e]ti:

6   ondaie ati hati8eɩinnen sθ' onteiennonniahak ɩaronhia din n' ondecha, a8eti de steniesθa iotierannon. aioɩenronj ati sti haat8ten de di8?

7   hoki ichien iɩen daat echi es[']okichatoɩeti aat._

8   i8aia θo onek te hierontra n'onɩ8ennonk8at: te k8atatoχa n' ondaie;

9   k8aata8eti iɩentron n' onɩ8ennonk8at ta ti θo iθondi io'ti de di8, ondecha8eti ihentron, oɩont ichien te hek8aɩenk,8ade hoki._

10 steniesθa te ɩandarek._ ondaie ichien hek8aɩente'θa de steniesθa hochonniannon chi hentron a'son te ondechatek, a'son te ɩaronhiatek, a'son onta chi te hentron?

11 taot ichien aia8endinnen, ahoteiennondinnen a8eti onta chi te hentron?

12 taoten eχa haoten ahaerat isen ichien st' ahachonniannon

In the following transcription of *De Religione,* colons in Pierson's Wendat text function simply as punctuation markers and do not indicate vowel length. The latter convention was not developed until much later. The notation /v indicates that an alternative phrase is being presented. An underline at the end of a sentence simply reproduces a line Pierson drew in that position.

THE NATURE OF GOD, PLANTS, ANIMALS, HUMANS, AND SPIRITS

Page 629

1   Those who would make the matter great, [who would] be believers, should think that the Great Voice in our lives,[2] he who is called God,[3] is one body.

2   However, God is three together: one is he who has them as children; one is he whom they have as child; the third is he who is a very true spirit.

3   He is not three gathered together. The Great Voice in our lives is one completely.

4   He is the Great Voice in our lives, he who has them as children. He is the Great Voice also, he whom they have as child. He is the Great Voice, too, he who is a very true spirit.

5   It is as if he is one in body, and they are one life-provider and one mind.[4] They all have the same mind and power.

6   They were all together as they made with skill the sky, the earth,[5] and all kinds of things. Would it be unimportant that God is such?

7   He is a spirit, a very true spirit.

8   In a small way, he and our medicine have a similar form.

9   Our medicine dwells in every part of us, even if we do not recognize it. That is like God dwelling over all of the earth; it is not important that we do not see him, as he is a spirit.

10 We know him by means of the many things he has made. At a time when he existed, the earth, the sky, all kinds of things did not exist.

11 How would he have created all things if he did not exist at the same time?

12 What would he use, as he made everything?

13 te hoerati te ιaentak andi ahatatia θo ara, chia θo aaꝹenk._
14 iskꝹerhe ati oιenron d' ahachonnia?
15 stan nondaie θo ara te hochondi de kꝹaιenhonk deχa te
    onιꝹaιakandennha, etsak etsak iθochien dꝹa
    hoteiennonniannon de te kꝹaιenk

Page 630

1 hoteiendaιate ndaoten haꝹendio sθ' oteiendichiaιi de sten
   ioterannon te Ꝺarati atiaondi ti ιaιe de hoteiennondi de sten
   akꝹten._
2 Ꝺa de aιonnhe ichien, oten dꝹa stan te aιonnhe._
3 oꝹhista,[6] ιariota te Ꝺennonnhe ιaronta ιaio n'onꝹe din n'ondaki
   ennonnhe.
4 achink ati iꝹatihꝹatsiraιe io'ti d' ennonnhe:
5 Ꝺa iθochien a te ꝹennonnhꝹtens aꝹeti, ιerohꝹi, achie, din de sten
   akarontꝹten, skat aιonkꝹatsironnia; ondaie ati
   skontonnhatierens._
6 ιahꝹentaιιaio Ꝺa skonkꝹatsirichias, aιerhon chia te
   ꝹennonnhataaꝹenk:
7 onιꝹe din d'hoki achink atonθa enditiokꝹichias de Ꝺa ionnhꝹten._
8 achink ati iꝹennonnhaιe d' aιonnhonkꝹannion, ιaꝹeti de sten
   iotierannon._
9 ιaronta de skat ionnhe; ιaio tendi atonθa din de ιahꝹenta,
   achink atonθa n'onꝹe din d' aιoki d'aιonnhe
10 Ꝺa iθochien a te onnhꝹten aꝹeti d' achink iιaιe.
11 Ꝺa ichien ionnon'kꝹachꝹten d' onnhe'kꝹi ιaronta, Ꝺa iθondi d'
   onnhekꝹi ιaio, Ꝺa iθondi ennond d' aιonnhekꝹi n'onιꝹe din
   d'aιoki / v Ꝺa iθondi onnonkꝹachennon._
12 chieιannen ionnonkꝹachandoron d'aιonnhe'kꝹi n'onιꝹe; te
   ιandoron θo aat ti onnonkꝹachꝹten de ιaio onnhekꝹi din de
   ιaronta._
13 ιaronta de ondaie iθochien onnonkꝹachaen d' atatentꝹ'ta chia
   d' atatrenhestakꝹa, stan te Ꝺatonk de chi aꝹatrontaιendist._
14 tsinnen atichien oka'kꝹi akataꝹa ιaronta chi oteꝹanhatie d'onn'
   aꝹachaιen d' achrontiatande?

13 There was nothing for him to make things with. He just spoke, and then something happened.

14 Do you think that it is of little importance, then, that which he made?

15 They are not the only things he made, the many things we see when our eyes move from side to side. Many other things he made we do not see.

Page 630

1 The Great Voice has an abundance of ability, as he made all kinds of things, too numerous to be counted.

2 Some live; others do not live.

3 Metal, stone do not live; trees, animals, humans, and spirits live.

4 It is as if there are three lineages of those who live.[7]

5 The lives of oak, ash, and every kind of tree make one lineage. They resemble each other in their lives.

6 Fish and animals make another family, as they have equal lives.

7 Humans and spirits make a third lineage, as another kind of life.

8 Three lives, then, are the life-providers for all things that are made.

9 Trees are one kind of life; animals and fish are a second, and humans and spirits are a third life.

10 Every kind of life is of three sorts.

11 It is a medicine of a particular nature, that which provides life for a tree. It is another way, that which provides life for an animal. They are different, too, those who provide life for humans and spirits; the medicine is different.

12 The life-provider of a human is a very valuable medicine. The life-provider of an animal or a tree is hardly a valuable medicine.

13 A tree's medicine makes it grow and lengthens its treetops. It is not possible for the tree to make itself go far away.

14 Who would see a tree withdraw from where it was standing, fleeing far when it sees the ax when you go to cut it?[8]

15   annen haonιe ati ataionsenχ8ik ιaronta sθ' achrao de ιaeronιe?
16   stan ichien te 8es ιaronta, stan ta te 8asenχ8as d'onn'
     a8atrontiaj._ oten de ιaio i8es ichien, ate8as d'onn' aιonatoia,
     te 8asenχ8as onn' aιonasteraj._

Page 631

1   ιandoron ati i8aiationnonk8ach8ten deιaio onnhe'k8i, 8ade
     arask8aθa n'ondaie, ιatoιaθa a8eti d'oιa8asennik chia d'
     otsi8as._
2   ιandoron ti aιonnhek8i n' onι8e chia d' aιoki._
3   nien aat ondaie chi tsonderati ιandoron ti 8ennonnh8ten
     n'ondaki ιaro ιandoron st' aιonnhe d' aιon8e._
4   ondaki de te oti8atsore, te 8endiheons, te ontonrichesθa te
     8atiatand8sta oten n' endi a8entenhaon onι8annonh8as,
     k8atonrichesθa, k8aatand8sta,
5   ahente ti k8es eχ' ondechate, aιerhon onχιιenk:
6   ondaki teιontιιenkιonek inde steniesθa te otiatori
     d'aιonatiatatoιat;
7   stan te otiatataιi de sten ak8aten d' aiaιenhaon χa ichien
     i8atiat8tens;
8   stan ichien ιatsihenstatsi te 8atiatontak8i, te 8atienteri
     n'ondientatsi aiotik; aiotsichratsi, otsing8aratsi a8eti, ara
     iθochien ti ondaki._
9   n'onι8ennonk8at skontierens, te ιonaιenk._
10   i8atiache de k8aeronιe, a8aton d' ationtatendiaj, a8aton d'
     ationtatiaχaska 8ade 8atsek te k8achitont dinde te
     k8aιonresont._
11   skat ara t'aiesachitiaj t'aιiateχaska n' ondaie de chieronιe._
12   te 8atonk steniesθa d' achieχaska d' oki ιaatataιe, onek ati ta te
     8achitont, ta te ιaonresont ara iθochien ti ιaata8eιi ti ιentron;
     skat iθochien ιaatonta'k8i._
13   etsak iaon tionnhe'k8i de tionι8e osk8enha, onda8a, a8eiachia,
     ιang8enia a8eti:
14   oten d' oki aonh8a iθochien ondiιonra onnhek8i, ara iθochien
     ondiιonra ti ιen d'oki._
15   onι8aataste de tion8e, [a]ι8andoronk ichien d8a de chi aι8eti,

15 When would a tree cry out as you cut down its body?
16 A tree does not walk, nor cry out when it is cut; however, an
    animal walks, flees when it is chased, and cries out when
    wounded.

Page 631

1   An animal's life-provider is a medicine of at least a little value,
    because it causes it to leave. One knows by means of it all
    that which tastes and smells good and, equally, that which
    tastes and smells bad.
2   The life-provider of humans is valuable, as, equally, are those
    of spirits.
3   It is extremely valuable, the life-provider of spirits, more
    valuable than the lives of humans.
4   Spirits are not covered with flesh. They do not die, starve, or
    get cold, whereas we are continually sick, starve, and are
    cold.
5   It is evident, as we walk around this earth, because we are seen.
6   Spirits are not seen because they are not covered with anything
    by which they are perceived.
7   They are not colored in any way so one would say, "They have
    this appearance."
8   They are not called charcoal [i.e., black] in appearance. They
    are not known to have been called snow [i.e., white], red, or
    green; they are only spirits.
9   They resemble our medicine in not being seen.
10 Our body goes to be cut, our fingers cut off. They are
    separated, our feet and our hands.
11 One of your feet would be cut off, separated from your body.
12 It is not possible for you to separate anything from the body of
    a spirit, because it does not have feet or hands. It is all
    together, existing as one.
13 Many things together provide life for we who are humans:
    liver, lungs, heart, and blood.
14 But the sole life-provider of a spirit is its mind; the mind only
    is the spirit.
15 We humans have heavy bodies; we find it difficult to go far
    away.

16 te e8atonk e8a d'a8eniete k8esichia ek8askoha θo, onta iaiete
    k8aatitaties;
17 oten n' ondaki i8atihensaienha: te otiataste i8aia._
18 atistiaronk ndaotente oatandore d'oskennonton, otichiaen,
    otironties oatakaen d'iok8as; ondaki atiaondi atistiaronk;
19 ondaie i8aia te iaerontra d'onn ak8endih8en, χa iθochien
    aondesa, chi aondech8trak iondecha8eti

Page 632

1 ondaie iθondi skatieren d' oki orak8annentaii chieiannen
   ontaiarak8ingenha d'onne tont8entaronh8en chi'atiorhatej
   iaon n' ondecha8eti st'ontaiarak8ingenha
2 a8enstran de chieiannen aontaiondechentaj, oiont ichien
   aoienka aiodechaienteson d' orak8t._
3 ontaiarak8ingenha θo ara, onne ondecha8eti aiarak8innion te
   onniandis._
4 i8aia n'ondaie θo atiaondi io'ti d' oki aioiaenk aθo ara d'
   annia'ten, onne ichien iaon de θo._
5 k8aatatentsi [d]e tion8e etsak iθochien oni8atiatandik d'onne
   chi eoni8aiaens 8ade oni8atonda8eiindik
6 anniaten ik8erhe θo sen te 8aieti din d' ek8erhon aiendi sen de
   chi atik8aatandiraha iθochien._
7 a8aton atichien iannonskon t'aetion d' a'son aiotennhotonk?
8 stan te saataechendi!
9 oten d' oki steniesθa te oataes, stan ta teiaatandiras stan
   steniesθa te otiatandik:
10 anniaten aioaienk oki chi aiontarati, chia aiotontarorik
   a8entenhaon, stan orast te ontontaraentandihend._
11 iannonskon aientrontaj d' oki chia chiennhotonnon,
12 achierhon aiotendoronk8en onsaiaiendi;
13 ichien stan ichien orast te onnonsk8eiindihend aonsaiaienha
   ichien oiont stan te iannhoandindi._
14 iannonskon achiatatia desa ontaiannonchia'ra'k8at de
   chie8enda; d'onn' achiak8endondat, aste ona'ti
   achie8ennoniok, ta ti te stonchiaraχend

16 It is not possible for us, also, to go on the water, for we would fall in if we were not traveling in a canoe.

17 But spirits are light, nimble; they are not even a little bit heavy.

18 They are very fast. Deer do not go fast; birds are slow; the wind is slow. Spirits are the ones who go fast.

19 It somewhat resembles the way light illuminates; in a short space of time it crosses the entire earth.

Page 632

1 A spirit and a sunray resemble each other greatly when day commences, because at the same time, it becomes light all over the earth when the sunray travels outward.

2 However great the earth would be, nevertheless, a sunray would go over all the earth.

3 When a sunray goes out, it is only a short time before it penetrates the whole world.

4 It is a little like that with a spirit, who would be anxious to go somewhere, and then, behold, it is there.

5 We humans have thick bodies. Frequently we are stopped when we are anxious to go, because a place is closed to us.

6 Sometimes we wish, "Let me go there," and we will wish, "Let us pass by before it becomes too narrow for us."

7 Would it be possible for us to enter a house when still the door is closed?

8 Would you not have run into something?

9 But a spirit does not run into anything. Nothing is too narrow for it, and nothing stops it.

10 Sometimes a spirit would go out, [and] cross to the far side of a lake, which would be continually agitated, not at rest.

11 Inside a house a spirit would be situated. At the same time, you have closed the door.

12 You would think, "It would be difficult for it to go out again."

13 Still, the house would not have been closed to it. It would go out again, nevertheless, the door not having moved.

14 In the house you spoke and your voice penetrated the house. When you spoke loudly, your voice penetrated to the outside, even though you would not have gone through the house.

15 aιarak8taha te ιannonchiaharen o8hista etio8histarah8i,
16 stan te orak8aes d'o8hista, ontaιarak8innion iθochien 8histaιon
 ta ti te 8histaιetsi:
17 θo ati io'ti d'oki ak8atatiatonιotak iθochien n'ondechon, de
 t'a8erhon ataιaton dechonιotak
18 stan te oataechend etiondecha chieιannen ondechatentsi._
19 χondaie i8atiat8ten n'ondaki chieιannen iιaonι8ah8ichennions
 de tion8e

Page 633

1 ak8etonk de k8aeronιe i8erhe aιatonnhia8ist i8aia
 aonsaionιienteha de χeena d' onn' e8aιiheonk;
2 i8erhe areisaιen de k8aeronιe aonsaιonnhontie i8aia eatataιe de
 χeena ennonchien eιatentonnia ιarih8a8eti._
3 oten n'ondaχi stan te ondakaratati d' ak8eton;
4 te 8endiheons aat de ondaie, d' a8enderhon tsa'ten sen te
 sk8aιonnhont d' e8aιiheonk;
5 stan te chi 8atindare n' ondaki st' a'son te ondechatek: di8
 ichien haonh8a aondechenhaon aθatien._
6 oten de chi aondechontie d' a8ask8ake ona'ti st'a8ennonhontie
 n'ondaki:
7 stan ιandaι8ra te ιen sti 8ennonhonιaste, stan steniesθa te
 otiohe._
8 ondaie iθochien ara ahaιondaι8raha daat ha8endio, te herhe, te
 ιaιechia[ι]isen;
9 ta ti n'ondaie te herhonde, 8ade eθorih8ichiaj, sθ' aιonatondi,
 ha8eri aat aιonton a8ennonnhek8ik aθo aondechenhaon;
10 chia te hoteiennondi ha8endio ιaronhia din n'ondaki,
 onditiok8annen ndaoten d' haιontichia[ι]i;
11 stan θo te onι8entio'k8a de tion8e._ a'son n'endi te k8andarek,
 onne ahaιonatichien n'ondaki._
12 aionιenronj atichien tihondiιonr8ten d' ha8endio st'
 ahaιonatichien?

15 A sunray appears, if a house had holes where glass is inserted.
16 The sunray does not strike against the glass when it enters inside the glass, even if the glass is not damaged.
17 It is like a spirit penetrating inside the earth by wishing, "I would penetrate the earth."
18 It would not have struck against the earth, even where it is of great thickness.
19 This is the nature of spirits; greatly do they surpass in force we who are humans.

Page 633

1 One who gives birth with our body wishes, "My life should be extended a little; my days should be carried again by my children when I have died."
2 It wishes, "My body should continue to live again, even a little, in the bodies of my children. Don't let my death be the whole matter."
3 But spirits do not have the caring responsibility of one who bears children.
4 They do not die wishing, "Let someone bring me back to life when I die."
5 Spirits did not exist while still there wasn't an earth. God alone is eternally placed there.
6 But after the world began, the lives of spirits began.
7 Because they have a strong life force, there is no power, nothing that will kill them.
8 The Great Voice only has power over them, if he wished, "Let me kill them."
9 However, he will not wish it, for when he finished making them he wished, "They should provide life forever."
10 The Great Voice created the sky and spirits at the same time. The group he created was very large.
11 We humans were not numbered in that group; still we did not exist when he created the spirits.
12 Would it be unimportant that the Great Voice's mind is such, as he created them?

13 aherhonska ti honditon'ra8asti, onditiok8a8eti atannonhonsθa
   n' ondaki tarih8a8eti sken aionk8as8a aondechenhaon;
14 chia ahenhaon d'ha8endio: χa ichien hatsier de sk8aki d'
   esk8erhon aiat8ak8as8a taronhiate:
15 8a de ahona8endrak8at, oten d8a stan te hona8endrak8i;
16 onditio'k8asχ8i n'ondaie de te honatrihotati, ondaie ondakate
   d' ahonatrihotat:
17 θo haonte θo ahatonationt taronhiate honatrihotati: oten
   n'ondaie de te hona8endrak8i, ondechon te hatonatsarandi:
   θo ati akonkontak ahondechenhaon te sk8atindiatenche._
18 taont8annonh8e taronhiateronnon, enderhe onne sen te
   atok8asti n'ont8e ti a8entron
19 e8a i8ondi aherhon ha8endio aatiatora8a θo n'ondaki de ont8e
   etaatokaratatihatieska st'a'son n'ondende eenska:

Page 634
1   a te k8atateskat oki oatatoteti n'ont8atiatannondande, t'achia t'
    ek8atonnia
2   di8 ichien ihannhas ihatonk seatannonsta8a d'echiaaha onh8a
    θo aat aontonnia;
3   senditonrontraha d' ora8en aieer, tatoten eonk8as8ataronhiate
    d' eaihej
4   seatia8enratindiha d'8kaot k8e n'ondechon t'aontetsirat
    d'eerih8anderaj._
5   θo ichien i8atierha n'ondaki taronhiateronnon stan te
    aont8atiatara8andik
6   a8entenhaon taonh8ahetsaronk, tandaton iontonk: etsaton sen,
    sa8arat achiak8as8a taronhiate d' echiatonnhaten._
7   8a ichien iotinditonr8ten n'ondechonronnon ondaki: te ondaen
    d' atatenditonrachiati;
8   stan tate onk8endias d' iontonk ont8andtonraton: chrih8anderaj
    atatotenk atichien d' hatitsihenstatsi hontendot ihontonk
    n'ondechon eontetsirat atorih8anderaskon._ ondaie io'ti st'
    a8entenhaon te taont8arih8aentonk8andik ondechonronnon
9   atont8atiechandik enderhe, o ichien n'ont8e eontien taronhiate
    st' aion8atientak de χ' endi onta te ont8arih8anderatinnen
    atennen._ aiat8araha atichien?

13 He was at the point of wishing, because he had a good, beautiful mind, "I should make all spirits family. Let them be happy forever."

14 At the same time, the Great Voice said, "This you spirits do for them, if you wish, 'We should be happy in the sky.'"

15 Some followed his word; however, others did not.

16 Those who did not listen to him were a small group; those who listened to him were many.

17 At that moment, he caused those who listened to him to enter the sky; but he pushed down into the earth forever those who did not follow his word; they will not escape.

18 The sky-dwellers love us; they wish, "Let humans be as happy as we are."

19 Also, the Great Voice wished, "I chose spirits to continue to take care of humans as they walk about on earth."

Page 634

1 Every one of us has a true spirit who takes care of us from the moment we are born.

2 God requests of it, "Preserve, protect the children from the moment they are born.

3 Put into their minds the good they should do, so they'll be truly happy in the sky when they die.

4 Forbid to them that which is bad, as those who will be mistaken would suffer inside the earth."

5 This the sky-dwelling spirits do; they do not separate from us.

6 Continually, they encourage us inside, saying, "Have courage. Do good deeds. You would be happy in the sky when your life ends."

7 Otherwise are the minds of the spirits who live inside the earth, a place of mutual bad temper.

8 Their words are not cut in two when they say inside our minds, "Be mistaken. Would it be true, the story the Charcoal tell, saying, 'In the earth those who frequently were mistaken will suffer?'"[9]

9 They envy us, thinking, "Oh, humans will be placed in the sky, where we would have been placed if we had not made mistakes. Should we consent to it?"

10 enderhe eaiaι8ariskon sen n'onι8e enderhe, ennonchien
onιionh8a θo ea,8atetsirat n'ondaki:

11 ndaoten te atiskenheaθa n'ondechonronnon._

12 chia te o'tihatie θo ondak8ichotontie ιaronhiaιronnon din
n'ondechonronnon te ιaon8aaatirontonk._

13 a te k8aataιe tendi te okichandeιenhatie, anniaten iesθa ik8es
skat ιaronhiaιeronnon, skat ondechonronnon._

14 aoeren, θasken te ιaonιo8ennontraties etionι8atonnhonti.

15 i8erhe ιaronhiaιeronnon te aιoθarati sen de χeakaratati
ιaronhiaιe aχeationt eaihej

16 i8erhe n' ondechonronnon te aιorih8anderaιi sen de χenga'te
ondechon aχeatatironten.

17 onne ichien esk8arih8ateha ti 8atiat8ten n'ondaki,

18 onn'esk8andiιonratoιenk ιaronhiaιe ondak8asti d' otiatatoιeti,
ondaie de hona8endrak8i d'ha8endio;

19 ondaie ati ιaonι8annonhonk iιen._

20 sk8arih8ateri onne ondechon eondasonnenti d' atinnonk8aesa
te hona8endrak8i d' ha8endio,

21 onh8a θo aat esk8aronj, d'aιihon

22 ondaie ιaonι8atonnheskannha n'ondechonronnon, enderhe te
onι8ariskon sen n' on8e n'ondechon etioteχa._

THE BODY-SOUL DIVISION IN HUMANS

Page 635

1 onh8a de k8arih8ichiaj sen ti k8aat8ten de tion8e te8ache ti
k8a[a]t8ten, skat onι8ennonk8at, skat k8aιeronιe._

2 ιaio ichien ιi8ιei de k8aeronιe, ondaie ichien ondariskontie._

3 ιaio de ias, askennonnia aa8entondihatie._

4 endi iθondi ik8as, askennonnia aon[ι]8entondihatie._

5 atesχ8eθa de ιaio 8ade onnonh8as, te sk8atieronχ8a
d'onn'a8atiatichien, d'onne atiotonharenron._

6 atesχ8eθa de k8aeronιe onnonh8as, aro θo ti oh8ichaιenheon
d'onn' aι8atiatichien._

7 ιaio de ιenheons, otsikens, otsinnonas; ιenheons iθondi de
k8aeronιe otsikens otsinnonas,

10 The spirits wish, "Let humans go with us. Let we who are
   spirits not suffer alone there."

11 The earth-dwellers are very frightening.

12 The forces of the sky-dwellers and of the earth-dwellers
   continue to be the same as they both draw us toward them.

13 Every one of us goes about with two spirits joined together
   wherever we go: one a sky-dweller, one an earth-dweller.

14 It is customary that both of them follow us from the time that
   we are given life.

15 The sky-dweller wishes, "Let those I take care of do good deeds,
   so I would cause them to enter the sky when they die."

16 The earth-dweller wishes, "Let those I am chasing be mistaken,
   so I would entice them inside the earth."

17 Now, you know the nature of those who are spirits.

18 You are sure that in the sky, those true ones who followed the
   Great Voice's word are happy.

19 They have us as family.

20 You know that those shamans who did not follow the Great
   Voice's word fell inside the earth.

21 In a short time, you will listen to what I said.

22 The earth-dwellers bear us ill will, wishing, "Let us go together
   with humans, inside the earth where it burns."

THE BODY-SOUL DIVISION IN HUMANS

Page 635

1 Now we conclude the matter of the nature of we who are
   humans. Our nature is twofold: one part is our medicine; one
   part is our body.

2 An animal and our body are grouped with each other. They go
   about together.

3 An animal eats and slowly grows.

4 We also eat and slowly grow.

5 An animal ages and gets sick. It is no longer strong when it is
   finished, between life and death.

6 Our body ages. It gets sick. Only one's life force dies when we
   are finished.

7 An animal dies. It decays and vermin eat it. Also, our body
   decays and vermin eat it.

8 atiaondi ondariskon ιarih8a8eti de ιaio chia de k8aeronιe._

9 aontaioнι8atondorek ndaoten; θo θo ara te k8aatetsi k8aeronιe
   ondaie θo ara te k8aatontak8i de k8aeronιe

10 stan i8aia te ιaek8aιennionhend de sten ak8atiat8ten ιaio onta
    te ιannont de k8ask8aιon n'onι8ennonk8at, 8ade okiιe
    ιiaat8ten;

11 ondaie aek8atontandichen n' onι8ennonk8at aιerhon di8
    s'orensθa.

12 ondaie aat onι8arenhesθa n'onι8ennonk8at ondaie ιaio
    k8ah8ichenniaθa

13 ondaie ιehen de k8a[e]ronιe 8toιeti θo st' 8kaot i8atonk onn'
    ek8enhej oten n'on[ι]8ennonk8at di8 ichien haatataιe
    etioatontie'ti

14 chia te haιonat8tensti ha8endio n'onι8ennonk8at, din d'oki
    d'onn' ahaιonatonnia chiaιiatat io'ti d'oki din
    n'onι8ennonk8at._

15 stan n'onι8ennonk8at k8atatoka, 8ade oki sk8atieren;

16 stan chiaιat teιen n'onι8ennonk8at dinde k8aeronιe;

17 ιi8eιi ichien onek st' a'son etionnhe;

18 di8 ichien aθaιaondasonten θo haonιe iθochien
    ateιiatendasonta8a, etionιionrichenha:

19 ennonchien esk8erhon ondaie n'onh8a n'on[ι]8ennonk8at
    ιaatsi d'oechenta a8eiachia ιang8enia ndia8eraten, stan
    n'ondaie te ιen

20 oechentaιon ιaatat n'onι8ennonk8at a8eiachiaιon ιang8eniaιon

21 8a kiatennond ιa8atsa8eti n' on[ι]8ak8atsi dinde
    onι8ennonk8at._

22 ιaata8eti ιaataron ti ιaatetsi de k8aeronιe: iιentron
    n'on[ι]8askotaιon iιentron de k8askaιon a8eti a te ιentron

Page 636

1 ιaata8eti iιannont k8achie, ιaata8eti iιentron onι8aske, ιaata8eti
    iιentron k8aiske;

2 onek inde te 8atias onι8ennonk8at, stan θora te ιah8ast[a]taion:

3 stan chieιannen teιanderetsi, stan chieιannen te 8a stan te
    o8ant, d'achierhon anniaten iθochien ion[t]s[i]
    n'onι8ennonk8at

8 Completely, an animal and our body go together in this whole matter.
9 We would be worthless if our body only were the extent of our being, if we were attached only to our body.
10 We would not have surpassed, even a little, all sorts of animals if we did not have our medicine inside us, as a spirit has a twofold nature.
11 We should feel passion for our medicine, because it resembles God.
12 Our medicine stretches our treetops. It is the means by which we surpass an animal in life force.
13 What used to be our natural body becomes corrupt when we die, but our medicine comes from the body of God.
14 The Great Voice made our medicine and a spirit of an equal nature when he made them. A spirit and our medicine are equally one.
15 We do not perceive our medicine, as it resembles a spirit.
16 Our medicine and our body are not equal.
17 They are together solely while one still lives.
18 God joined them; then they are separated when our breath falls.
19 Don't think that our medicine is our brain, heart, or blood. It is not any one of those.
20 Our medicine is inside our brain. It is inside the heart and inside the blood.
21 The flesh that covers us all over and our medicine are different.
22 It is dispersed throughout the length of our body. It dwells inside our head; it dwells inside our body; it dwells everywhere.

Page 636
1 It is inside our feet; it dwells in all of our breasts. It dwells in all of our arms.
2 Because our medicine is not cut off, it is not distributed in several places.
3 Our medicine is not of the length or the width you sometimes thought it to be.

4   aoιaske iȣat, χa θo itsontsiha, endiaιe iskȣat._

5   ennonchien eskȣerhon ondaie ιȣannen d' iȣat aιoskotaιon; stan
    ichien θo te ιarihȣten._

6   ιaataȣeti iιentron deχa dind eχa stan ta te ȣatiataχaskaȣas;

7   ondaie iȣaia te ierontra kȣaȣenda;

8   θo ichien st' aιokate n' onχiatrihotas

9   oιont ichien a te onhontaιe aȣendaȣeti aιȣendinnion de
    kȣaȣenda stan chia te ιaȣendetsi θo ara te ιaȣendinnions de:
    skat dinde skat

10 θo ati io'ti n' onιȣennonkȣat

11 stan chia te ιaatetsi te iιentron kȣahȣatsaιon d' achaȣi ona'ti
    dind' etaιe ona'ti:

12 stan ichien chia te skaatetsi te skentron nien aat ιaataȣeti
    iιentron d' achaȣi ona'ti din d'etaιe

13 kȣaienhȣiti ona'ti iιentron ιaataȣeti din de tsikȣangȣati;

14 chia te iιentron kȣahȣatsaιon ιaataȣeti; ate onneaιe, a te
    otsinnonhiataιe ate endiaιe a te ohiaȣiraιe ιaataȣeti; dind
    ationtatendiaj, stan teȣatiaχend onιȣennonkȣat aȣatiataraȣa
    aȣatiatateȣa iθochien de θo aotaιe ιentrontak._

15 taot ichien haoten onιȣennonkȣat ιaatsi._

16 aȣaton ati[?]t[i] kȣatonk χondaie iιaatȣten; te eιenk ichien ondi!

17 ondaie iθochien te kȣaatoretakȣa ti ιandaιȣr kȣaataȣeti,
    n'ondaie kȣatoiannonχȣa:

18 ikȣerhe, kahachia! oki n'onιȣennonkȣat: ȣade
    ondaiekȣendiιonraentonkȣa, ondaie tsikȣehieratakȣa,
    ondaie kȣatoιaθa kȣaraskȣaθa, kȣatonieθa kȣahachonsθa
    aȣeti._

19 θo iθochien itionnhetsi, ti ondetsi de ιaatat e kȣaskaιon:

20 aιaatingenhaθo ara onne ichien ekȣa'sen: stante tsikȣatatiakιte
    tsikȣaronχa steniesθa te tsikȣateskȣaθa

21 anniaten aonιȣannonhȣaj ondaie ionniak kȣasaonkȣichiaj
    n'ontatetsentakȣa:

22 ikȣerhe aiaιȣaristen sen n' onιȣennonkȣat, kȣe de t' aιaaιenha:
    onek inde ta te tsonιȣaιakandendandend._

23 de te oaιendi, ιarihondi iθochien ιaιakarent ιahȣarinda: stan te
    skaιenk:

4   It is inside one's breast; this is again so long that at one's fingers it is again inside.

5   Don't think it is largely inside one's head. It is not such.

6   All over the body it dwells, here and there. It is not divided.

7   It appears a little like our voice.

8   There is an abundance of those who listen to us.

9   Every one of their ears is penetrated by all of our voice. The voice does not penetrate just halfway, one by one.

10   It is like how it is with our medicine.

11   It does not dwell in half the length of our body. It is inside our flesh at the top and the bottom.

12   It does not live in the middle. It dwells all over the body: at the top and at the bottom.

13   On our right it dwells, and on our left.

14   It dwells equally in all of our flesh: every nerve or vein, every finger, every toe, all over the body. And if one's fingers were cut, our medicine would not have been cut. It would have withdrawn from the place where it used to dwell.

15   What is the nature of our medicine?

16   What is said, then? We say this, "It is a body that one does not see.

17   Its power is that through which we examine it; all of our body is moved by it."

18   We think, "Our medicine is a spirit!" For with it we think, remember, know, walk away, breathe with it, and move.

19   For the length of our lives it is inside our body.

20   It leaves only when we die, when we no longer speak, hear, or smell things.

21   Whenever we are sick, it makes for us a medicine with which to cure.

22   We wish, "Let us retain our medicine so that it doesn't go out [leave], because then it would no longer go to have a look at us."

23   If it went out, it is for nothing that the eyes of a corpse are open. It does not still see.

Page 637

1 ιarihondi iθochien te 8achitont, stan te 8arask8as stanta te
sk8endioiannonk;

2 din d'achiendiatens a8aronj? aontaia8eiachenk atichien te
ιonandiandichonk8annion? a8atonnharen
t'aιonaronhiaenton! [?] steniesθa achient, aiochiatoren?

3 ιanda8ate atiaondi:

4 taot ex' io'ti n'ondaie![?]

5 ondaie de te skannont aιonnonk8at;

6 aonsa8atoiannon atichien oh8arindaιon?

7 aonsaiontatonesk8en d' aιa8enheon eeronιe?

8 ndioharon, iskatsi8aιen, itsotiatatondi d'onne ιah8arinda oton
ara iθo ti χ8ask8ahens, ara iθo ti k8atandi

9 tsinnen atichien aiaιoronhiaenton n'ontateιen ιehen, d'onn'
aιa8enheon?

10 aonsaionraθon atichien n' ontennonha ιehen?

11 aιaraha atichien d'ok8eton? te ontonk sa seindandeten de
cheena ιehen, θoia e8entaιenk?

12 taiaon ataionnonhiandij, a8erhon eonetsikenchoka._

13 aaihej iθochien n'on8e, onn'ontatesk8ahenk; k8atennontandi
iθochien aontatiatingenk, aontatennontra8hes:

14 θo atichien aier d' orast te ιannont d' aιonnonk8at._

15 ondaie ati, ti tsiatoret, ti ιandoron onι8ennonk8at;

16 aonχinnonh8eha n'on8e: ondaie onχinnonh8eθa?

17 d'ason ιi8eιi n'onι8ennonk8at k8aeronιe:

18 akiateχaska de chi onχisk8ahendi a8eti n'onχinnonhonk ιehen
a8eti d'aι8arase ιehen, d' aι8atandironha ιehen din d'
aι8atatiena ιehen._

19 stan tsaten te tsonι8annonh8e, d'onne aonι8aatonti
n'on[ι]8ennonk8at ιehen, ondaie aιondiιonrationditak
n'onι8e d'onn' onχiendiιonraentonk8ak:

20 a8atiatora8a iθochien de k8aeronιe onne ichien onχindiιonrhendi
stan te tsennonh8e de k8a8atson d' o8atsaιon._

21 aiora8en, te tsaonesk8at de k8a8atsa ιehen d'onn' aonh8a
a8aton:

Page 637

1 It is for nothing that it has feet, because it does not walk away. It no longer moves its fingers.

2 And if you called it by name, would it listen? Would it be angry if I said many insulting things to you? Would it rejoice if I flattered you? If you hit it with many things, would it feel pain?

3 Completely, not at all.

4 What is it like?

5 One's medicine is no longer inside.

6 Would it move again inside a corpse?

7 Would they again be pleased when their bodies have died?

8 Go away; it smells very bad. It was frightening when it became a corpse: we only hate it; we only fear it.

9 Who would praise those who were their same-sex siblings when they die?

10 Would those who used to be spouses again lie together?

11 Would one who has given birth consent to it if one said, "You should enfold your dead children into your robe for several days"?

12 One would be seized with fear, thinking, "They will spread their corruption to me."

13 A human being dies. Then that one is hated, hurriedly put outside and buried.

14 Would our medicine act when still it is not inside?

15 Examine our medicine, for it is valuable.

16 Humans loved us; at what time do they love us?

17 When our medicine and our body are still together.

18 After those two become separated, all those who were related to us hate us, all those who were our cousins, our opposite-sex siblings, and our children.

19 No one loves us any longer when our medicine leaves us. It took away the minds of humans when they thought of us.

20 It separated from our body and they forgot us. They no longer love our flesh: it is empty flesh.

21 That our flesh would be good would no longer please, when it becomes alone.

22 onı8ennonk8at ıehen aotachonniahak k8aeronıe ıehen ason
   ıi8eıinnen: θo θo aat a8atiataıarennia n'onı8ennonk8at, onn'
   a8atiatachat de k8aeronıe ıehen,

23 onna otsikenk, onn' aotsinnonas, onn' aıaata8iha._

Page 638

1 sk8atoχa ichien n'onh8a, ti okaochachen de k8aeronıe;
   sk8atoχa iθondi ti oatandera8ati n'on[ı]8ennonk8at;

2 sk8atrihote ti oki, ondaie ichien askennonha d' aondechenhaon
   eonnhej,

3 stan steniesθa te aon8eθa steniesθa te oios; stan atiaondi
   a8enheon te ıen._

4 aıendionratoıendi te ıenheons n'onı8ennonk8at, aıendiıon-
   ratoıendi st' eı8eθa d'onn' aχiateχaska de k8aeronıe ıehen:

HEAVEN AND HELL

5 a'son iθochien d8a te sk8arih8ateri, ti ıarih8ten deχa
   sk8a[ı]eron._

6 statrihotat ati n'onh8a, onn' aı8atendoton st' oiheratia
   n'onı8ennonk8at onn' aoatonti de k8aeronıe ıehen.

7 stan skat te ondarate d' aıonnonk8at ıehen d'onn'
   aontonnhaten n'onı8e:

8 onek ati tsaıondiıonrat te ıen st' a'son aonnhe 8ade ıaronhiaıe
   eent oten d8a n'ondechon eaıosonnent:

9 ondaie ıaronhiaıe eontienda d'aıorih8iostinnen st'
   aıonnhontiend ondaie de honachiendaentatiend ha8endio,
   a8eti de hona8endrak8ak steniesθa erih8anderask8a:

10 ondaie ıaronhiaıe eonderaθa d' aokaratatihatiend ti
    ha8end8ten de haon8entsichiaıi:

11 ondaie ıaronhiaıe eent, haaıotenrihatiend d' eesask8a, stan te
    haaıonnonkontak aıon8e, te haaıok8aeron, te haaıok8enraıi,
    te haaıonetandi, te haaıa8eiachasenni:

12 ondaie θo ara ıaronhiaıe eontondechen de ıarih8a8eti
    etsaıotatre8atik 8kaot st' a'son aıonnhek

13 aioıenronj ati st' eonk8as8a de θo a8eti eontatiataaeriθon de
    steniesθa aiontonk8andihon:

22 Our medicine completed our body when the two were still together. Immediately as our medicine withdrew, our body went bad.

23 It became rotten, and vermin ate it because it was rotten.

Page 638

1 You know now that our body is bad, corrupted. You know that our medicine is admirable.

2 You listen, as a spirit, peacefully it will live forever.

3 Nothing discourages it; nothing kills it; it does not completely die.

4 I am certain that our medicine does not die. I am certain that they two will go to such a place when they are separated.

HEAVEN AND HELL

5 Still you do not know the other matter, you who are assembled here.

6 Listen, then, while I tell you of how our medicine went straight when it left our body behind.

7 Medicines do not dwell in one place when humans' lives end.

8 They are not only of one mind as they still live, so some will go into the sky, whereas others will fall inside the earth.

9 They will be put in the sky, those who believed while they continued living, all those who honored the name of the Great Voice, and those who were with his word concerning making all kinds of mistakes.

10 They will be great in number in the sky, those who kept the word of he who created the earth.

11 They will go into the sky: those who had pity on the poor; those who did not scorn humans; those who did not kill, steal, commit adultery, or get angry.

12 They only will be put in the country in the sky, those who totally restrained themselves from being bad while still they lived.

13 Would it be unimportant, then, that they will be happy there, supplied with all that is necessary, all the things they would come to desire?

14 tsa'ten aȣatondotiest n' ondechaȣeti aıoenton daat
     aıokiıȣannen chia skat aıaen aȣenstran aiotonronton de sten
     akenkȣarȣten daat ıenkȣaraȣasti, aȣenstran aiotonronton d'
     oȣhistandoron, d' onnonkȣarȣta aȣeti._

15 stan ichien orast te ıȣannen, stan ichien deχa te
     chiechiennonnianden, ondaie aat aesanderaȣa._

16 de ıaronhiaıe a te eataıe eaıotondotaraha d' aıorihȣiostinnen
     ondaie atiaondi achiaskand de ıaronhiaıe a te eataıe
     eaıoenton._

17 chieıannen astonkonten n'ondechaȣeti ot[e]ndotarichon
     aıaoneskȣandikonȣe:

18 d'aȣentenhon te ontatechiendaenk; d' aȣentenhaon te
     ontatronhiaentonk._

Page 639

1   annen atichien acheatorenha d' aȣentenhaon
     aiesaronhiatenton?

2   stan te aıoteȣa'tandihend: ıaronhiaıe θo ara θo ontatierha._

3   te ondaen kȣ-atatennonronkȣannion, te
     ondaend'atatennonhȣendi, te ondaen d'atatechiendaen;

4   haonhȣa ichien saıoronhiaentonk haȣendio d' aıoatatoıeti
     ıehen; stan haiennentas, aȣentenhaon hachiennondiak ti
     aıonȣesennen, st'aaıotenrhak eesaskȣa._

5   aȣentenhaon sarihȣtaskaȣas ti onθaratak honachiendaenhak;
     θo ati te saıonnonronkȣannionk: ihatonk, stan te
     ȣrihȣensennihe aondechenhaon ti skaθaratandi st' a'son
     ichionnhek_

6   nda, ehenhaon, tsendaon χondaie skoneritindik: din de chi
     orachȣt at[e]ndota dindechi &._

7   ndio ȣase ehenhaon χa sen satien ti ıitron ti tiatrandeıen aat: te
     ȣastaθo chi echiatien;

8   isa ichien onsaıonchiaendaen ehenhaon onek ati de sonhȣa te
     chiakenrentak; skechiendaentatiend aȣentenhaon._

9   eıentakȣi esaıohetsaron haȣendio eıentakȣi esaıaonnharen;

10 ehenhaon onne ichien ıȣannonhonsti daak ıatoıen aat:

14 The possessions are assembled of all the earth, all the many things that they have, the very large-spirited ["rich"], and they have it as one; it would possibly be abundant, all kinds of beautiful cloth, gold, and wampum.

15 It is still not much; you would not have honored the name of that which you admired.

16 In the sky everyone who believed will put possessions up.

17 Greatly you scorn that all over the earth are spread out the possessions that please humans.

18 Continually they honor each other. Continually they praise each other.

Page 639

1 Where would you find those who would continually put you in the sky, praise you?

2 They would not tire of it in the sky, doing things only for each other.

3 There is a place of mutual greeting with respect, of mutual love, of mutual praise.[10]

4 The Great Voice alone flatters those who were true, not stopping continual praise for the generous who had pity on those in a poor state.

5 Continually it is shown to you that as they did good deeds and praised him, he greets them with respect, saying, "I will never forget your doing good for me while still you were living.

6 Come on," he will say, "Take this I am paying you back with, and far to the sky the possessions will be.

7 Come on," he will say, "Put yourself here where I reside. Let's join together. Do not put yourself far away.

8 I again praise your name," he will say. "You alone were not diminished in continually going about praising my name."

9 Continually the Great Voice will encourage them. Continually he will make them rejoice.

10 He will say, "I truly have made you related."

11 aondechenhaon ek8a8eιihatie; stan annia'ten te 8entrache te
    ι8atiatara8andihe; ao't ichien esk8aιonchiaιen, aot
    eι8annonh8eha, ao't iθondi esk8annonh8eha; aot
    esk8atratsistandihi, steniesθa aat eι8a8endaeriθe;
12 stan te sk8ate8a'tandihe aondechenhaon d'
    eι8atenrachonnionde, stan iθondi d' aιonh8a te
    8aιιιondasennihe d'eι8annontenharon;
13 steniesθa a8eti sk8achiatorhek, areisaιen, st' ason n'ondende
    itsonnhek, onh8a de te tsisk8achiatorande ehenhaon:
14 ochende sk8aθorask8a, e8aιennheιe te sk8a[at]arihenchonhonk;
    stan θo te tsisk8aata8enche, ehenhaon, stan te tsisk8aιentie
    d'aθo din d' otarihati:
15 achennonk eo'tihatie aondechenhaon θo iθochien
    esk8aatanda8ank ti onnianni stan te tsisk8aatand8stande
    stan iθondi te ondera'ti te sk8atarihatande esk8ennontie θo
    ara aondechenhaon etsak ehenhaon d'ha8endio._
16 sk8atonrichestak sk8ask8arahatak, sk8andachiatensk8a;onne
    ichien aιeιarennia nondaie; a8eti esk8annonaj θo ara chi
    eιetoj, θo haonιe θo eι8aenhas._
17 stan 8atsek te sk8andiennonhe de sten esk8atonk8en; a8eti
    ichien oerindi ti ιitron:
18 χa ichien te sk8a'k8ande, a8eti ta ti te sk8achiase;

Page 640
1   sk8akeronsk8a ehenhaon st' ondende sk8esk8a; etsiatandihik
    de sk8atriosk8a,
2   ennon te tsisk8annonhiandij, stan χa t'etietsiatichiaχon
    d'etsiesatannonhonk
3   echi onati t'etieonk aat eχa d' aιotieronnonskon;
4   ondaie iθochien etiontatiationθa ιaronhiaιe d' etsik8andiιonrak
    ιehen, ondaie d' etsionnonh8e chia de endi χennonh8e._
5   andea atichien t'aesk8arikennia n'ondaie, taot ichien
    aesk8ariho'k8en, stan χa te skandare d' otechien'ti.
6   ιande8ate atiaondi d' atatiechandi orih8a'ton d'atateiachasenni
    oteιarennion atate8end8tandi orih8endi atatak8endihatandi

11 "Always we will go about together; never will the day arrive
    when I will abandon you. Always, you will see my face.
    Always, I will love you. Always, as well, you will love me.
    Always, you will desire of me many things that I will
    furnish according to my word to you."
12 "You will never weary me when I prepare a palisade for you. It
    also will not seem much to me to give things to you."
13 "All kinds of pain you felt while you still lived on earth. Now
    you will no longer feel pain," he will say.
14 "In winter, you were cold; every summer you sweated; it will
    no longer happen to you," he will say, "You will no longer
    go about seeing cold and heat."
15 "In the middle it will continue forever. It will be warm a long
    time. You will no longer ever be cold, or be made excessively
    hot as you go about." The Great Voice will say this
    frequently.
16 "You were hungry, had a dearth [of food], were thirsty. I send it
    away; all you will desire, when I know it, I will offer it to
    you."
17 "You will not ask for anything else, for all things that you will
    desire are furnished where I live."
18 "You will intend to take all of this; however, you will not finish."

Page 640
1   "You were afraid," he will say, "while you walked on earth.
    You feared those you killed."
2   "Do not again move your scalp in fear. Those who mistreated
    you do not search for you here."
3   This is far from where they arrive, those who were frequently
    destructive.
4   They are admitted into the sky, those who were of one mind,
    those who love me and those I love.
5   Would it ever be possible that you would quarrel? What matter
    would you be divided on, for it exists here no longer, that
    which is bad, harmful?
6   Completely nonexistent is envy. It is lost, anger. It is sent away,
    speaking against others. It has ceased, blaming others.

7   ondaie iθochien aιorih8aen eronhiaιeronnon atateronhiaenton,
    atatechiendaen k8atatennonronk8annion e8a
    iontatonetsindik de steniesθa aaιoraha:

8   θo iθochien echiatonnharen de sten ehonannont de tsataχen de
    sonh8a aiesannontonhonk, aιerhon skat esk8entaj ea8enk θo
    io'ti de tseh8atsirat aιenk._

9   areisaιen ehenhaon d' ha8endio, a'son te sk8achonhatienn
    d'ora8en ti tsonn[h]ek;

10 andea iθochien stonesk8andihik ti sk8ensk8a n'ondende,
    ondaie ι8annen sk8aenterinnen d' 8kaot, i8aia θo onek
    sk8aιenhak d'onnianni, st' a'son sk8aesask8a n'ondende,

11 stanιarih8a8eti te sk8atieraχondihik d' ora8en, te
    ιiatondihendihik io'tinnen._

12 aonniannik ichien steniesθa estonesk8en aιandi8ak iθochien
    onsesatron8as:

13 aonsaonniannik aθo onne 8a ennond onsesonesk8en;
    aonda8aha θo a8ennion ichien ondaie._

14 θo iθochien aa8enche de sten aιonι8araha deχ'ondechate:
    steniesθa te ondiri steniesθa te orenh8i._

15 e8a andea [ι]entiok8a8eti te onι8entiok8arandi d'
    onniannihaton skarih8arati, onek aonι8arih8araha d'
    anniaten aonι8entenr._

16 oten deιaronhiaιe a8eti ιarih8a8eti skat eonι8atontiesten d'
    ora8en, stan skat tetio'tonk eιenk, te ιiatakonchiok ea8enk de
    tionnhesa:

17 d'ek8aak8astiska, chia te onι8araha ιannonchia8asti d'
    at[e]ndota8asti ιandiahaιa8i,

18 eskat eondatarostik / v atiaondi θo io'ti d' aiotirih8ichiaιik a8eti
    d'onniannihaton de ιaιa8i de ιa8asti eskat

19 eaonι8aronhiaenton aondechenhaon, stan t'e8atiennentache

Page 641

1   n'ondaie iondech8ten de ιaronhiaιe:

2   oeri stan te endoronk8a d8a ti ondech8ten de ιaronhiaιe te
    onskannha stan andea θo te aιondiιonraen erihondiasθa

7 It is the matter for the sky-dwellers, mutual flattery, honoring of names, greeting with respect, also mutual thanks, all kinds of things that have happened with them.

8 There you will rejoice at the things they will give you, brother. They would have given it to you, because you will have it as one. It is as if there would be one lineage.

9 The Great Voice will say, "You would not have experienced that which is good while you lived.

10 Rarely were you pleased while you walked about on earth. Greatly you were familiar with that which is bad. Too little, you saw that which is good, while you were in a poor state on earth.

11 The whole matter of that which is good was mixed for you. It was as if there were alternates.

12 It would be a long time all kinds of things would please you. Suddenly, it disappeared on you.

13 It would again be a long time when some other different things pleased you again. It passed in a short space of time."

14 All kinds of things are going to happen to us in this country. Nothing is firm; nothing is stable.

15 Also, rarely as a group did good happen to us. The only matter that happened to us was that one had pity on us.

16 However, in the sky, the whole matter is one. It will rush at us, that which is good. Not one thing will be missing. They two will see each other as reflections, the lengths of our lives.

17 We will continue to be beautiful in body. At the same time, other things will happen to us: a beautiful house, beautiful possessions, and good-tasting food.

18 Friends will continue to be completely as one. It is as if they would have decided that all which goes to be good, that which tastes good, that which is beautiful, is one.

19 They will praise us forever. Their capacity to do so will not end.

Page 641

1 That is the nature of the country in the sky.

2 Others do not value the nature of the sky-country. They do not desire it, and never think of it.

3 innonh8a deχa ιatendot sk8arihonniannonk te sk8arih8iosθa ti
ιarih8ten._

4 aiontaioνι8arask8ank atichien d' aι8atsihenstatsi chieιannen
etion8eti de ιarihondi te ιen?

5 ondaie chon oνι8aatenh8i deχa tsondechen: oνι8eri
aierih8ateha n' oνι8e d'aonh8a ιandoron._

6 aontaion ι8entrontak etionιiondechen d' otrihondi te ιen ti
ιarih8ten:

7 aioνι8ationk atichien n'oνι8at[e]ndota8an ιehen
t'aioνι8ateχaska8ank ati d'onχinnonhonk? ιanda'k8a de
aioνι8atiatra8ank atichien? aioνι8atatiesatik atichien
ιarih8a8eti din d'a['] k8as din d'iech, chia de
ιannonchia8astik, onta te oνι8andiιonratoιendi eonk8asθa
ιatoιen ιaronhiaιe d' aιoθarati n'oνι8e ιarih8a8eti
[e]ontatronhiaten aondechenhaon te tsaιochiatorande &

8 onn' arihondej st'eotiata8enk onnennonk8ak ιehen
d'ondaθaratinnen d'otirih8iostinnen._

9 annen ati nonh8a e8endet d8a te otirih8iostinnen?

10 ondechon ichien etioteχa de te 8asχ8as._

11 stan θo te ιatsi[s]t8ten n'ondechon 8teχa ti ιatsi[s]t8ten
d'etsitsistoresθa etsindask8aentonk;

12 chieιannen etiotsistannentaιi de sk8ateιaθa stan ιatsistateιen
deχa ιatsistont, ondaie aat ιatsist8tie n'ondechon 8teχa:

13 askennonia iθochien a8atsaιaiahe de sk8ateιaθa; heιenk
iθochien andiare ιaechas oecha, aonniannik ichien ιandaιon
aιahachontarhenha:

14 anniaten iθochien aotaιe onta8akonten de χa ιatsistont, χa
ichien andiare aιa8atsarit, d' a8esk8ak ichien 8atsek
aιa8atsaχe; stan andea te kachiatande, θo te ιaataιasθa
d'eeronιe,

15 d'anniaten aontatetsistorej askennonia iθochien andaιon
aιatsistontie de chi, din de chi, askennonia andaιon
aιatsistinnionhe:

16 oten n'ondechon 8teχa aoienka eata8eti atiaιoataienteson, a8eti
atiaιonneotrak a te onneaιe;

17 t'achia θ' aotsistannentaχa d'annia'ten [i]e[n][t]ron
etiaιototrande θo d'aaιotsistaraha._

18 i8aia θo onek aιatsistaen de chieronιe chia t'aιatsistariha
chiata8eti, chia aesaatateιat ataesatiatoνιotak atiaondi

3   They treat it as a made-up story. Perhaps you treat my story as made-up, not believing it is so.

4   Would we Charcoal have continued to leave from a place far away if it were just a story?

5   It brings us to your country, our wishing: "Humans should know that such a matter alone is valuable."

6   Would we live in our country if it were only a made-up story?

7   Would we arrive, separated from our possessions and those to whom we are related? Would we separate ourselves from sex, mistreat ourselves in the whole matter of that which covers [clothes] and that which one eats and one's beautiful house if we were not sure that humans who did good deeds will be truly happy in the sky, praising each other forever and no longer feeling pain?

8   I have now finished my discourse concerning what will happen to the medicines of those who performed good deeds and believe.

9   Where do they go to, the others who are not believers?

10 Inside the earth, where it burns, not being extinguished.

11 It is not such a fire there inside the earth as the fire with which you cover prisoners.

12 It is very far from the fire with which you burn. It is not the fire attached here. It burns sharply, the fire burning inside the earth.

13 Slowly, that which you burn with eats the flesh. At first, on the outside, one's skin is eaten. In a short time, the flame enters inside.

14 Sometimes, part by part this fire proceeds; first, it causes flesh to cook. Afterwards, elsewhere, flesh is about to be eaten; it will never be used up. One's body is not consumed.

15 At some time, they are covered with fire; slowly, the fire is going to continue, here and there. Gradually, the fire is going to penetrate inside.

16 However, inside the earth there is burning immediately all over one's body, going from one end to the other of every bone.

17 At the beginning, when the fire is attached, it will go from one end to the other.

18 It is little only, the fire on your body; at the same time, as the fire spreads all over your body, it would burn you, penetrating your body completely.

Page 642

1 stan t'etionda8enrente eιenk chia t'aesaatateχa a8eti de heιenk de andaιon._

2 stan θo aat te otsist8tie n'onι8at[eιa]ti._

3 etsak iθochien ondoronk n' onk8ennonχ8as oentannonen aek8aentonχ8a, ak8eθa etiohachak: oten n'ondechon 8teχa steniesθa te aon8eti._

4 ennonchien echierhon ondaie θo ara atiohachak daat otsah8i, n'ondechon

5 t'aιaentaha; chia t'aiotik aθo d'orannonen steniesθa te aιotiesde θo, aoienka aiok8ateιannon._

6 8asχ8as de χa k8ateιaθa, chieιannen aiohachand8tenk aιahach8taj, anniaten a8atonichien orast d'aionsk8at, ι8annen, iθochien aiaιondekonti a8en, onne ichien a8asχ8a._

7 oten n'ondechon etioteχa te aιondekonties aontaιanderatak ichien

8 a8enstran de ιontara8eti etiontara te aontarendi ondechon, stan ichien oιont te ιatoιandend 8teχa?

9 nien aat aιatsenh8annha aιanderatande θo t'aiohacha'k8ande:

10 din de θora te onnontacha d'ondienta te onsonnenθa d'ondechon aioιetsik atichien d' 8teχa?

11 stan te 8asχ8achend, satita8a'ten, aonh8a ichien aiondientatej n'ondienta, aonh8a aiontaratej; de ontara ιehen, din de onnonta ιehen._

12 isk8erhe ati oιenron ti ιahach8ten?

13 χa iθochien aιahachetsiska aontaιahachingenha n'ondechon, onne ichien aionιiondechaιaiahon onιiondecha8eti aoienka aiotinnontateιannon deχa onnont8tonnion._

14 hatsistannenchonk onek ha8endio, ondaie io'ti st' a'son te onιiondechaιaias._

15 oten d'i8aia θo t'ahannenchon8a ιa8atatennonten iθochien aontaιaaιenha χa iθochien aiondesa chi'aonιiondechatej stan t'ets8tej aιenk en steniesθa

16 aoha[cha]sχ8ache n'onι8ateιati, st' aosaιihatie d' onnhatont a8atennhataιasθa θo ara: onne ichien a8asχ8a d' 8teχak:

17 θo atichien aio'tik n'ondechon 8teχa?

Page 642

1 No place will be missing, as they burn you all over equally, outside and inside.
2 It is not a very piercing fire, that with which one burns us.
3 Often it is difficult to put wet firewood in a fire. We would put a stick in the fire and it will only catch fire with difficulty. But nothing stops that which burns inside the earth; it is not closed off.
4 Do not think that only very dry wood catches fire if it falls to the ground inside the earth.
5 It would be equal if wet things were left there. They would burn all over at once.
6 What we burn with here extinguishes. If a flame would have stood very high, still, at some time, one would put it out by throwing large amounts of water on it. Then it would be extinguished.
7 But where it burns inside the earth, if one threw water on it, it would augment it.
8 If a whole lake fell inside the earth, would burning not be perceived?
9 A very much augmented hearth would catch fire then.
10 And if several mountains of snow descended inside the earth, would the burning diminish?
11 It would not have been extinguished. Give up hope: snow would burn; the lake and the mountain would burn.
12 Do you think, then, the flame is insignificant?
13 The flame would be long and would go out from inside the earth. It would eat all of our country; at once, mountains would burn all over.
14 The Great Voice covers it with fire. It is as if it is still not eating our country.
15 But if he uncovered it even a little, and it would be hurried out of here, in a short time our country would be burned, and many things would not burn again.
16 The flame reaches the point of extinction when we burn those who are dead. Only the wood in the fire is consumed; that which was burning is extinguished.
17 Would it be such with the burning inside the earth?

18 aoteιande θo stan te ȣatetsistaιasθa._

19 dinde steniesθa te onkȣennonχȣachend, aιatsistȣtenk ichien
       oιont._

20 te oskenheati ti ιatsistȣten!

21 steniesθa achionχȣa de θo, aȣasen atichien?

22 stan atiaondi: ιaenta t'achientonχȣa chia ioentatej iaon, onek
       ichien ȣatienta ιaiahend aondechenhaon aioentateιande ta ti
       te ȣatientaιastandend._

Page 643

1   din n'onιȣe aieskontaha, chia aiaιoatatej ichien eataȣeti;

2   onek ichien otontandi ti ιatsistȣten te ontiataιastande
       aondechenhaon;

3   eeataȣeιik eaιoatateιannon te ondiιonhiaχe,

4   θo ioti d'aionchonχȣa, aoienka aochatarihenk, onne θo
       aochatej, atiaondi ιatsista aȣaton: ta ti te ȣatachaιasa;

5   aȣachȣtenk ichien θora t'aιaιennhiaj, stan te ochaιe't[s]ik eιenk,
       din de t'achiachorast aȣachaȣeιik ichien stan iȣaia ta te
       otierontraȣan._

6   skȣanderaȣas ti otetsistontandi n'ondechon ȣteχa!

7   oeri ondi te etoχa n'onιȣe._ θo aιoatonnentihatie d'
       aιorihȣanderaskon aιonnonkȣak ιehen:

8   θo areisaιen aȣe'tande de sennonkȣat d'anniaten chiatreȣaθa te
       chras d' iιatonk._

9   etsaιon sen, hesachiendaen haȣendio ti chionnhe, ahitenr
       echiatonnhaten._

10 θo aȣe'tande de sennonkȣat de tsa'ten cheakȣenras,
       cheakȣaeronk, cheendae'tandik._

11 ennonchien echierhon eιarihȣa'ton aion
       d'echiatieronnonionhonk ti chionnhontiend:

12 haatate ichien ιatoιen haatate daat haȣendio, te hiaιannrak
       chrihȣanderaχonnionhonk [!]

18 At the point of burning, the fire will not be consumed.
19 Nothing would have been firewood for such a fire.
20 The nature of the fire is astonishing.
21 Would it be that many things you would put in the fire would be finished?
22 You would not put a stick completely in the fire before it would burn. In vain, the stick was eaten. Forever, it would be going to burn; nevertheless, the stick would not have been consumed.

Page 643

1 And when humans would get into the fire, they would burn all over.
2 It alone is frightening that the fire is such that they will not be consumed.
3 It will not be without purpose that they will be together burning all over.
4 It is as if one would put an ax in the fire. At once it becomes warm, the ax is burned, completely becomes fire. Nevertheless, the ax will not be consumed.
5 The ax would be such that several summers passed and the ax will not have been diminished. When you took the ax out of the fire, it would be all together, not even a little bit disfigured.
6 Do you admire the frightening fire that burns inside the earth?
7 Humans do not know that the medicines of those who are frequently mistaken descend there.
8 Your medicine is about to go there, because sometimes you speak against that which I say.
9 Have courage; honor the name of the Great Voice of your life. He would have pity on you when your life ends.
10 Your medicine is at the point of going there. Stop stealing, killing, and committing adultery.
11 Do you think that the many damaging things you continued to do while you were living will be forgotten?
12 He exists, it is true, the very Great Voice exists. He looked at you as you made many mistakes.

13 ichierhe ati ehask8eιik, te t'a8endratiese, d' eιaaιenha de
 sennonk8at ιehen?

14 θo ichien ateιataha ti hentron d'ha8endio hannenraentandik io'ti._

15 θo haonιe ati ehenhaon, onne χa i8e d' oki otieronnonskon
 ndaoten a8eiachiat._

16 taot eχ' io'ti, ehenhaon ske8enda esatihatiend a8entenhaon?

17 atiaondi eskeιentak8ak:ιatonhonk endi ti tsatennonh8eha de
 tsonι8e ennon esk8atendindehes: oten desa
 chiak8aesatak8ak ti ιe8end8ten ara θo ti cheatoιaθak
 cheeronnionnionhonk cheiachasennihik;
 cheatonnheskannhak._

18 oki satonnen onh8a de ehenhaon, oki θo tsariskon de
 staιerandihik._

19 ti seta8a ndio chi asa'kaochontie't;

20 ndioharon sen n'ondechon ti satratat: stan te ιonnonh8e aat ti
 sakaoch8ten;

21 θo ichien aset etioteχa de te 8asχ8as:

22 ondaie ichien esare8at d' a8entenhaon, stonkontak ondaie
 tandendi de sonι8esk8andihik chrih8anderask8a ti
 chionnhek._

23 te otennonhianditi d' asechienten ha8endio te otennonhianditi
 n'ondechon 8teχa, de saιore8atak8a n' onachientandik._

Page 644

1 tsinnen te 8atandik ιatsist8ten?

2 tsinnen atask8ahens, i8erhe onnianni θo: d' aondechenhaon
 e8aiataιaia ti ιahach8ten?

3 achiate[i]a[θ]aska, stan ta te chiasenχ8achend nondaie te
 saatateιaθa?

4 aιendionratoιendi ihennonha d' hatirih8annens deχa
 sk8andare d' ihontonk, onn' ahon'ki onnianni θo:
 d'eonχitsistore d' aι8atrios d' eonχindenniannik._

5 ondaie i8ochien ahontonhonj, te ιandoron n'onχieratandik
 ιatsista d' esk8atrios chieιannen a te ιiatre ti ιatsist8ten, chia
 n'ondaie d' etioteχa n'ondechon._

6 tsa'ten d' achiaki chiatonnhonιannonniak, ichiatonk onnianni
 θo, d'eιonιetsistorej

7 sandιonratoιendi te ondetsi d'onn' aontatetsistorej n'on8e._

13 Do you think that he will close his mouth, will not go about speaking, when your medicine goes out?

14 The Great Voice stood up where he dwells. It is as if he ambushes it.

15 Then he will say, "Here walks a spirit that frequently did damage all over. It was bad-natured.

16 Why is it," he will say, "you continually went about abusing my word?

17 You will continually irritate me with it. I said, 'Love each other, you humans. Do not trick each other,' but you mocked my word. You only molested, damaged them, were angry at them, and bore them ill will.

18 You became a spirit," he will say, "A spirit and you go together. You copied it.

19 Come on, withdraw from where you are standing. Leave badness far behind.

20 Jump out of inside the earth. I do not love your great badness.

21 Move away from where it burns without extinguishing.

22 It will continually punish you for scorning it with mistakes that pleased you while you lived."

23 For those offending the Great Voice, the burning inside the earth with which he punishes is terrifying.

Page 644

1 Who doesn't fear such a fire?

2 Who hates oneself that much that one wishes, "A long time, forever, flame will eat my body"?

3 Would you continue to be brave, not cry out, if it burned you?

4 I am certain that the elders here where you live are together when they say, "They went on a raid for a long time. Those we fight who will overcome us will cover us with fire."

5 They would continue to say, "It is not difficult to deal with the fire your enemies use. Greatly it is distant from the fire that burns inside the earth."

6 You are on a raid, and make a resolution, saying, "It is a long time they will cover me with fire."

7 You know for certain that it is not a long space of time that humans cover each other with fire.

8 chieskechien dȣa ichierhe; eonderaȣa ti ιateiaθa ta te
ιasenχȣache, eonιechiennonnia eondechontie._

9 θo atichien aesandιonratoιenk ιatsistaιe te saskontandi
n'ondechon ȣteχa: te chiatentachend, te
esachiennondandend._

10 aiontitaȣa'ten iθochien d'aiaιenrhon anniaten haonιe
eιatiataιasθa, anniaten haonιe eaι[o]teȣaten n'
onιiatatsiraθa._

11 orihȣa'ton iθondi n'ondechon atatenderaȣan, atatenchiendaen:

12 aiointatechiendaen atichien de saιoskȣahens haȣendio? stan te
ȣatondend._

13 anniaten ichitron de saatannonenχȣa n'ondechon
eιarihȣandiontatie θo atatennonkonten, atateiachasenni
atateskȣahendi:

14 stan tsa'ten aondechenhaon t'etsisannonhȣeche din d' aιoki din
n'onιȣe ehiaskȣahenk iθochien d' haȣendio onne ichien aȣeti
ichien eesakaochaȣeiachas._

15 hi ehendihon n'ondechonronnon, hi hotiatatontandi:
ndioharon ho'kaochachen;

16 aȣeti eesatonȣes ondaki d'eιesatonten: ara θo
t'eιesakȣendoretandihi d'echionnhonιenha: ondaie ichien
askennonha te ιachiatiatontaȣandihe aondechenhaon
d'eιesatontaj, eιesaesataj._

17 tsaθas asken, tsaθas n'ondechon ȣteχa:

18 endi de ιatandik ichien n'ondaie aonnonhȣara'ton isen chien,
ta te ιatandihend._

19 stan ta teȣannonhiandijχend, de t'aeskȣenhaon; onn'
aesatsistorej;

20 stan te ιrakȣa deχa skȣateιati innonkonθa atiaondi.

21 ιaro atichien aontonιetik n'ondaie te ιatandik?

22 stan tsaten te ȣaιatsarandi te aȣen θo se,

23 stan ichien t'etiondaskȣenhaȣind χa tsondechen d'aιotierontie;

24 aιonhȣa aιendιιonraen, de ιaro ekȣaιe'ti chi-iιitak atiaondi
ιannionιenhake ontaιaraskȣa:

25 chi ιrihȣateri ti skȣaatȣten, skȣannonate n'onȣe ιaio
skȣaentendi d' atatetsistorej aȣeti de skȣaȣatsari[ιi] n'onιȣe
ιehen

8   You think, "Others will admire my being brave. I will not cry out; they will make my name great as long as the world will continue."

9   Would you be certain if you were in the fire that burns inside the earth that your body would not be finished? Your name would not have been made great.

10   They should lose hope, those who would think, "At some point my body will be consumed; at some point those who torture me will tire of it."

11   Also, lost inside the earth are mutual admiration and mutual praise.

12   Would those the Great Voice hates be praised? It would not have been possible.

13   Wherever you dwell, you will sink into the earth, where mutual contempt, anger, and hatred will go hanging about.

14   No one will love you any longer, spirits or humans. The Great Voice will hate you. All will be angry at your badness.

15   "Oh," the earth-dwellers will say. "Oh, he is frightening. Go away! His corruption is bad."

16   The spirits will rejoice in tying you up; they will reproach you when you suffer. You will not peacefully escape from them. They will continue to tie you up and mistreat you forever.

17   Fear it! Fear that which burns inside the earth.

18   I fear it. One's brain is certainly lost if I would not have feared it.

19   I would not have been afraid if you would say, "They covered you with fire."

20   I would not worry about your burning. I scorn it completely.

21   Would I have come to such a place if I feared it?

22   No one pushed me. No one said, "Go there!"

23   Those who go about doing damage would not have brought me as a prisoner to your country.

24   I alone wished that I come here. I talked it over completely when I was at the place of the French from where I left.[11]

25   At the same time, I knew your nature, your custom of killing humans, your covering each other with fire.

Page 645

1   chi [ι]rih8ateri n'ondaie orast ichien ontaιarask8a: aιerhon oeri
    ichien n'ondaie d'aionιetsistorej ιoeri ichien d'aionιiataιaia,
    stan n'ondaie te ιatandik._

2   onek inde te ondetsi te 8aιechiatorandend, θo te onιierha._

3   ondechon aak [ι]atandik, aondechenhaon te ιendiιonhiaχend;
    ondaie aonh8a ιatakakeronsennik d' aionιetsistorej
    n'ondechonronnon: ondaie iθondi aonh8a ι8akeronsennik._

4   din d'aiaιenhaon ondechon echeatorast deχa aιotio'k8ate
    ιatsistaιe de t'aesaatonti de chi 8teχa;

5   aιraha atiaondi aιerhon oeri ichien d'aionιetsistorej,
    itsonda8a'ka isen chien d'aonιechiatoren;

6   ondaie ichien 8toιe'ti aιerhon d' aχeatannonstat de chi
    aιotiok8ate d' aonh8entsannenhaon aiaιoatate ιannon stan te
    eatentachend._

THE REJOINING OF BODY AND SPIRIT AFTER DEATH

7   k8ioti t'esk8askenheatandik onn' aιatendot st' eotiata8enk
    onnennonk8ak ιehen d' eιaonationti d' atieronιe ιehen?

8   eιanderat ichien te tsisk8askenheaten, d'esk8aronj
    st'eonι8aata8enk e8atondechaten._

9   ennonchien esk8erhon honnennonk8achaιon onek ιaronhia[ι]e
    ehonk8asθa d'hotiatatoιeti ιehen din d'hondatieronnonskon
    ιehen ennonchien esk8erhon honnennonk8achaιon iθochien
    ehontetsirat ondechon

10 anniaten esaθaratik esarih8iostik, stan aonh8a θo ara
    te8ak8astande ιaronhiaιe de sennonk8at ιehen;
    eharonhiaenton iθondi ha8endio de chieronιe ιehen:

11 oten de tsa'ten echrih8anderaχonnion stan n'ondaie θo ara
    t'e8atetsiratande sennonk8ak ιehen, ehare8at ha8endio de
    chieronιe ιehen:

12 8ade ondatsi ιehen de chieronιe chia de sennonk8at, donne
    sten ichiatierhak dora8en din d' 8kaot; eski8eιi, iθondi,
    anniaten haonιe din d'ora8en din d'8kaot etsesaerista'k8en
    d'echiatonnhaten._

Page 645

1 I knew the matter; still, when I left, I thought, "Those who cover me with fire, those who eat me, I do not fear.

2 It is because it is not long I would have felt pain. There they do not treat me badly."

3 Inside the earth I fear very much. I would not ever lose consciousness. It alone I am afraid of for myself, the earth-dwellers covering me with fire. It alone, also I am afraid of for you.

4 And I would say, "Inside the earth you will take out of the fire this group if they would abandon you, leave you behind far from where it burns."

5 I would consent to it completely, thinking, "They would cover me with fire. Certainly, a very short time I would feel pain."

6 "It is fortunate," I thought, "I should keep the group far away forever from burning all over and not being consumed, used up."

THE REJOINING OF BODY AND SPIRIT AFTER DEATH

7 Are you surprised as I tell about what will happen to one's medicines when they abandon their bodies?

8 You will no longer be greatly surprised when you listen to what will happen to us when the world ends.

9 Don't think that only the medicines of those who are true will be happy in the sky. And those who frequently damage, don't think that only their medicines will be made to suffer inside the earth.

10 Sometime you will have done good, and you will have believed. Your medicine won't be alone in being happy in the sky. The Great Voice will also treat your body well, putting it in the sky.

11 But if you are one who will make many mistakes, not only your medicine will suffer. The Great Voice will punish your body.

12 As your body and your medicine were associated when you did many things, good and bad, they will be together again at some time when they will make recompense for you, for both the good and the bad, when your life will end.

13 θo iθochien iondetsi te ιatoχa de kȣaeronιe, st'a'son
ιandaιenchaιon iιannont, ȣade te ondateχaskaȣan
n'onιȣennonkȣat, de ιatoιatak de kȣaeronιeιehen._

14 stan ichien aondechenhaon ιandaenchaιon t'eotasetik eιenk
kȣaeronιe ιehen; stan aondechenhaon ȣatsek ta t'eιiatiende
n'onιȣennonkȣat ιehen chia de kȣaeronιe ιehen.

15 eȣentaentaj d'etsikȣatonnhont: θo haonιe ati te tsoat[a]k
onιȣannonkȣat e kȣaeronιe ιehen chia onιȣaatorak etsikȣet
ιaronhiaιe ndiaȣeraten ondechon._

16 tsatrihotat stan te hondiιonrasχȣi haȣendio eharonhiaenton
ndaoten de kȣaeronιe d' anniaten eonιȣaθaratik: stan
nondaie θo ara te hannon[h]ȣeche n' on[ι]ȣennonkȣat,

17 eherhon [ti hondiιonrȣannen haȣendio] aιiȣeιik aθo, aιiakȣasθa
d'hatieronιe din n' onnennonkȣat aιerhon te ιiakontachat
onιechiendaenhak aȣentenhaon, st' ason te ιiatendasonθak
ondende;

Page 646

1 orasendik atiaondi ti haerha._
2 oten d' oki hotirihȣanderaskonnen aȣaton ati?
3 te herhe ondaie θo ara [t]aιaronhiaιen d' aonnonkȣat ιehen
4 tendinnen sen chien de chieronιe ιehen din de sennonkȣat
ιehen, d'onne chrihȣanderaskȣa; ateιon te ιiatonskȣa sθ-
onachientandihik haȣendio; tasken aθo te θonaιentakȣak:
5 aiorihierik atichien de skat ara te hareȣaθa d' haȣendio?
6 stan kaatore'ti te haienhȣichend, θo te haerha; ahorihonnhij
atiaondi onta tasken ta te hareȣatandend._
7 tsirihȣateha eθorihȣichiaιi haȣendio
8 skȣaeronιe aondiaras eskȣennonkȣat d'onn'aȣaskand d' ȣkaot;
eιiariskon ichien n'ondechon
9 oten de ιieronιe eorihȣaȣas aιennonkȣat d' oraȣen, anniaten
eȣendiιonraentak: eskiȣeιik eιiakȣasθa ιaronhiaιe;

13 One does not know how long our body is inside the pit, as they are separated, our medicine that did the perceiving, and our body.

14 Not forever will our body be hidden inside the pit. Not forever is it elsewhere. Not forever will our medicine and our body be placed apart.

15 Days will pass, then we will be brought back to life. At that time our medicine will again seize our body, either in the sky or inside the earth.

16 Pay attention; the mind of the Great Voice is not small. He will treat our body well, put it in the sky, if at some time we have performed good acts. He will not love our medicine only.

17 The Great Voice will wish, because he is wise, "Let their body and their medicine be happy together, for since they came into being, they honored me continually, while still they were joined on earth."

Page 646

1 It is of the same sentiment, completely, that which he does.

2 But what would become of the spirit of those who frequently were mistaken?

3 He doesn't wish one's medicine would be the only one to suffer.

4 Your body and your medicine were certainly two together when you were mistaken. They were two together every time they offended the Great Voice; both irritated him then.

5 Would it be a reasonable, correct matter if the Great Voice punished only one?

6 He would not have learned from examining it if he does that. He would be completely ignoring the matter if he would not have punished both.

7 Familiarize yourselves with the Great Voice's decision in the matter.

8 Your body aided your medicine when it desired that which is bad. They will go together inside the earth.

9 But my body will take the matter of my medicine concerning that which is good, when it will think about such a thing. They two will be together again, happy in the sky.

10 ondaie io'ti st' iherhe haȣendio, aonsaiontonnhont iherhe
    aιoatorak aonsaiontatieriesen de sten iontierhak oraȣan d'
    aιoatatoιeti ιehen, iherhe aιoatorak aiontatereȣat ondechon
    de sten iontieronnionhonk aιorihȣanderaskon ιehen.

11 eonniannik ιandaιenchaιon eιannontaj de kȣaeronιe ιehen ara
    θo ti [e]ιaataȣiha oιenra eȣaton;

12 chi hentakȣa d' haȣendio stan te saιaonn[h]estande θo st' aaihej
    n'onιȣe,

13 ondaie d' iherhe aȣahentenk asken ti ιaheken d' hati[e]ronιe
    n'onιȣe d'onne akiateχaska n onnennonkȣat: ara iθo ti
    ιa[h]ȣa[r]indaen, ara iθo ti otsikenchaen ara iθo ti oιenra ti
    sken_

14 ondaie ondiahak echi onati achahatonskȣa deχa ιa[h]ȣarindaen
    de ιaskȣa,[o]n ιannontak onnonkȣak ιehen._

15 oten n'onhȣa aonsaȣatoiannon te skiȣeιi onnonkȣak ιehen?

16 onne ichien tonsa[s]aιonda[s]onten haȣendio n'onιȣennonkȣat
    ιehen chia de kȣaeronιeθo haonιe θo e[ȣe]ndeohas kȣaeronιe
    de sten eoatorik on[ι]ȣennonkȣat ιehen,

17 ιaronhiaιe taontaȣe't de sennonkȣak ιehen ara iθo t' aιandiaιon
    ondaie ichien eondiaιonchoka de chieronιe ιehen st'
    onsaιiȣeχa:

18 ondechon taontaιaatingenha de sennonkȣat ιehen ara iθo t'
    aiokaochatsiȣaιen ondaie θo aokaochȣten eokaocho'ka de
    chieronιe ιehen:

19 aiotonnharatie de sennonkȣak ιehen aonsaιaatinnion de
    chieronιe, onne iθondi aȣatonnharen de chieronιe:

20 aiochiatorande θo de sennonkȣak ιehen aonsaιaatontarhenha
    de chieȣatsaιon ιehen chia t'aiochiatoren iθondi de
    chieȣatsaιehen:

21 aioataiatik oraȣen de sennonkȣak ιehen aonsaȣatennontrak
    chieskȣaιon ιehen chia t'aioatotrak aȣeti de chieronιe ιehen
    de sten otieratihatie._

Page 647

1   ιatsista aiokȣatsihatie sennonkȣat ιehen aonsaȣennontarhenha
    de chieronιe ιehen chia t'aiohachak iaon de chieronιe
    ιehen._

10 It is as if the Great Voice wishes, "They should be brought back to life"; he wishes, "Those who were true should be recompensed intact for the many things they have done that are good"; he wishes, "Those who were frequently mistaken should be punished intact inside the earth for the many damaging things that they did."

11 Our body will have been a long time inside a pit. It will just rot and become dust.

12 The Great Voice does it deliberately. He will not prolong there the lives of humans who have died.

13 He wishes, "Let the human body appear to be lazy when the body and the medicine are separated." It is only a lying corpse, only lying rotten. Only dust it is again.

14 The medicine inside the body used to, at first, move this lying corpse.

15 But would one's medicine move it again in many places when the two are together again?

16 The Great Voice joined them again, our medicine and our body. At that time, all kinds of things will spread from our body to what was our medicine.

17 Your medicine would come back from the sky. Just its good nature will spread to your body, when they two are going together again.

18 When your medicine would go out from inside the earth, it would smell bad. All its badness would spread to your body.

19 Your medicine would go about rejoicing, as it would again penetrate your body. Your body also rejoiced.

20 Your medicine would feel pain when it would reenter your flesh. At the same time, your flesh would also feel pain.

21 Your medicine would have caused goodness to enter your body when it would go inside again. Equally, it would go through all of your body, going about doing many things.

Page 647

1 Your medicine would go about being covered with fire. When it would again be inside your body, your body would catch fire.

2   chiata8eti atiaondi ata8atsistonιon'tak, ti ιatsist8ten aoienka θo
    aesaataienteson, stan te tiaonda8enrente d'
    aesaatateιannon._

3   k8io'ti eskiatatennonh8eha d'orih8anderaskon ιaeronιe ιehen
    chia d'onnonk8ak ιehen, d'eski8eιik? a8aton atichien?

4   astonh8eha ιandahia te sandijas te saιonrets[ai]as te sachitias
    chiata8eti sa8atsoron8as?

5   astonh8eha ιatsista de saιachiateιaθa a8eti de cheiaske
    chieιonske chiennhechiaιe satsistorechonnionk?

6   achiateiataska achietsistannonh8ek ti ιatsist8ten:

7   oki ιehaon a8asaonk8tenk aieseιannhonχ8a, tiongentsik,
    otsiιa8achia osta8enchont tionnhonsk8aen otsihati a8eti
    taiesaeraten:

8   aesaιa8as atichien ti ateιatontandi?

9   atiaondi te8atonk, achiesk8ahenk: stan te chiesk8ahenchend
    ιandahia d'aesaatiaχonnion chieronιe; te chiesk8ahenchend
    ιatsista chiata8eti d'aesaataιastannon; stan te
    chiesk8ahenchend d'oki otsi8aιen osta8enchont otsiι8achia
    d'aesatsonratsirat aieseιannhonχ8a?_

10 ondaie aat echi eskanderat eιiatateiachas chieronιe chia de
    sennonk8at ιehen te skiatenda'sonten, esatonnhont onta
    nonh8a te chrih8iostande._

THE END OF THE WORLD AND THE RESURRECTION

11 tsatrihotat asken ti ιarih8ten d' aonh8a ιarih8aen;
    tsirh8ateh8aten, tsirih8andoronk8at: stan anniaten te
    sk8atrih8atieren de θo aiotik._

12 astehierak8ik ichien, ιatoιen etsik8atonnhont, ιatoιen
    on[ι]8aatorak eaι8ak8asθa ιaronhiaιe n'onι8arih8iosti;
    ιatoιen sk8aatorak te sk8atonnhontaion8a, stan te
    sk8arih8iostande:

13 ondaie sken aιarihonιok te 8atiesen chia te sk8eiachiati,
    ennonchien e8aιerik onsahotirih8andiιonrhenk iaon d'
    etsik8atonnhont._

14 stan inn aιatier aiorih8andirha ti ιarih8ten:

15 iιerhe aιrih8etsik θo i8aia aιrih8aient st' ea8ent etsontonnhont.

2   The fire would penetrate you completely. It is such a fire that at
      once it would go the length of you; no place would be
      missing; your body would burn all over.

3   Will the body and medicine of one who frequently made
      mistakes love each other again when they will be together
      again? Would it be possible?

4   Would you love a knife that cuts your fingers, hands, and feet
      in two, strips your whole body of flesh?

5   Would you love a fire that burns your breast, arms, face,
      thighs, that covers you with fire?

6   You would be brave to have loved such a fire.

7   From a spirit it would be medicine of such a nature. They
      would put a liquid in your mouth: snakes, bile, rattlesnakes,
      toads would be the mixture they would make for you.

8   Would it taste good to you, as it is a frightening liquid?

9   Is it not entirely possible that you would hate the knife that
      would cut your body in many places, the fire that would
      consume all of your body, the spirit that would put into
      your mouth the bad-tasting liquid made of rattlesnakes and
      bile, that would make your bowels suffer?

10   If you will not now believe, the anger of your body and your
      medicine with each other will be to a great extreme when
      they will be joined together again when you will receive life.

THE END OF THE WORLD AND THE RESURRECTION

11   Let it be that you listen to it, as it alone is a matter of
      importance. Save the matter; consider it valuable. At no time
      would they two resemble each other.

12   Always remember: it is true that we will be revived; it is true
      that we who are believers will be intact and happy in the
      sky; it is true, as intact bodies you will be tortured, you who
      won't believe.

13   Let the matter easily penetrate the middle of your hearts. Do
      not let me think, "They forgot that we will be revived."

14   What should I do so that it would be a firm matter?

15   I wish, "My matter should be a short recounting of what will
      happen when they are revived."

16 ennonchien 8atsek esk8andiιonrontie't ιandoron ndaoten
ontonιenhatie

17 tsakak8a sti otierannon deχ' ondechate tsakensehon
orak8annentaιι a8eti d' hatironnon ti tsakannren deχa
ιanda8atonnon, chia de ιontaronk8annion, otrahondihaton
a8eti chia te otierenhatie a te oιennhaιete tiotondechondi
a'son te ondarhontie

Page 648

1 isk8erhe iθochien d8a stan iaon te 8atiennentache
aondechenhaon; isk8erhe eo'tik eιarakontie, eιandaontie,
isk8erhe eotik eonk8eton n' onι8e ιaio a8eti & sk8arihonnhis,
stan θo te a8enche._

2 esk8atron8a e8entaentaj, de sten ioterannon deχ' ondechate:
eιarak8aton deχa iιar ehatiatentaha de tichion
esk8atronhiaron8a ιaronhia8eti, e8entandennia de deχ'
ondechate d' eondechentaha;

3 eθondarandi ha8endio deχa ιanda8atonnon θo iθochien
ea8enche chi eιastek a8eti d' oherok8aenton din d' anniaten
achonk8annion.

4 ιatsista etiondechachiat eondechaιaia n' onιiondecha8eti chia
t'eohachak, e sk8entat a te ondeche χa aondesa onne
otondechaιasti:

5 θo ati onn'a8atenda8aten ιanda8a ιaihona din de ontara onne
ichien eιontentonnia ιaio atironties ιah8enta a8eti, onne
ichien te skarhate, te skarendate, te tsonnont8t anniaten
onne iθondi aon'sen a8eti n'onι8e onh8a de aaiheonche
n'on8e aontonniande iθochiend8a,

6 te k8atennontraties io'ti: oten de θo haonιe stan te
tsontatak8etonde stan ta te tsontennontratiese; eskat
eontentonnia aιotio'k8a8eti n'on8e te ιandiaιendi._

7 taot ichien aia8enk aonsaionk8eton?

8 tsinnen aat a8erhon a8atondechaten θo?

9 di8 ichien haonh8a ehendiιonraen:

10 taot ichien? ha8endio endi ati ahek8are8at te k8andiar ondi de
hon8entsenh8a haonh8a ιehen eθaonh8entsichiaιι,

16 Do not let your thoughts go elsewhere, as the direction in which I go about speaking is very valuable.

17 Look at the many things done on this earth. Consider the sun and the stars. Look at the rivers, lakes, and forest: every summer, when the earth is made again, still they do not go about at rest.

Page 648

1 You think that others' ability will never cease. You think it will be like the sun's continuing to rise, running its course, and rivers' continuing to flow. You think it will be like humans and animals having children. You do not know that it will not happen like that.

2 All kinds of things done on earth will disappear as days pass. The sun that rises will disappear. The bodies of stars will end. All the sky will disappear. A day will arrive when the earth will end.

3 The Great Voice designated a time that these rivers will dry up, as well as all marshes and water in many places.

4 Fire will strike the earth in a blow that will eat all of the earth. At the same time, every country will one day catch fire. In this short period of time, the earth will be consumed.

5 Then, the flowing waters of rivers, streams, and lakes will be stopped. Animals, birds, and fish will perish. No forests, rocks, or hills will exist anymore. All humans will die, those at the point of death and those at the point of birth.

6 We go about following each other in sequence; but at that time, humans will no longer have children, no longer will follow each other in sequence. The whole group of humans will perish as one; no one will escape.

7 Why would it happen that they would again have children?

8 Who would wish the earth would end?

9 God, alone, will put his mind to it.

10 Why would we act against the Great Voice, not help, as he carries the world that he alone made?

11 haonh8a haonh8entsanditihatie, haonh8a ehendiιonraen
  d'eherhon onh8a de aonιondechonti θo te ιondechenh8a._
12 onι8a8an te ιen d' aek8enhaon, taot eχa asonι8atonten?
13 eθa8entaιatsi de hondiιonraιon ha8eri ondaie θo ara
  a8atentonta8a chia eskondecharon8a
14 eθoteraka8i ti 8ent8ten d'ara ιehen etserak8aιen ti 8ent8ten chi
  [ha8]entak8i sonι8entase'tandi d' ek8arak8ingenha
15 stan nendi te sonι8atsatandi ha8endio ha8eri aiaιehieratie
  a8entenhaon aiaιenrhon ιateiensθa sen n'onh8a, k8e de
  taιendi8ak aθo onne θo aonι8aatarenk._
16 ondaie iθochien 8to[ι]e'ti d' iha8en daat ha8endio,
  astehierak8ik asken de tsonι8e, 8ade θo ichien
  ontesk8aata8enche ont'etsondecha'tonde achie._
17 ahek8andachiondat atichien?
18 te harih8aen ιandachiondandi, stan te 8atondend 8atsek
  ahakonten._
19 ιara ιehen d'etsorhenha e8atentonnia a8eti de sten ioterannon:
  θo ati n'on8e ιehen esaιaonnhont ha8endio
20 stan ichien 8a eatennond te saιotonniande

Page 649

1 nien aat esaatichiahon de k8aeronιe ιehen, chia θo esaationt n'
  onι8ennonk8at ιehen θo haonιe etsik8atonnhont._
2 oki ehannhaha ιaronhiaιeronnon, ehenh[a]on, ti sahenretanda:
  aonsaiontonnhont on8e ιehen; θo sken aionditi o'k8ichien
  chi onnont8t._
3 onne ichien a8arask8a d' oki ιaronhiahenk akataha,
  onn'atiohenret chieιannen aιa8endaha aιenhaon sa
  tsatonnhont ndio tsonι8e ιehen! astenditiok8ichien
  ahendiιonraen onna ha8endio d' esk8atientaj
  aondechenhaon:
4 o8endaιarendi ndaoten e8ak8enda8aton8a ea8enk
  ιaronhiaιeronnon daat echi esk8end8annen a te ondeche ati
  eιa8endaιaonte θaa8enk [ι]a8end[and]eronniannion de
  hinnon aιandi8ak iθochien aaonh8entsaιaonte
  n'ondecha8eti._

11 He alone goes about supporting the earth; he alone will deliberate, thinking, "I should abandon the earth then. I will not carry it."

12 It is not ours so that we would say, "Why did he lose it for us?"

13 He designated the day; inside his mind, he thought, "The day will come when I will destroy the earth."

14 He marked what will be the last day when one will see the sun again. He deliberately hid the day from us when one will see the sun leave us.

15 The Great Voice does not show it to us; he thought, "They should go about continually on guard. They should wish, 'Let me learn so that I am not surprised when we come to rest.'

16 It is fortunate," he said, the very Great Voice. "Be forever on your guard, you who are humans, because you are going to lose your country."

17 Would he lie to us?

18 It is not his matter, lying. It would not have been possible that he would begin to speak outside [the truth].

19 When day will dawn for the last time, all kinds of things will perish. Then the Great Voice will revive those who were humans.

20 Others that have different bodies he will not create.

Page 649

1 He will remake our body and reintroduce it to our medicine: at that time, we will be revived.

2 He will speak to a sky-dwelling spirit, saying, "Go cry out that humans will be revived. Let them be created as a group in the far hills."

3 The spirit will leave, standing up in the middle of the sky; it will cry out with a large voice, saying, "Return to life. Come on, you humans. Form a group where the Great Voice wished that you will be placed forever."

4 The voice will make a noise as if through a curved object [i.e., a trumpet]. The sky-dweller will have a very augmented voice: in every country, the voice will make a loud sound. The voice will thunder, and suddenly the earth will resound all over.

5   θo θo aat eka8endingenha ɩaronhiaɩeronnon
    onn'ationtatennonten aonsaontonnhonton n'onɩ8e ɩehen._

6   etsak echiakak8a a8enɩe ontaontesko8a, 8a de ɩandaɩenchaɩon
    ontaontatennontak8a, ɩarhaɩon θo d8a ontaɩentiokontie;

7   echeenteha de ɩatsista aɩoataɩastinnen [o]ɩonɩe iθondi eon'sen
    de ɩaio aaɩoataɩaiennen: echeɩen d' aθo aɩoionnen
    onde[onrendich]; dind'ond8taɩe[']te; echeɩonchiateha te
    chieɩannrak ontatiatontak ontatetsistoresk8a ontateskosk8a
    ontatiataɩaiahenk

8   stan te tsaɩoataɩetsi i8aia stenies8a tetio'ton d'eeronɩe ɩehen
    tseata8eɩi atiaondi θo ichien itseat8ten ti eat8tennen st' a'son
    aɩonnhek._

9   te saskenheaten echiakak8a aoienka tonsaontenneannhontron,
    d'anniaten onnearichonk._

10 a te onneaɩe ak8atandisk8ahon a8echiaχe n'ondaie de te
    ɩiatr[a]ndeɩennen v/ te ɩiatenneandeɩennen tonsaɩiatraha θo
    ara, onne ichien tonsaɩiatenneaχason:

11 onne θo i8e d'otsinnonhia'θa ɩatsinnonhiatichias iθondi
    n'ondatsi ɩehen tonsaɩiatakonchiok ichien onne
    tonsaɩiatetsinnonhiatannhontren, aioenka aonsaɩiatatienteha
    aioenka onsaondatenros8a tonsaɩiatrandeen;

12 θo iθochien aa8enche d' otsonra osk8enha, onda8a, a8eiachia
    a8eti sk8atindatichiaχe io'ti d' eɩonkerontak8ak
    onsa8endorenha onne θo onsaɩonterh8s8a._

13 eoteiendaɩate ndaoten sti otierannon de k8aeronɩe ta ti
    stenies8a ta te ɩandatanderaχe,

14 stan te k8akak8ache 8atsek iaon aa8eiachiontarhenha
    n'onɩ8eiachiontak8innen χa ichien esk8eiachiondiontaha
    chia te onɩ8aiach[i]ati:

Page 650

1   teskontrandeɩenchon θo d' osk8enha, onda8a, otsiɩa8achia:

2   θo ichien etso'tik sti ɩaeren nonh8a:

3   χa ichien ek8atennonronten st' onɩ8askotont; θo iθondi
    etsik8achitonten te k8achitont θo etsik8akonresonten,
    etsik8ateiachionten te tik8aɩonrestontak tetik8aiachiontak;

5 Scarcely will the voice go out from the sky-dweller when they will be hurried, those humans who would be revived.

6 Many times you will look at bodies being withdrawn from inside the water. Some will be taken out of a burial pit; others will be traveling from the forest.

7 You will become familiar with those who were consumed publicly by fire, also those who died fighting and were eaten. You will see those killed by cold, famine, and war; you will become familiar with the faces you have looked at of those taken prisoner, covered with fire, and boiled.

8 They will no longer be diminishing, not even a little; nothing will be missing from their bodies. They will be completely together again. They will be as they were while they were still living.

9 It will astonish you when you look. At once, they are joined again, the bones of those who had their bones spread out.

10 Every bone that went up against another is going to search for the other; two that were once joined together will meet again. These bones will be joined together again in many places.

11 A nerve will go searching for a nerve it had been associated with. They will look at each other again. At once, they would know each other again. At once, they are companions rejoined.

12 Then it will happen that bowels, lungs, livers, and hearts will again search for a place. It is as if they will be assembled at that place, again being put into something.

13 It is with an abundance of skill that many things will be done to our body. Nothing will be in a mistaken place.

14 We will not see anything outside: hearts will be put inside where they were attached; they will be suspended here, between our arms.

Page 650

1 Liver, lungs, and gall bladders will be joined together again.

2 Then they will again be as they are now.

3 Here, our scalp will be attached to our head. Then, also we will again have our feet attached where they are attached now. Then our hands will again be attached to our arms where they are attached now.

4   a teıon atiaondi eskaerik de k8aeronıe ıehen:

5   onh8ati chi oıak8enda'tonnen te k8aıakarent, stan te
     tsisk8aıenhak te tsonı8aıakandend ichien:

6   onh8ati chi otonnen te k8ahontaıarent etsik8aronıannon;

7   etionıionrichendi onı8ask8eıihatiend, te tsik8a8endandarek;
     etsik8a8ennonten etsik8atatiahaj ichien;

8   anniaten iaon de ıaıi, stan te tsisachoniesk8a de sten
     akandiah8ten chie8endio n'onh8a eıenk d' echierhon, χa
     i[ı]es haoten aonıechonia;

9   otentondinnen d'aiontoiannon d' aionrask8a, d'aiaıaonesk8en
     steniesθa din d'aiaıochens, tetion[ı]8enheonnen;

10   tetsik8ak ichien n' ondaie a8eti, etsik8achahatons etsik8eska,
     etsonıionesk8en steniesθa din de etsonı8achiens._

11   stan skat te aıonnhek aıotiok8a8eti n'on8e, stan sk8entat, te
     aıotondiati stan sk8entat te aıa8enheati, stan sk8entat
     ondechon te aıonnontarhendi._

12   oten d' etsik8atonnhont eskat etsonıonrich8taj, eskat ondechon
     te tionıiondechandeı[a]ra eskat ıandaıenchaıon
     etik8aatingenha; esk8entat etsik8atiatichien._

13   haıotsindachia chia te es'ontonnhont haıonea [hotrea] ıehen
     chia te tisk8eontondik echiaaha ıehen d'anniaten
     satesk8eθak; 8ade esk8entat etsik8aton._

14   aonh8a ıarih8aen atiaondi ti ıarih8ten._

15   a8enstran eonı8andera8a, d' ek8aka'k8a eaı8as ichien
     n'onχichi8ta ıehen onχiatrea ıehen, a8eti de chi etiaıosaıi
     tetiotondechondi n' onı8e ıehen

16   stan inn ek8erhon d'ek8akak8a atsihise ona'ti ontaıannenrontie
     te 8arati n'on8e ıehen;

17   chia te aıotiok8a θo k8atrak8at ontaıentiokontie; te 8atoχ8aθa
     ona'ti onta aonh8entsaren8anhatie ndaoten;

18   skat a de ontaraıe tontaaıotesko8anhatie d'aıo8arindinnen
     ondechen d8a ontaen aıotа8ake θo aıosaıannenıe ıandastoıe
     aıonnonchiondiıe 8endake & a te ondeche

19   eskat tetiaıotenst on8e ıehen d' etsontonnhont Josaphat te
     onnontaen; [te onnontoıen]

4 Every time, our bodies will again be completely right.

5 A long time before that, eyeballs were lost from our eye openings. We were no longer seeing. Our eyes would no longer move back and forth.

6 A long time before that, our ear openings were lost. We no longer heard.

7 When we died, we went about mute; our voice no longer existed. We will again have a voice. Again we will talk.

8 Concerning eating, you tasted all kinds of food; you are Great Voice, it will not be that you will wish, "This that I eat would be such that I would taste it."

9 It perished when we died, that which would move or walk, all that which would be pleasing and be hateful.

10 We will again seize it. Again we will move. We will continue to walk again, be pleased by many things and hate some things.

11 Not one would have lived of all humans. One day, not one was born. One day, not one died. One day, not one went inside the earth.

12 However, one day, we will be revived. Our breath will again stand. One day, we will rise out from inside the pit. One day, we will be created again.

13 An old man and his grandson will be revived at the same time. At the same time, there will be a day when one who was a child and one who was very old will again become human.

14 It alone is such.

15 Just as much as we will admire looking at our grandparents, we who were their grandchildren, so equally at all those humans who died earlier, when the earth was first made.

16 What will we think when we look at the uncountable number of humans coming from the south?

17 They are of an equal number, the group that is coming from the east and the very many who go about wandering from the west side.

18 From every lake, those who were shipwrecked will come out of the water: they will come from the countries of the Ottawa, Abenaki, Andaste, Iroquois, and Wendat; they will come from every country.

19 Humans will be of one measure. They will be revived in the valley of Josaphat.

20 eeiherak8at k8atennontandi eennhaha χa iθochien eondesa
    eιe[n]tiok8aerik._

Page 651

1   a8enstran de chieιannen a te ontrek d8a chieιannen
    etieatontiend chia te eon ichien orast atiaondi skat te
    ontakonchiok;

2   aiaιenrhon chi aιotiok8a8eιihatiend iaon de skandaιenchat.

3   skat ati ontaaιosa'tihatie ιandaιenchaιon aiaιenrhon ondaie
    eonnia st' eonditiok8andorat aθo skat eonditiok8ichien

4   d' iherhe daat ha8endio ondecha8eti aiontrihotat ti
    [i]8aιendiιonr8ten de χeatichia[ι]i n'on8e;

5   iherhe daat ha8endio aietoj asken a8eti ti χeronhiaentonk
    aιotatoιe'ti n'onι8e onιechiendaentak, chia de χere8aθa
    aιotieronnonskon ιehen;

6   iherhe daat ha8endio ataiondechek aiontatienteha d'
    aιoatatoιe'ti ondecha8eti aierennent aiechennonndiannon / v
    aiontonesonnion etsiχeerisen,

7   iherhe daat ha8endio ataiondechek aierih8ateha sti eerhak
    erih8anderask8a d'aιotieronnonskon ιehen; aionιras asken
    d' etsiχere8at._

8   aiaιondera8a, d'eχeak8endihaten n'ondechon te χeatsarak8en:

9   χondaie ihondiιonr8ten d'ha8endio d'iherhe skat
    aiontiestannon de tsontonnhonton n'on8e ιehen._

10 tsatrihotat ti haiend8ten d' ha8endio: θo θo aat ek8enhej
    esonι8arih8ichien st' ek8atientak aondechenhaon din
    n'ondechon aient din de ιaronhiaιe

11 θoia θo iaιon d'aιotrihote de θo haonιe oki iθochien ιaatra
    ιaronhiaιeronnon de tionι8annhek; chia de ondechonronnon
    de ιarih8taskahon8as d' onι8arih8anderaskon i8erhe
    aχeatonn[h]eskandi:

12 θo haonιe de onι8ennonk8achaιon iθochien eιonaatatoιe'ti
    aonh8a iθochien eιon[a]ationt ιaronhiaιe ndia8era'ten
    n'ondechon; a'son ati de k8aeronιe t'eιaataratiese / v a'son
    de k8aeronιe te konaatrak8ande._

20 They will go straight to a place, for they will be requested to hurry. It will be a short time that they will be a complete group.

Page 651

1 No matter how far they were distant from each other, and how great the distance they will be coming from, they will arrive at the same time, they will still see each other face-to-face as one.
2 They would think that at the same time they had gone on as a group in one burial pit.
3 As one, then, they were dead inside the pit. They would think that they would have rapidly formed one group.
4 The Great Voice wishes, "Over all the world, the humans I created should listen to my thoughts."
5 The Great Voice wishes, "They should know that I treat well those true humans who praised me, and that I punish those who frequently did damaging things."
6 The Great Voice wishes, "Those who are true should know each other in every land. Over all the earth they should shout approval, praise, give thanks that I will make recompense for them."
7 The very Great Voice wishes, "In every country they should know what they did, those who were mistaken by frequently doing damaging things.
8 They should admire that I will reproach them, pushing them down inside the earth."
9 The mind of the Great Voice wishes, "Those who are revived should be assembled as one."
10 Listen to him, as the Great Voice's skill is such: scarcely will we die when he will decide for us that we will be placed forever either inside the earth or in the sky.
11 A few will be together there listening; at that point, a spirit representing the sky-dwellers protects, defends us. At the same time, the earth-dweller makes declarations concerning the many matters in which we are mistaken and thinks, "I should bear them ill will."
12 At that time, they designate inside our medicine whether they will cause it to go to the sky or inside the earth. Still, our body will not accompany it. Still, they will not make our body participate.

13 oten d'es['] arihierihat ti ιarih8ten ha8endio d'etsik8atonnhont,
    tasken a te θaatrak8at de k8aeronιe din de onι8ennonk8at
    d'eharih8atoιet d'aondechenhaon a te k8akontak._
14 iιaatra isen chien de k8aereonιe de sten ek8aerhak a'son
    itionnhek:
15 8toιeti θo iherhe daat ha8endio chia t'aιotiata8enk aθo
    aonh8entsennenhaon din d'ora8en din d' 8kaot aιenk._
16 ennonchien esk8erhon chieskechien ara ιehen te s'aat [?]
    etsik8atonnhont! eherhon aonιi sen onnianni ti 8arih8tensti
    t'achia aιa8enheon?

Page 652

1   i8aιen ιaronhiaιe echiatien desa, oten chi tsitron ondechon
    esaokaochonnent._
2   stan n'ondaie te herhonde; eιarih8aιont de θorih8ichiaιi
    n'onι8e t'achia θaonton[n]haten:
3   stan anniaten ta te s'aatoreθa d' ha8endio
4   d' aherhon aonsaιron8a 8atsek e8aιierenk
5   endi iθochien de tionι8e tsonι8aron8askon de sten karih8ichias,
    8ade etsak ik8aatatonk ik8erhe χa ichien aia8enk
    aionniannisθa ek8andirak ichien te onnianni.
6   stan θo te ha8ens ha8endio, onek ichien steniesθa te
    hotonnhitandik
7   a8eti hatoχa de sten ik8atierannonk, k8endiιonraentonk a
    hatoχa steniesθa k8atatiak!
8   haronχa onteseiachenk anniaten din de sonesk8en sten haoten
    chi hotoιen._
9   taot ichien aia8enk t'ehatoιandandend?
10 ehaatatek8i de chiesk8aιon chiata8eti eθiachiati ti hentron
    ondaie ichien ehentrontak8i k8ask8aιon,
11 d' iherhe aonιendiιonratoιenk ti eiend8ten aonιi sen eonθarat
    eonιechiendaen dinde t'eonθaratande, onne ichien
    ek8atonnhaten anniaten iιenhatie._
12 taot ichien aιenk ahorihonnhij de sten aionι8arenk
13 stan ta te sonι8akannrandihik sti tionnhontiend:

13 But the Great Voice will speak the truth that we will be revived. He will make both our body and our medicine participants. He will designate forever what state we will enter into.

14 Our body is certainly represented concerning many things we will have done while we lived.

15 It is fortunate, then, that the Great Voice wishes, "Let it equally happen to them forever, either that which is good or that which is bad."

16 Do not think that he will examine it once more when we will be revived, wondering "Is it good that I determined the nature of the matter as soon as they die?"

Page 652

1 "I said, 'In the sky you will be put, but far away you dwell, your badness will descend into the earth.'"

2 He will not think that it is forever, that which he created for humans for the moment their lives end.

3 The Great Voice never reexamines a body.

4 He thought, "I would make disappear that which is outside what I will have done."

5 We humans frequently take back things that are done because frequently we are lost; we wish, "It would happen that it would get better. We will strengthen that which is not good."

6 It does not happen to the Great Voice. He overlooks nothing.

7 He knows all things that we do and think. He knows all kinds of things we say.

8 He hears when you become angry and when you are pleased. All things of such a nature he knows at the time.

9 What could happen that he would not have known it?

10 He is ever present inside your body, for he dwells completely, permanently in our bodies.

11 He thinks, "They should make me certain of their nature by doing good, by praising me, or by not doing good by the time they stop living."

12 What would he overlook in all the things we would have done?

13 He did not avert his eyes from us while we went about living.

14 taot ichien t'ahonditonrhatandihi de sten asontꙸataer?
15 chi tarihꙸichiati ondechon eontetsirat atorihꙸanderaskon de
    stan te tsontonnhonta'kꙸache._
16 chi tarihꙸichiati iθondi taronhiate eonkꙸasθa d' atotatoteti
17 atonditonranditihatie ason θo iens eχondechate aterhon chi
    ꙸahente ti atonditonrꙸtenhatie st' atonnhontie;
18 chi te haatoretihatie d' haꙸendio d' oraꙸen din d' ꙸkaot eonton
    eaihej;
19 ondaie ati io'ti st' itatonk, stan ꙸa te sontꙸarihꙸtenstandihe
    haꙸendio ara tehen esontꙸaataiannonton etsikꙸaatonnhont;
20 ondaie ichien chiatat es'arihꙸandiθa de θorihꙸichia[t]i
    ontꙸatonnha[ta]ke
21 eherhon ichien onek tarihondat[i] asken aiatotrihotaj
    ondechaꙸeti n'ontꙸe din d' atoki; eherhon atotiokꙸaꙸeti
    ahonatichiendaen n' ontechiendaentatiend st' atonnhek,
22 aiatonditonratotenk asken ti endoronkꙸak tarihꙸiosti, ti
    ontandihik atatakꙸ[a]eron, ti tarihꙸanderati ti
    ontetsikastonhonk eesaskꙸa, ti eskꙸahenskꙸa ontreꙸatak
    atatakꙸenrati atatendaetandi atateꙸendꙸtandi:
23 eherhon ati daat haꙸendio aiontatechiennonnia nondaie
    aiontataskand, aiatenhaon kahachia tandeia de ontꙸe; θo sen
    te tiatꙸtennen st' ason itonnhek
24 eherhon iθondi haꙸendio de tentiokꙸaton esatoatꙸtaska aꙸeti
    n'ontꙸe tehen atehenchaꙸannek aθo aiontehenk
    atotieronnonskon n' onteꙸendaesatak

Page 653
1 skꙸarihꙸateri ti aoneskꙸat d'aiontatrihondat tannonchite
2 χondaie haatsi d' asatondenniandi, χondaie de skat haatsi
    d'achienk asatoendaon, χondaie de skat haatsi d'
    asatondatꙸta[ꙸa]ha n'onχiesaθak;
3 atiaondi te ꙸatonk ti ataoneskꙸandik n'ondaie aontatias
    aontatrihondat:

14 Why would he doubt the things he did for us?

15 At the same time, both were created, that those who frequently were mistaken and would not take the life out of it will suffer.

16 And that those who were true will be happy in the sky.

17 They go about strengthened in mind while they still go about on earth, because they go about with such while they continue to live.

18 At the same time, the Great Voice goes about examining what is good and what is bad concerning what they will become when they die.

19 It is, then, as I say: the Great Voice will not go about putting in order for us other than the last time, when he will examine us when we are brought back to life.

20 He will again strengthen the matter he created at the end of our lives.

21 He will wish, "Let the matter be made public, so that humans and spirits would listen all over the earth." He will wish, "Let their whole group praise those who praised my name while they were alive."

22 Let them be certain that they should value believing, fear being mistaken, be patient with those in a poor state, scorn the spirit, hate killing, punish stealing, adultery, and speaking against others."

23 The Great Voice will wish, "They should praise, desire it. Humans should say, 'Oh, it is good! Let such be my nature while still I was living.'"

24 The Great Voice will wish, also, that he will make it appear to the whole human group, "Let those who frequently did damage by mistreating me with words feel great shame."

Page 653

1 You know that it causes one to be pleased, that one would be praised, augmented in reputation in a full house.

2 · In this he is called, "He won over them." In another of the three he is called "He seized them." In the other he called, "He knocked over the villages of those who mistreated us."

3 Nothing is as pleasing to people as being named, being enhanced in reputation.

4   θo atichien aioιenronj d'aiaιoneskʒen aιoatatoιeti
     d'esaιochiennonnia haʒendio?

5   ehenhaon χa ichien te hat daat hoθaratinnen horihʒiostinnen
     haonhʒa χa handarek ti hatenditenrhak haonhʒa hentrontak
     ti hatreʒaθa orihʒanderatande ahaenterik atakʒenraιi,
     atateiachasenni atatiatoιati? ara iθo ti hoteienstihatiend ti
     honnhek, ara iθo ti atrendaent hondiιontakʒihatiend:

6   θo ichien ehaʒendʒtenk haʒendio, t'esaιonnonronkʒannionnon
     d' aιoθaratinnen aιorihʒiostinnen, θo iθochien ehaerande,
     ehatotrak ιentionkʒaʒeti d' aιorihʒiostinnen,

7   chia ehenhaon d' iesʒs tsatrihotat tsondechaʒeti deχa skʒatiesti
     onne ichien onsaχeerisen d'aιoatatoιe'ti de chi aιotiokʒate
     n'onιechiendaentak st'ason aιonnhek, ondaie ichien
     onsaχeerista'kʒen d'aχennonhonsθa chia aιʒaatat onn'
     aʒaton eskat eaιʒendaιarat ιaronhiaιe eskat eaιʒaska eskat
     eaιʒakʒasθa

8   ehenhaon aʒenstran echiatronhiaenton aιien d' ehiatsaten desa
     eθiatrakʒat otiokʒatoιetiιe d' asaιonn[on]honsθa

9   chieιannen etiorannentaιi de ιannonchi[ι]e aiotatechiennonia,
     te ʒatrondrakʒi n'ondaie oten deχa aonhʒa, ιarihien ti
     aoneskʒat d' asaιonnonhonsθa d' haʒendio ʒade
     aondechenhaon esaιoataeriθon de sten eonskan

10   t'ehaʒennentache d' esaιochiennonnia, t'ehaiennentache
     d'esaιoronhiatenton

11   chia t'eotik aθo d' ehontehenk aιotieronnonskon de
     saιoatʒtaska haʒendio;

12   tseatat iθochien aesandandij aesatehentak, atiaondi te
     tsisatondik; aoienka

13   ontachieιonchienha:ichierhe taihen! te oskenheati onιatehaθa ta
     ti?

14   esaton de ιarihʒaʒeti etiesachiaten daat echi etsotehati?

15   stan tesatat θo ara te ιen ʒkaochaʒeti eesakaochaχʒehon._

16   ondechaʒeti iaon etsesaent de steniesθa satieronnon
     sarihʒanderaχonnion a te ondeche a te eataιe eesandiaton

17   eaιenhaon tsakakʒa chi hokaochate sonιʒaesatak [χondaie
     eatsinnen d' esaιokʒaeron]

4   Would it be unimportant that it would please true people to have the Great Voice praise their names?

5   He will say, "Here he stands, he who did very good deeds. He was a believer. He solely existed in having compassion. He alone dwelt in resisting being mistaken. He went about learning as he lived. He went about with a mind for praying."

6   The Great Voice will have such a word. He will honor those believers who performed good deeds. He will go over, count all of the believers.

7   At the same time Jesus will say, "Listen, all of you who are assembled here in your country.[12] I have made recompense for those who are true and who at the same time were in the group that praised me while still they lived. I made recompense for them by adopting them into my family. We are equal in living in one place, the sky, and we will be one in happiness."

8   He will say, "You will be happy, my child." He will make you a member of a true group that he adopted.

9   One is very far from the house where one would be praised without gain. It alone is pleasing that the Great Voice adopted them, because forever he will furnish all that they will desire.

10 He will not conclude his words with praising their name. He will not conclude his skill with putting them in the sky, flattering them.

11 Let those who frequently were destructive feel shame when the Great Voice reveals all to them.

12 They are one, those who insulted you, caused you to feel shame. Nothing is possible for you; suddenly, your face fell.

13 Do you think, "It is astonishing that they made me feel shame?"

14 Will the great shame be lost to you, the whole matter that they will speak strongly against you?

15 They are not one only, those who will reproach you for your badness.

16 All the world will strike you again for the many things you did when you were mistaken. In every country, every one will wound you.

17 They will say, "Look at his earlier badness, at his mistreatment of us." This is what they called, "He will kill them."

Page 654

1   endi, ehenhaon de s[']aatat; ndioharon sen n'ondechon
      ahokaochonnent ondi ondera'ti honnonk8aesa!

2   stan inn esandionr8tenk ıentiok8a8eti esatontiesten
      esakaochaχ8ehonnion?

3   daat otrih8atontandi etsearih8atonhons de chrih8anderatak sti
      chionnhek

4   ara iθo t' echiatonteha ara iθo ti t'esondachenk ara iθo
      t'echiatone't anniaten ies8a achiakonchiaıa'ten d'
      echiatonkonchiok d'eesannonkonton;

5   chi ona'ti achiaton8a8a chieıannen aıotio'k8a echitiok8aıen
      d'eesannhaiahon; etiesendachi88a etisak8endoretandik

6   stan skat t'etiaıoata8enrente, d' esask8ahens a8eti esatones

7   ho ho iontonk oerisen aat esonı8aerisen sonı8aesatak oerisen te
      hatakonhen d' asaıok8aeron d' asaıok8enraıi d'
      asaıoata'k8a;

8   oeri-sen aat aondechenhaon ehonaraıenichon d'ondaki
      ıatsistaıe de te 8ask8as; ondaie te s[']arih8acha8at
      harih8aesaθak ıarih8iosti._

9   onh8a de erih8ateθa n' onı8e d'anniaten onχinnonkonθa
      etiaıo8endaten

10   θo d8a ıandaıon iθochien onχeiachasennik etiontone'θa oıonıe
      aiontatia aiaıenhaon, χa ichien haat8ten de chi atehat,

11   aıenrhe ehaıesk8ahenk, ehiat8taska ehaırioha:

12   oten d'etsisk8atonnhont stan t' etsontatandihe d' ennonk8aesa;

13   oıonıe iθochien eontatehat: ies8s esaıonnonkonten,
      esaıotehentak;

14   ehati8endiontatie honditiok8a8eti [ı]aronhiaıeronnon n' ondaki
      a8eti d' ennonı8eıehen, te honachi[a]ıon
      ehonask[r]otonchonhj;

15   eaıenhaon d' oki kahachia ahotahekenk aonıi,

16   taot echiatier de θo haonıe?

Page 654

1   He, who is one [of them], will say, "Go away. Inside the earth
    his badness fell, he who is a great shaman."

2   What will your thoughts be concerning the group, all of whom
    will rush at you, and who will reproach you regarding your
    badness?

3   It is very frightening that the mistakes you made while you
    lived will again appear to you.

4   You will only be impatient with the space of time. You will
    only be discouraged those times when you look at your face
    in reflection of their scorn for you.

5   When you turn to face their great group you will see those who
    insult you as they stick their tongues out at you and
    examine your words for faults.

6   Not one is missing. They all hate you and are thankful for your
    position.

7   "Ho, ho," they will say, "Hurrah, he will make recompense to us
    whom he mistreated. Hurrah, he is taking the place of those
    he killed, those he stole from, and those whom he ravaged.

8   Hurrah, forever spirits will roll him over and over in the fire
    that does not extinguish." He will make satisfaction for
    mistreating belief.

9   Humans sometimes will scorn us when they are familiar with
    the matter. Their words will rise up.

10 Others are angry at us inside. When they changed their mind,
    they would talk openly, saying, "Here he of such a nature is
    standing."

11 They think, "He will hate me. When I will appear to him, he
    will go to fight me."

12 But when you will be brought back to life, those who are
    shamans will no longer be feared.

13 They will be publicly made to feel shame. Jesus will scorn
    them and will cause them to feel shame.

14 All of the sky-spirits of those who were humans will go about
    arriving with such words. If they had him in their mouths,
    they would spit him out.

15 One spirit will say, "Oh, was he ever treated appropriately!"

16 What will you do at that time?

17 echeras atiaondi d' esannonkonton: echierhon orih[i]erihen
ondaie n'onꞇiesaθa isk8aꞇakaochachen isk8aꞇatieronnonskon
aonꞇitahekenk ichien

18 echierhon, χondaie ea8enk d' etsik8atonnhont

19 ꞇatoꞇen aat θo ea8enk ennonchien t'esk8andiꞇonrhatenk._

20 onꞇ8andiꞇonratoꞇendi k8a8eti etsik8atonnhont din d' esa din
n'endi din d'a8esk8ak on8e eonton; onꞇ8andiꞇonratoꞇendi
esk8entat esonꞇ8arih8ichien d'ies8s k8a8eti de tion8e;
onꞇ8andiꞇonratoꞇendi ies8s te saꞇokaska a8eti n'on8e;

21 .8atsek andiare esaꞇotron d' aꞇoatatoꞇeti 8atsek iθondi
d'aꞇorih8anderaskon:

22 onne θo esaꞇondiatens aꞇoatatoꞇe'ti ehenhaon ndio aste desa de
esk8achiendaentak ꞇaronhiaꞇe ek8a8eꞇik aondechenhaon
oten desa de sk8atieronnonskon [ꞇ]ehen ti tsata8a ndio
ondechon ondi tsakaochontie' [illegible word omitted]
ꞇatsistaꞇe de te 8ask8as;

Page 655

1 a'son iθochien n'ondaie eha8enhatie chi' ate8atonh8entsoren,
θo ati eaꞇosonnent [e]nnonk8ae'sa ꞇahachaꞇon; eeaton[ta]ha
a te onkonten:

2 k8ioθti sk8arihondias8θa ti ꞇarih8ten?

3 stan nendi te ꞇrihiondias8θa atiaondi iꞇerhe ꞇatoꞇen θo ea8enk,
8ade θo ichien ihorih8tensti ha8endio,

4 tsinnen atichien aonsaꞇaron8a d' horih8ichiaꞇi?

5 tsirih8iost a8o tsirih8iost taꞇ8andaꞇeren d'aꞇ8atsihenstatsi,
saꞇ8a8endateri ti ha8end8ten,

6 taꞇ8atrihotat asken d'aꞇ8atonk, etsik8atonnhont de tionꞇ8e
ꞇatoꞇen etsik8atonnhont._

7 taot eχ' ioti te sk8andiꞇonrentons, stan iθochien ea8enk te
8atonde d'aonsaꞇiontonnhont:

8 sk8arihonniannonk ta te sk8aatoreθa ti handaꞇ8r ha8endio d'
esonꞇionnhont

17 You will approve, completely, of their scorn for you. You will think, "They are correct in their mistreatment of my great badness, my frequently creating great damage. They treated me as I deserved."

18 You will think, "This will happen when we will be resurrected."

19 It is true that it will happen. Do not doubt me.

20 All of our minds are certain that we will be resuscitated, whether you or I or those who will become humans afterwards. Our minds are certain that one day Jesus will complete the matter of all of us who are humans. Our minds are certain that Jesus will separate all humans.

21 He will first put those who are true in one place, putting elsewhere those who are frequently mistaken.

22 He will call the true ones by name, saying, "Come here you who have praised my name. We will be together forever in the sky; but you who frequently caused damage, leave it inside the earth. Leave your badness behind in the fire that does not extinguish."

Page 655

1 Still, he will go about saying, "The world is split in two." Then, those who are shamans will descend into the flames. They will commence to be in the fire forever.

2 Why do you treat the matter as if it were made up, a story just for amusement?

3 I do not treat it as a made-up story. I completely believe that it is true that it will happen, for the Great Voice determined it to be such.

4 Who would destroy that which he created?

5 Believe it, believe it; copy we who are called Charcoal. We know the nature of his word.

6 Listen to us when we say, "We who are humans will be revived. It is true. We will be revived."

7 Why is it that your thoughts swing back and forth that it will not happen that we would be resuscitated?

8 You tell many made-up stories. You do not examine, consider that the Great Voice has the power to cause us to live.

9 tsinderaⴗa sen ti hoki d' hoteiennondi deχ' ondechate aⴗeti
deχa ιaronhiate ondaie ichien chia haatat d' esonιionnhont

10 isa atichien ahiatandoron de chionιⴗeha d'eherhon
aonsahiatichien ondaie ichien de te haondechandoron
etiondecha?_

11 chi hiaιienhⴗindi, d' ason te tsitrontak:

12 aonsahionniska atichien d' eherhon aonsahiatonnia

13 sen a'son te endarek aιonⴗe, ioton ichien d'onne haⴗeri onⴗe
aiondaιrat

14 taot ichien aιenk te ⴗatondend d'eherhon onιⴗe
aonsaiondaιrat?

15 ndiaⴗeron ιandoron d' aiaιondechonnia chieιannen iondecha
steniesθa te eeratandend, chia de onιⴗe aonsaiontatiatonnia
d'onna iιaen d' aieerat?

16 ondaie isen chien ιandoron ιachondi d' a'son te ιaen d' aieerat,
stan te ιandoron onsaιachondi d'onne iaιen d' aieerat

17 iιaen de kⴗaeronιe ιehen, haatonniatinnen haⴗendio oιenra
hoerati de saιoatondi daat okontakⴗi n'onⴗe ιehen

18 tsoιenraen iθondi d' aonsahaerat aonsasaιoatonnia;

19 aonsahontendoronkⴗen atichien?

20 ondaie n'onhⴗa io'ti te skⴗandiιonrhatandik, d' iskⴗerhe
otendoronkⴗi ndaoten d' a te ιaιe aonsaieestannon de
kⴗaeronιe iskⴗerheιandoron d'a te onneaιe
aonsaienneannhontron a te otsinnonhiataιe
aonsaietsinnonhiatontarak

21 aiaιotendoronkⴗen ιatoιen n'onιⴗe te echionniak oten
d'haⴗendio taot ichien aiaⴗenk ahotendoronkⴗen ti hochondi
isen chien de kⴗaeronιe;

22 anniaten aesahonichiaik, chi aⴗakonronⴗa ta ti aesandoron d'
achierhon aonsaιhonachondia?

23 chi sachondi n'ondaie haⴗendio hoteiendichiaιi kⴗaeronιe
onsaⴗatronⴗa n'ondaie d'onn'ekⴗenhej

24 serhon θo ara esateiendichien haⴗendio d'esonιionnhont

25 θo θo esakontatie d' esachonnia sti hoeren st'achia hochiaιi
stan steniesθa ta t'esanderaxe,

9 Let it be that you admire that he is a spirit that has the ability to make the earth and all the sky; he is the same one who will make us live.

10 Would he find you difficult to make again, you who are a mere human, if he wishes it to be such, if he does not find a country to be difficult.

11 He knew how to make you when still you did not exist.

12 Could he make you if he would wish to make you?

13 While still humans did not exist, it was possible for him to wish that a human would be caused to exist.

14 Why would it not become so if he would wish a human to again be caused to be?

15 Which is difficult, that the earth would be made of great size out of nothing, or that humans would be made again where there is something to make them out of?

16 It is certainly difficult, preparing something when still one has nothing to do it with. It is not difficult, preparing something again when one has something to do it with.

17 There is our body; the Great Voice made it out of something. At the very beginning, he made humans out of dust.

18 Again dust is there; he would also do it again with that. He would again make them.

19 Would it be difficult for him to do it over again?

20 You now doubt it; you believe that it is very difficult to assemble every one of our bodies. You think that it is difficult to join every bone, every nerve.

21 It would certainly be difficult for humans to do it. But the Great Voice, why would it be difficult for him to prepare our body?

22 Sometime you would make a canoe and then it would break. Would it be difficult for you to think, "I would make the canoe again"?

23 It is the same with the way you are made. The Great Voice made with his skill our body that is destroyed when we die.

24 Think only that you will be made with skill. The Great Voice will bring us to life.

25 You will continue being prepared as he has done it from the moment he completed it. No part of you will be mistaken any longer.

Page 656

1 steniesθa atiaondi t'esannonθe θo θo esaakonten aȣerochia
   tetiorerochiontak:

2 χa ichien eo'tik esaskotonten ιachaȣi etaιe ati esachitonten stan
   ichien ondihιtonhiaιι te kȣateȣennonniande

3 stan iaon te ȣataionde, d' otsinnonhiata otsonra, oskȣenha
   ondaȣa aȣeiachia, aȣeti θo iθochien eskȣatijherakȣat
   etiotindata ιehen,

4 aonsahondιtonrhenk atichien d' haȣendio stan [on]t[a]kȣak?
   stan te sondιtonrhens

5 θo θo eseiachiandionten st'aȣeiachiontakȣak: θo θo
   esaιonchionten ekaιonchiontak[ȣak] θo aat esaiachionten
   ekaiachiontak; a te ιaιe esandataenhas n'ondataιehenιstan
   skat te hendιtonroiande:

6 haenteri te kaen d' onnonra d' atietsinnonrakȣen de
   skȣatrioskȣa; haenteri te kaen n' onȣe ιaȣatsa d'
   eskȣaȣatsaιaien;

7 haȣatsaιenk skȣaskȣaιon, ehȣatsatakȣa ati es'eskȣaȣas

8 ondaie esaιoȣoatsieraten d' etsiskok onιȣe ιehen stan ichien
   skȣaȣente ιen;

9 oten de ιaio skȣaȣatsaιaien otiatennion de skȣaskȣaιon isa
   skȣaȣatsa oton, skȣaȣen n'ondaie eιenk._

10 stan t'etsetsiȣandihe: ondaie θo ara eetsiȣatsoronȣas n'onȣe
   ιaȣatsa ιehen onek inde te haȣeri haȣendio aiontatiataιaia n'
   onȣe d'onna' asaιoatichien:

11 cheȣatsannneskȣan io'ti n'onȣe de cheataιaien etsontatierisen
   n'ondaie d' etsontonnhont etsesaȣatsaskȣa eaȣenk:

12 achiatonhonj atichien taot eχa aonιeχȣa?

13 echieȣatsasχȣahenk iaon d'endaskȣa eeronιe ιehen; echierhon
   ndaoten aιatieron n'onȣe aχeataιaia;

14 skȣatrihote d' iιatonk, aȣeti ihondιtonratoιendi haȣendio: te
   kaen de kȣaeronιe ιehen onnea ιehen aȣeti d' otsinnonhiata
   ιehen din de steniesθa iotierennen honȣe ιehen

Page 656

1 Nothing of yours will be missed; your hair will be suspended where it was attached.

2 It will be like this. Your head will be attached on top; at the bottom, then, your feet will be attached; we will not be wrongly turned around.

3 They will not be lumped together inside, the veins, bowels, liver, lungs, and the heart; they will go straight to where they used to be.

4 Would the Great Voice forget where it used to be attached? He does not forget.

5 So your heart will be suspended where it used to be attached. He will not forget one place. Your face will be attached where it used to be attached; your arm will be attached where it used to be attached; everyone will be in its former place in you.

6 He knows where the scalp that you seized from your enemies still lies. He knows where it still lies, the human flesh that you consumed.

7 He sees the flesh in your internal cavity; he will take the flesh out. He will take it out of you.

8 He will add the flesh that is missing from those humans that you put in the pot. It does not belong to you.

9 But the bodies of the animals you eat the flesh of will pass into your internal cavity, will become your flesh. Yours it will be.

10 You will not take flesh from humans, because, when he created them, the Great Voice did not wish that humans would consume each other.

11 It is as if you peeled off their flesh in a circle, those humans you consumed. They will have recompense made. When they will be brought back to life, they will smell of your flesh.

12 Would you say, "Why would they ravage me?"

13 You will hate the flesh of the prisoners' bodies. You will think, "Greatly I caused damage when I consumed humans."

14 You listen to that which I say; the Great Voice is sure about it all: where they lie in our body, the flesh, bones, all the nerves, and all kinds of things that humans were made of.

15 ondaie ati sterhonhonj te s'ak de diȣ,ondaie esaιonnhont d'
     aιoȣenιehen, stan te hondiιonh[i]aιi θo te honniande;
16 a te eataιe esaιoerisen d' aιaonhȣa eeronιe ιehen stan ta
     t'esanneohietande desa sannea ιehen din n' endi ιehen;
17 ondaie θo eskiȣeιik aιenneannhontron, ondaie θo tesχiataχa
     deιaȣatsa din d' onnea de chi te ιιχennen iotinnen;
18 ondaie θo te skiatrandeιen d'otsinnonhiata d'otirandeιennen
     st'ason itionnhek:
19 ondaie tsirihȣenhȣa ondaie tsatrendaen sterhon ιatoιen
     etsaιȣaataȣeιik etsaιȣatonnhont,
20 χa ichien atiaondi etso'tik θo θo a te tsaιȣaιakarenten onhȣa te
     aιȣaιakarent.

Page 657
1 θo a te tsaιȣachitonten, de onhȣa t'eaȣachitont θo a te
     tsaιȣaiachionten st' aιȣaiachiontakȣi n'onhȣa; χa ichien
     etsonιȣaskotonten st' onιȣaskotont;
2 stan ȣa te sonιȣaatȣtentande stan ta te sonιȣaatatennionhe._
3 etsonχienteha n' onχienterinnen; eaιenrhon ondaie ichien
     χondaie haatsinnen de chi i're

THE NATURE OF THE DEVIL

4 stirihȣateha, d' anniaten te skȣandiιonrhaten eskȣerhon aonιi
     sen ιatoιen etsontonnhont oki ichien skȣahonchoies; iȣerhe
     ennonchien eendoronkȣat ιarihȣiosti
5 aonhȣa de ondechonronnon ondiιonratoιendi atiaondi
     etsontonnhont; isa iθochien tsonnhitandik θo aat de
     skȣarihȣiosti;
6 iȣerhe χa iθochien aiaιondiιonretsik st' ondende iens; iȣerhe
     n'ondaie aχeatandoιaret d' aιonhȣa aiatandoιaron de
     ιaronhiaιe aιokȣasti._
7 taot ati iιaerha d' iȣerhe aχeatandoιaret d'aionkȣasθa
     ιaronhiaιe:

15 Continue to think that God will again seize it. He will bring
   back to life that which belonged to them. He will not be
   confused in his making.
16 Everybody will be made complete. Your bones will not be
   mixed with mine.
17 My bones that were joined will be together. Flesh and bones will
   be joined again in the same places in which they were joined.
18 The veins that were joined while still we lived will be reunited.
19 Bring the matter to prayer; believe it is true that we will be
   together again, that we will be resuscitated.
20 It will completely be such again here, when every one of us
   will again have eyes where we now have eyes.

Page 657

1 Then every one of us will again have feet attached where we
   now have feet. Then we will again have arms attached were
   we have them attached now. We will again have our head
   attached where our head is attached now.
2 He will not cause us to be other than we are. He will not
   change us.
3 They will again know us, those who knew us; they will think,
   "This is he who was called _____ when he walked."[13]

THE NATURE OF THE DEVIL

4 Know the matter for certain; if sometime you will doubt,
   wondering whether it is true that one will be brought back
   to life, the spirit is disturbing your ears, wishing, "Let it not
   be that they value believing."
5 The earth-dweller is certain, completely, that one will be
   brought back to life. It causes you to ignore it at the moment
   of your believing.
6 It thinks, "They should persist in their thinking as they walk
   on earth." It thinks, "I should cause them bad fortune. I
   bring bad luck to those who are happy in the sky."
7 What does it do when it wishes, "I should cause them bad
   luck, those who would be happy in the sky"?

8   i8atonk ati ondiıonr8annen ıarihondi d' ihontonk
     hatitsihen[s]tatsi ondechon eontetsirat d' eaihej
     aıotieronnonskon, onek hatirihonniak d'ihontonk ıaronhiaıe
     eonk8asθa d'aıoatatoıeti ıehen:

9   te ıatoıen nondaie i8atonk d' oki: esk8enhej θo ara i8atonk,
     onne ichien a8atrih8aten dinde tsonesk8andihik, dinde
     sk8achiatorhak

10   taot ichien aonsaietoj d' eaihej._

11   etsaıon sen i8atonk oki onh8a isen θo sak8astik te 8atiesen
     onh8a isen θo sonesk8en de ıandak8aıe haon

12   taot ichien tachatatendahatinnen n'ondaie?

13   aiora8en te tsisachoniese d' echiehej,

14   taot ichien t'achiatandihi ıarih8anderaıi?

15   te ıatoıen aat te ontatere8aθa d'onn' aaihej,
     d'aıorih8anderaıihatiend st' ason aıonnhek._

16   χa ichien iıaerha d' oki, i8erhe aiaıenrhon te ıatoıen te
     aıotetsirati n'ondechon

17   ondiıonratoıendi n'ondechonronnon stan t'erih8anderaχend
     aion8e, det'aierih8iost ondaie io'ti;

18   st' ak8ichotonk i8erhe aırihondias8θa aθo n' ondaie

19   ıatoχa d' oki ondechonronnon stan te tsisk8arih8anderaχend te
     sk8erhe eaı8atetsirat aondechenhaon d' eaı8arih8anderas:

20   ıatoχa d' oki i8erhe eonθarat iaon a8entenhaon te aıenrhe
     eaı8ak8asθa ıatoıen aondechenhaon d'ora8en
     eonı8akaratatihatie eaıionnhonti

21   ıatoχa d'oki i8erhe aiaıondiıonrasχ8ik aionı8e, ondaie
     aonsaieıenten d'aionda8aha aiaıaonesk8en st'ason [a]ıonnhe
     ondaie ichien te endoronk8endend d' aondechenhaon
     aiaıotonnharak ıaronhiaıe din d'aiontatennhaha d'8kaot,
     aiaıenhaon eıonesat ta t'echrache

8   Because it has a great mind, it says, "It is a made-up story, that which the Charcoal tell, that inside the earth those who do many damaging things will suffer when they die. It is only a made-up story they tell, when they say that those who were true will be happy.

9   It is not true." The spirit says, "You will die only." It says, "Both what you found pleasing and what you felt was painful are ended."

10 What would one experience again, when one does?

11 "Have courage," says the spirit. "Be happy now if it is easy. Take pleasure from sex."

12 How would you not have caused your own loss?

13 It would be good not to experience it when you die.

14 Why would you not fear making mistakes?

15 It is not true that they are not punished when they die, those who committed mistakes while still they live.

16 That is what the spirit does. It wishes, "They should think that it is not true, that they do not suffer inside the earth."

17 The earth-dweller knows for certain that humans would not have committed mistakes if they would believe that it is so.

18 While its force stands, it wishes, "Let me make it into a made-up story."

19 The earth-dwelling spirit knows that you would not make mistakes again if you think, "We will be caused to suffer forever when we will make mistakes."

20 The spirit knows, thinking, "They will do good continually if they think, 'We will be truly happy forever if we go about taking care of that which is good as we continue to live.'"

21 The spirit knows, thinking, "Human minds would be too small. They would prefer a short time of pleasure while still they live. They would not have valued that forever they would rejoice in the sky, and they would incite each other to badness, saying, 'I will mistreat you and you will not approve of it.'"

Page 658

1 aiaιondiιonrannenk, ondaie aionθasdeχa θo aiondetsiha
   aiaιochiatoren ondaie ichien aat aionθas aiaιenrhon
   aondechenhaon te ιatonnhon taionȣa n'ondechon θo
   eȣaιieient eιihej._

2 ondiιonratoιendi d' oki θo ichien iȣaens onn'aerihȣiost te
   tsennhatenk erihȣanderaθa aionȣe aιenrhe aonιoneskȣen
   ȣade ondaie aat echi etsondera'ti onskannha
   d'aondechenhaon eonkȣasθa

3 aiaonnhiska atichien d' oki ti ιarihȣten

4 ondaie ati iondiak skȣaskȣaιon ιandachiondaθa iȣatonk te
   ιatoιen deχa handakarotatie hoa'taton'hatie d'
   hatsihenstatsi._

5 aȣaton atichien d' aonsaiontonnhont onȣe ιehen ȣade
   otsikencha θo eιenk

6 oten dȣa eontatiataιaienk aonsaiontatiataerit atichien n'
   ondaie?

7 taot ichien aiaȣenk aonsaiontatiatichien θo θo
   aonsaiontatiatȣenst ti eatȣtennen st'aιonnhek?

8 θo ichien iιaerha d' oki ιandaιon skȣandiιonrachaθa inn?

9 etsak iθochien θo iȣaιierha iθondi d' aιonhȣa chia
   teιonιȣatonnheskannha

10 onek ichien n' endi te ιatrihotas d' aιahonchoies, stan te
   ιaronιasennik aιendiιonra iθochien iιerhe ιatoιen te
   ιiateχaska d' aιennonkȣat din de ιieronιe onn' eιihej;

The Resurrection of the Body

11 diȣ [i]chien te haι[e]ondasontak t'achia ιehen aιatondia

12 taot ichien es[h]otendoronkȣen d'eherhon t'aondandasonten
   d'etsontonnhont onȣe ιehen?

13 ιatoιen aιon θo eorichon aιonnea ιehen, oιont ichien te
   haιannronnionk aȣentenhaon de diȣ es[h]aenteha

14 n'ondaie d'eherhon aonsaιonneannhontron, eskat
   aonsaιenneiest de haeronιe ιehen

15 onek [i]θochien aionιenneateιatik a[ι]ȣatrios ondaie ichien
   ȣtoιeti eȣataten d'oιenra,

Page 658

1 They would be weak-minded. They would fear that for a short time they would feel pain. They should greatly fear, thinking, "Forever I will be tortured inside the earth, which will follow me when I die.'"

2 The spirit is sure, then, that "it happens that once they believe, humans will very much regret their mistakes, thinking, 'It would please me,' because greatly they desire to be happy forever."

3 Would the spirit ignore the nature of the matter?

4 It is done inside of you; it lies, saying, "This is not true. They go about obscuring." It makes he who is called Charcoal disappear.

5 "Would it be possible that humans would be resuscitated, as it will involve rotten material?

6 But others whose bodies will have been eaten, would they be again furnished with what is necessary?

7 How would it happen that they would be created again so that they would be made as they were while they lived?"

8 What does the spirit do to corrupt your mind?

9 Frequently, it does to me what it does to all of us, bearing us ill will. It is for nothing.

10 I do not listen. I move my ears. I do not hear it even a little. Inside my mind, I think, "It is true that my medicine and my body will be separated when I die.

THE RESURRECTION OF THE BODY

11 God joined me at the beginning, when I was born.

12 How would he find it difficult to do again when he will wish, 'I would again join it' and humans would be brought back to life"?

13 It is true, then, that one's bones will be spread over many places; nevertheless, God will be at many places continually and he will again know.

14 He will wish, "The bones will be joined again as one. I will assemble them in his body."

15 My enemies would only burn my bones. It is fortunate that they will burn to ashes.

16   ondaie ati es'aerat haȣendio de [e]s[h]aenneichien din de eonneaȣindik ondechon ndiaȣera'ten aȣenιe?

17   oeri ichien n'ondaie es[h]atariest ti ιatarȣten d'aιennea ιehen ιata oton ondaie θo es[h]aιenneichiat aoienka,

18   stan iȣaia te ȣaιendιιonrȣtakȣas d'aιerhon kȣe de t'onιiataιaia ιanniennon eιihej

Page 659

1   stan iθochien eoataȣenk de ιieronιe ιehen taot ichien [e]t[h]aιateiachiȣtak de onde?

2   haondechichiaιι isen chien haȣendio etiondecha stan te hoerati, stan te ιaentak d'ahoeratinnen

3   ondaie atichien te s[h]aatichiahend de ιieronιe ιehen d'onne ιaen d' ahaerat

4   stan n'onhȣa ta te skȣaatore'θa ti haiendȣten haȣendio a te oιennhaιe te ȣarati de sten akȣten n' onsahonnhont aaȣenk haȣendio.

5   etsak orontoιenheon ochende te tsȣtsitsont te tsohiont, te tsondratont aȣeti io'ton d'onnhekȣinnen io'tinnen de ιaronta ιehen

6   onsaιa[ι]enra θo ara onne ichien tonsaιak n'ondaie aȣeti, aιandiȣak iθochien onsaιandratonten onsaιatsitsaraχon onsaȣahionten onne atiaondi onsaȣatonnhont ιarihȣaȣeti de ιaronta ιehen

7   te skȣanderaȣas sen sti aȣens onn' eskȣandaj ondechon

8   skȣannenhas'θa aιonniannik iθochien aonnenhaȣiha t'aaȣenk aonnenhaιenhej

9   θoia θo onsaȣentaȣa tontaιandiok ichien tontaȣatonnhonθe onnenha ιehen

10 onne θo ιannendae onsaȣaton chia onsaȣ[at]ennenhichien de kȣaιannionkȣa, aȣeti de kȣandatarontakȣa.

11 skat ichien n'endi onderati anderaȣas ιandatara aιej ȣθaj ndiaȣeraten din de sten akandiahȣten aιaentaha θo ara ιeskȣaιon

12 onn' aιaȣiha taot ichien te ȣatatennionȣes

13 de ondaie ιangȣenia iθochien aȣaton ιandatara ιehen dinde ιaȣatsa ιehen d'aιeιinnen. o ichien kȣaienhȣi n'endi de kȣaȣatsatennions ιangȣenia θo itionniak onιȣentonraιon,

16 The Great Voice will do it again. He will make the bones again, whether the bones will be rotting inside the earth or in water.

17 Oh! He will assemble again the clay that my bones became. He will make my bones again quickly.

18 Not even a little will I worry if I thought, "Perhaps dogs will consume my body when I die."

Page 659

1 Why would he have a hard time with what will happen to my body equal to that of a country?

2 The Great Voice made the country, certainly, and when he did, he did not make it with anything, as there wasn't anything he would have used with which to make it.

3 Would he not have made my body again when there is something he could use with which to make it?

4 You are not examined for flaws, for the skill of the Great Voice is such that every year he gives life to innumerable things.

5 Frequently a tree "dies" in winter; blossoms, fruit, leaves are no longer attached. All have disappeared that provided life. It was like a dead tree.

6 When again it is spring, it all comes back. Suddenly, leaves are again attached. Blossoms again open up. Fruits are again attached. All of the tree that was is brought back to life.

7 Let it be that you admire it, just as when you will plant corn hidden inside the ground.

8 After a long time, the corn rotted and died.

9 Several days again pass before the seeds sprout, when the corn is brought back to life.

10 Fall again appears and corn is again made, completed. We cook with it in a pot and bake bread with it. That which rotted made the corn become like clay.

11 I, for one, greatly admire the bread I have eaten, as well as the corn soup, or any other kind of food that was outside then inside of my body.

12 When it rots, what does it change into?

13 The bread and flesh that I ate became blood. Ah, we have the ability to change flesh into blood. We make it inside our stomachs.

14 stan iθochien onι8aki te ιen,
15 di8 atien achia ahaonnhi v/ ahondoron d'eherhon
   a8at[e]ιenratendi ιa8atsa θo aonsa8aton de k8aeronιe ιehen
   oιenra ιehen
16 stan ichien tehotendoronk8andihe n'ondaie._
17 taoten ιehen d' o8hisθa aι8a8histonniaθa d' aι8annionιenhak
18 ιata ιehen aι8ataratennions ati, d'ara θo ti aιιonι8eha d'o8hista
   aιionniak,
19 ta ti te handaι8rachend di8 daat echi es'oki aat d' eherhon
   a8atoat[at]endi θo d' oιenra on8e sen aonsa8aton?
20 ehonaιr8aha echa, te hotendoronk8andik aat en steniesθa._

Page 660
1 tsirih8iost aθo ara sterhon ιatoιen etsaι8atonnhont.
2 tsirih8iost iθondi sterhon θo θo etsaι8atonnhont onι8aatorak
   ιaronhiaιe d8a eaι8et, oten d8a n'ondechon eent.
3 [ts]irih8ios[t] sterhon aondechenhaon eonk8asθa
   ιaronhiaιeronnon, aondechenhaon eontetsirat
   ondechonronnon
4 onh8a de stondara8a st' a'son itsonnhe, d' esk8atientak
   ndia8eron sk8ara8as ndi8aron sk8a'tsaθa, onh8a θo
   tsirih8erik [!]
5 stan ta te ondiιonrhati ιaronhiaιe ona'ti sk8annondandik
   sk8a8eti, ichien isk8atandik ondechon.
6 estenniaιon ati steniesθa a8entenhaon atsierenk d'ora8en
7 ondaie d' aioio de ιaronhiaιe aιok8asti, atrendaent ioios de
   ιaronhiaιe aιok8asti onsa8atatre8ati d'8kaot ioios de
   ιaronhiaιe aιok8asti, a8eti d'aontetsikaston d'onn'
   aaιonnonh8aj aaιonnhonιenha, aeesaha ondaie ichien
   tendennions de ιaronhiaιe aιok8asti
8 sk8arih8ichias i n'onh8a taot aieer chia aieon ιaronhiaιe?
9 onh8ati etietsiatendotondinnen ti ιarih8ten onta te
   skondak8annen de ιaro onati / v dechi a8eti._

14 It is not that we are spirits.
15 God is placed before. Would he ignore it, find it difficult when he will wish, "Dust should change into flesh," our body out of dust.
16 It will not be difficult for him.
17 What did it used to be, the metal we French make things out of?
18 It was earth: we who are only mere humans who make metal changed earth.
19 God, the very great spirit, will not have exercised power when he will wish, "The body should be changed. Dust should become humans again."
20 He will be so powerful that all kinds of things are not difficult for him.

Page 660

1 Believe it! Think only that it is true that we will be brought back to life.
2 Believe, also that our body will be intact at the very moment we will be brought back to life. Some of us will go to the sky, but others will go inside the earth.
3 Believe that forever sky-dwellers will be happy and that forever those who live inside the earth will suffer.
4 Now choose a place while you still live, the place where you will be put. Either you are left out or you are designated. Now do the right thing.
5 It is not to be doubted that on the side of the sky, they take care of all of you, and that all of you fear inside the earth.
6 Have courage, then; continually do all kinds of good.
7 It would be worth happiness in the sky: praying is worth being happy in the sky; restraining oneself from badness is worth being happy in the sky; for those who were patient with those who were sick, suffered, who entered a poor state, that is worth their being happy in the sky.
8 Do you search for a matter now of what one would do before arriving in the sky?
9 A long time ago, they told you a story that there were no longer two places, here on all of this side.

THE JESUITS AND THE IROQUOIS MISSION

10 oeri ondi θora onne ioιennhaιe etionι8aιaens eχ'ondechen / v
etitsondechen onh8ati etiaιannondandik etisk8andare / v
eχa sk8andare,

11 ondaie d'aι8erhe te aχirih8aienstandi asen st'aieer chia
aionk8asθa ιaronhiaιe d'onn' aaihej:

12 onh8ati chi aι8atrendaenk aιatonk, θo sen te onι8endaraθon
aιonnonchiondiιe aiaι8arih8aenha8it iθo ιarih8iosti

13 isa ichien sk8ahaha8eιindi:

14 θora onne a te onι8atati desa onι8eri askennonia sken
a8atondechatat deχa te onιiondechenton a teιon
ichientsisk8arih8iaχon

15 ondesonk ιehen ehorhaιenchonnen ιannie[n]ιe eθonandiarenti

16 onnontaιe eon[ι]8ennonnen ιannienta aaι8andatonnia stan
iθochien te onniannindi de θo aa8atien chi aonχichien te
hotiaιi onnei8tronnon ιannontaιeronnon te aιonnen._

17 onne θo onsaιaιenra haondechete ontahondechenha8i
d'[h]atinnia8enten aherhonska eskat aθo ahondarat
onontaιeronnon ιatoιen ehoatindaιeren d'[h]atinnia8enten
hotirih8iosti de hontrendaen._

18 taot aek8aer haoten?

19 ahatende honatichia[ι]i n'ondaie;

20 etsak onsahonrask8a ιannionahake d' hatitsihenstatsi ondaie
onsahotiatenha8i atatrih8aienstandihon

21 henderhonhonk areisaιen, a te ondeche esaι8a8ennenha8it
ha8endio a8eti d' aιonnonchiondiιe ιandastoιe dinde riιe.

Page 661

1 haesk8aio ichien n'ondaie Ataratiri ιehen tendi te
haesak8atsistore Hechon ιehen, [H]atironta ιehen;

2 te annaosteiaj ιehen skat ohonra8enta hesk8aio'ti Arontoιennen
haatsinnen;

THE JESUITS AND THE IROQUOIS MISSION

10 For several summers we were ready to go to your country, a long time before some good happens to us where you live.

11 We wish, "Let it be that we teach them what they should do so they would be happy in the sky when they would die."

12 A long time ago we prayed, saying, "Let it be that we go to establish ourselves at [(the country of) Those Who Make a House (the Iroquois)]. We should bring believing there."

13 You closed the path to us.

14 Every time we talk, we wish, "Let peace be present in this country." We didn't go the country, because every time you cut off the matter.

15 Father Isaac Jogues was ambushed in Mohawk country, where they cut off his fingers.

16 In Onondaga country we went and made Flint our village. It was not a long time we were there before they searched for us at Montreal, the Oneidas and Onondagas together.

17 Spring returned and Father Paul Ragueneau carried the Bear Nation of the Wendat. He continued to wish, "Let the Onondagas truly imitate the Bears in believing and praying."

18 What would be the nature of what we should do?

19 He was at the ending point of their killing them.

20 Several of the Charcoal left again from the country of the French. They again were brought over to teach all over.

21 They wished, "Ah, we will bring the word of the Great Voice to every country, that of the Iroquois, that of the Andaste, and the Erie."

Page 661

1 You killed them at Ataratiri. You covered with fire Hechon [Father Jean de Brébeuf] and Hatironta [Father Gabriel Lalemant].[14]

2 At Te annaosteiaj you killed Arontoιennen [Father Antoine Daniel] with a gun.[15]

3   Eθarita ιehen skat iθondi te heskȣa'kȣati ohonraȣenta
    heskȣaenti ȣracha haatsinnen; okȣentondiιe skat jaques
    haatsinnen te hotiaιi achienk ahaeskȣaio chi hoatenhȣa
    haȣendio ondechrase:
4   te ȣastaθo eθaιiatrakȣa't onnontsira ιehen θentenhaȣiθa ιehen
    n' [h]onatindaskȣenhaonnen ιannienιe ιarihȣaȣeti
    honatiesati,
5   te ȣastato n' ondaie ehaιiatendoton aιerhon tsonχiataȣi,
6   stan ichien te skȣerhonhonk onne skȣaioskȣa d'aιȣatsihenstatsi
    ondaie haιonȣentenrandend, de haaιȣaesaθa; stante
    skȣerhonhonk ondaie-iaon ahaonιȣaationtinnen ιaronhiaιe
    daat etiaιokȣasti
7   te onnianninnen te hennonhek, chieιannen a te ι[i]atrek de
    skȣandiιonra ιehen, chia de endi onιȣandiιonra
8   aιȣerhonnonk haondechrenhaon sen te hennonnhe d'
    hotinnonchiondi, oten desa iskȣerhonhonk onne sen
    hondasaιi aȣeti d'hatitsihenstatsi,
9   endi nde a te ȣentaιe etsiatrendaentandihik aιȣatonhonk: Diȣ
    sa chi[ieȣendio] [st] aιionnhe setenr asken d'
    aιonnonchiondi, sendiιonrontrak asken aierihȣiost kȣe n'
    ondechon t' aontetsirat d' eaihej;
10 etietsiatannonstaskȣa etietsinnhehek st' aιȣatrendaenhak oten
    desa skȣeiachasennihik aȣentenhaon iskȣatonhonk
    aιȣandȣsenȣanȣan de skȣatsihenstatsi te etsindaskȣaenk
    asen aietsiskok ichien ndaoten;
11 chi aιȣarihȣateri aιȣataχen ti skȣandiιonrȣten,

Page 662
1   ta ti te aιȣerhonhonk iȣaia ndio sen ondi aiaιindaιeren,
    honnonhȣa de hatiataesen hatindiaιaste θo sken ondi
    aiaιȣatatiatȣtenst onχindiaχonk onkitsistorech; aiaχindiaχon
    iθondi n'endi aiaχitsistorej,
2   stan andea n'ondaie te onιȣeri, θora iȣasen aaχiatonten
    d'etsienhȣaten, stan skat oιont ta te aχendiaιi,
3   stan [te] tsonnonkȣaro'tataθo te aχi'kȣan d'aιotieratinnen
    eataȣeιi ichien ateιon tsaιoaιendi

3　At Etharita, also, you knocked over 8racha [Father Charles
　　Garnier] with a gun. At Ok8entondile [Trois Rivieres] one
　　[was killed], Jacques he was called. You killed three in Te
　　hotiali [Montreal]: Chihoatenhwa ['he is brought from afar'],
　　Ha8endio [Great Voice], and Ondechrase [New Country].[16]
4　Let it not be that he will not include me with Onnontsira
　　['head'] and θentenha8iθa ['where he brings a field'], who
　　were taken as prisoners and mistreated.[17]
5　Let it not be that he will tell a story, they again gave us.
6　You did not think when you killed we who are called Charcoal,
　　"They had pity on we who mistreat them." You didn't think,
　　"They would have introduced us to the sky where they are
　　very happy."
7　It was not a long time ago that your mind and our mind lived
　　far apart.
8　We wished, "Let the Iroquois live forever," but you wished,
　　"Let all the Charcoal be dead."
9　Every day we prayed for you, saying, "God, you are Great
　　Voice of our lives. Have pity on those who are Iroquois. Put
　　inside their minds that they would believe, for fear that they
　　would be caused to suffer inside the earth when they die."
10　We were taking care of you, protecting you while we were
　　praying for you, but you were continually angry at us,
　　saying, "We speak insultingly against you who are called
　　Charcoal. Let it be that we take you as prisoners; we would
　　put you in water [i.e., in a pot.]"
11　We knew, my brothers, that your minds are such.

Page 662
1　However, we did not think, not even a little, "Let it be that we
　　should copy them. They mistreat us, are cruel. Let us be
　　made as those who cut our fingers and cover us with fire.
　　We should cut their fingers, cover them with fire, too."
2　Never would we wish, "Several tens of your nephews and
　　nieces we should tie up." Not once would I cut their fingers.
3　Not one wampum belt did we seize that they used to come
　　together with every time that one goes out again.

4   etsak iθochien d'oki onɪꙅandɪꞇonrontraskꙅa atonhonk, ndio sen
    ondi tsio d'aꙅentenhaon etsiesaθa

5   stan te aɪꙅatrihotaskꙅa, ondaie ichien areisaɪen
    etsiakeronsennihi n'ondechon ꙅteχa d' aeskꙅaatateɪennen
    aondechenhaon d'ason te skꙅarihꙅiostinnen aɪennen chia
    aietsionnen

6   oeri ichien aɪꙅerhonhon'k] n'onχitsistorech iꙅasχꙅach d'
    otitsistaꙅan ondaie te otennonhianditi n'ondechon ꙅteχa d'
    aondechrenhaon te ꙅasχꙅache,

7   stan ɪarihꙅate ɪen n'onχioch aɪꙅerhonhonk aioraꙅan
    esonχionnhont haꙅendio d'eꙅatondechate

8   ndioharon hast aɪꙅataχen tsirihonti de skꙅandiaɪaste

9   onne i-aon skꙅaꙅatsaχꙅindi etsiataɪaien n' onɪꙅe ɪehen

10 tsiɪondasennik asken te ꙅatiesen atatendennianni

11 sterhon onne iaon onnianni sti ꙅa d' aχiondechatonti d'
    aɪꙅatrioskꙅa.

12 taot isenchien aonsaietsiataet n'onꙅe, chia aeskꙅateꙅaten d'
    etsiatiataesatandik?

13 annen aotaɪe aonsiestsiasteraaj d'etsindoɪareskꙅa chia
    aonseskꙅaerik d'etiskꙅeiachenskꙅa;

14 te tsendare ondi de skꙅatatiendaonskꙅa, stan skat te
    skandataen de skꙅatatien'tannonhonk stan skat eꙅa te
    skahꙅatsiraen d' aɪahꙅatsiraꙅeɪik,

15 ara iθo ti otsikꙅeniarichon t'etiendarek eskꙅatrioskꙅa,
    tsotrahichiaj onne t'etiaɪoenχꙅinnen; ɪaio iθochien aɪondarat
    t'etiaɪoteɪatinnen

16 annen atichien aieatontieskꙅ[a] n'onꙅe ꙅendake ɪehen,
    etionnontate ɪehen ɪeraɪenrek ɪehen Trakꙅae ɪehen Rie ɪehen,
    askikꙅannhe ɪehen, ehonkeɪehen?

17 aꙅeti atiaondi etsiatentonniati,

18 taot ichien aiaꙅenk aeskꙅannonaj orast atatondiasti
    atatendatꙅtaꙅan atatondechatonti?

19 onne ichien ondi tsondecharahaχꙅihatie a te ɪondeche
    d'etsieiachasennihik, stan skat te tsaondechaꙅenrente,

20 χa sen te aɪotiesti, otiokꙅaꙅeti d' estiotiokꙅaɪasti n'onꙅe, θo
    ichien aiohꙅarindandꙅtenk ti onnontandꙅte de chi
    onnontara;

21 oɪonɪe sen te tsonstaronk d' aɪotonnenskꙅa ɪehen
    d'etsindaskꙅaioṣenni!

4   Frequently, the spirit entered our minds, saying, "Come on, kill those who continually mistreat you."

5   We didn't listen. We were afraid for you, that you would have continually burned inside the earth, because still you would not have been believers and would have been killing.

6   We thought, "They cover us with a fire that extinguishes. It is frightening, inside the earth, where it burns forever without being extinguished.

7   It is not such a matter that they kill us," we thought. "It would be good, because the Great Voice will give us life that a country that will appear."

8   Go outside of it, my brothers. Quit your cruelty.

9   You ate your fill of flesh with your eating of humans.

10 Let it seem large to you, not easy, vanquishing, knocking over villages and taking scalps.

11 Believe, "It is a long time to destroy the country of our enemies."

12 Would you mistreat humans again when you would grow tired of mistreating them?

13 When would you wound again, when you were right [emotionally], those you brought bad fortune to when you were angry?

14 Those you seized and were seized by are no longer. Not one village exists any longer of those you many times struck and were struck by; not one lineage would be together.

15 Only blackened embers are spread all over where once your enemies were. A forest is again made, where once they had a field. Animals come from where once they were burned.

16 Where would they have gone to, the humans that were Huron, Petun, Neutral, Trakwae, Erie, Nipissing, and Algonquin?[18]

17 You caused them all to perish completely.

18 Why would it happen that you would still desire to torment, to knock over villages and to wipe out countries?

19 You go about turning over countries—every country you were angry at. Not one is missing.

20 If they were assembled in a group together, the corpses of the humans you consumed would be as high as the top of a high hill.

21 It is evident that they cry in mourning, those who were widows of those you killed as prisoners.

22 skat asen te tsonk8endieraχon n' on'renθa ontatiatannhatenk
    etsichiaj de haaιonnonhonk ιehen!
23 stan iιerhe te sk8atondihend n'ontesk8atratasen
    aesk8atanditenr, d'i8aia tson8e eιenk
24 χa sen te ιanda8indesonk d'etsichiaj n'on8e ιehen ιang8enia
    ιehen a8atontarichiaen iaon chi[e]ιannen aιontaraska
25 stirenk aθo nondaie te tsontarichiahon ιang8enia stenda'tiaj
    aθo de sk8a8atsaιaien non8e ιehen, χa ioh8arindand8tek,
    tsa'tandik asken aιaontaj,

Page 663

1 ennonchien etsisk8a8atsannonaj, ennonchien
    etsisk8ang8eniannonaj n'on8e aesk8andiatae'taska, d' orast
    ta te sk8ata'chonk eιenk;
2 ndio sen ondi tsati'ta8aten n'on8e ιaio, n' on8e atatiataιaen
    n'on8e atatetsistore; tsachonti ndio etsienθa,
3 onh8a θo aat ehesk8are8a't ha8endio onta te sk8a'ka8an n'on8e
    etsisk8ahens; ehetsondechaton't atiaondi de
    sk8atatendraten,
4 isk8erhe ati s'otindiιonrhendi hatiskend de sk8atriosk8a ti
    haesk8aeren haesk8aesati?
5 stante s'otindiιonrhendi, a8entenhaon iθochien
    honennontandik ha8endio d'ha[ι]onatichiai ihontonk sa
    s'een't asken, ιaroιe n' onχiesati sasee'risen n'onχiatate'ati,
    n'onχiskok n' onχinneoιannen;
6 χondaie ihatierha de haesk8achiaιi
7 stehiaraha de sk8annonchiondi stehiaraha onne tioske[n]hen
    isk8e te kandaιenchata d' esk8aatannonenk8at:
8 tsiataten tsiataten, satsaka a8entenhaon sk8atechen'tannonk,
9 esk8asen ichien onna onta te sk8atrihotaθe
10 taι8a8endrak8at asken aι8ataχen taι8a8endrak8at d'
    aι8atsihenstatsi aι8aatsi
11 chi atsachonti de sk8atoιena n'on8e etsienθa tsasχ8at asken
    d'8teχa n'on8e etsiskontak8a, tsindatsen'tan'non n'on8e
    etiskok8a ti tsatennonh8eha n' ondecha8eti endare n'on8e,
    askennonia θo ondi ti tsatateιenhaj aetsonnhej

22 Their voices are again mixed as one with the regretful cries of those who are related to those you killed.

23 I do not wish that you would have lost when you jumped, pounced, but that you would have had even a little pity on those who will be humans.

24 It does not just make a river's flow, the blood of the humans you killed. It made a large lake.

25 Let it be that you stop making lakes of blood. Let it be that you are satiated with eating the human flesh of this pile of corpses. Let it be that you begin to be satiated forever.

Page 663

1 Do not desire the flesh and blood of humans. You would unload your throat if still you will not be satiated.

2 Come on, give up killing humans, eating humans and covering humans with fire. Come on, leave behind the ax you hit them with.

3 Soon the Great Voice will punish you if you don't quit hating humans. He will cause you to lose your country and to fall like dry leaves.

4 Do you think that the spirits of the dead of the enemies you mistreated have forgotten?

5 They have not forgotten; continually they press the Great Voice who made them, saying, "Let it be that you hit quickly those who mistreat us. Pay back those who burned our bodies, put us in water and rendered our bones into liquid."

6 This is that which they say, those whom you have killed.

7 Remember, you who are Iroquois; remember, it is close to the time when you go to sink into an endless pit.

8 Stop, stop! Take back continually striking many times.

9 You will perish if you do not listen.

10 Follow our words, my brothers. Follow the words of we who are called Charcoal.

11 Leave the ax far away, the ax that you use to hit humans with. Let it be that you cause to be extinguished the fire that you put humans in. Knock over those pots you put humans in. Love all countries where people live. Look at each other peacefully as you would live.

12 hatinnionienhak ade hatienh8i iθondi n'on8e iaio te
   etsiatandik, chi henditak8a henderhe [e]hennonhej aθo k8e
   de t' ahatirih8iost de chi ehennonnhontie
13 chrih8ateha sken iannienie chrih8ateha sken onnei8t d'iiatonk
   chi-henditak8a d' hatinnionienhak te haesk8achiach,
   henderhe ahennonnhej chieskechien ehatirih8iost
14 iannendaie hotinnenrinnonnen etisk8andare,
15 aiotonnen te honderinnen aiaχingat d' aiote8annen
   aiondatontionnen te iaent[a]k aat atendacha a te iannonske
   iannonchichonk: oiaresa iannenhenta8i, onnionchia a8eti,
16 ta ti te haaiongaton, onek inde atatrio te hotiatenhaonnen,
   henderhonk ichien t'onsaiaχiatak aiorih8iosti
   aonsaierih8iost aonsaionθarat,
17 oten de iannienieronnon te haaioendaonnen stan skat te
   aiheonchend, a8eti aiontatonnhontinnen
   aiontatrih8iostinnen iarih8iosti,
18 ondaie io'ti ai8ataχen ai8arikennhak iarih8iosti, ondaie ioti
   st'oni8annenrarede iannienie oni8eri aiaχire8a't aθo d'
   erih8annianniθa iarih8iosti askennonnia sen aiontien
   d'eienhatie
19 ennonchien etsonχionda'χ8a d'aiaχirih8aienstandihi n'on8e
   ondechra8eti ondaie θo ara atiaondi oni8eri
20 sk8andiiont iierhe ai8ataken, stan ichien te iatoien ta te
   sk8andiiont

Page 664
1 te ien, onek ichien ason te 8ahente aiaienrhon [t]ate
   etsiatoreθa,
2 stan ichien ondi te hotindiiont, ondaie atichien asechiennonnia
   aiaienhaon χahachia hondi[i]onr8annen de θo θo
   ahondiionretsik d'a8entenhaon ahachontata n'on8e
   saioskonk8a?
3 stan i8aia te ierhe ondaie iandiionrondandi iaatsi,
4 annen atichien aietrontaj n'on8e, ondaie haoten te eentechend,

12 The French have the ability to kill humans; they deliberately
   wish, "Let them live so that they would believe as they
   continue to live."
13 Let it be that you know it, Mohawks, that you know it,
   Oneidas, that which I say when I say that the French do not
   deliberately set out to kill you; they wish, "They should live
   in order that they will believe."
14 In the fall, they went in an army to where you live.
15 It would have been possible [to do it], if they had wished, "We
   should go after those who fled and left their villages" where
   great provisions were lying in every house, full houses with
   beans, buried corn, and squash.
16 However, they are not going after them, because they did not
   come as enemies: they thought, "We would again seize those
   who believe, so they would believe again, and do good again."
17 But the Mohawks were not seized. No one would have died. All
   would have been given life that would have been believers.
18 It is such, my brothers, that we disputed regarding believing; it
   is such that we came in a group to Mohawk country,
   wishing, "Let us regulate those who have kept for a long
   time the matter of believing. Let them be peacefully settled
   in the process."
19 Do not again ravage the places of those humans we teach in all
   the countries. That is our only wish.
20 You have sense. I think, my brothers, that it is not true that you
   have no sense.

Page 664
1 It is only that it is still not evident. One would think that we do
   not examine you for faults.
2 They had no sense. Would people praise his name, saying,
   "Ah, he had a great mind, persevering in his thoughts that
   continually he should shake an ax at humans and put them
   in a fire?"
3 I don't think, even a little, that it is called a growing mind.
4 Where would humans dwell, who would not have known the
   nature of it?

5   ondaie i n'onh8a hondiιonr8annen hesk8aas de saιoios on8e,
    a8eti saιonneariχonk?

6   ιaio ichien chia te otindiιont 8ade ιaienh8i iθondi ιaio
    d'atatiataιaien n'on8e

7   k8aio'ti de on8e te haratas ndaoten ιarhaιon a8entenhaon te
    hate'nda8ha etsak aθa-[ι]enriaj stan ιandea te haata'tonk

8   aon[ι]i n'ondaie hondiιonr8annen, te chiatoreθa?

9   ιaio ichien onderati ondiιonr8annen 8ade ιaienh8i k8-aratati
    a8entenhaon ιarhaientesonnionk e8a te ιaata'tonk

10 aonιi sen isk8erhe ondaie hondiιonr8annen d'aoienka
    aθanda8iaj de chi aιanda8ati ehoιaens?

11 ιaio ichien hondiιonkennion, n' ondaie tsitaioka, ιah8enta
    a8eti, ondaie ostore te 8atinda8iach stan ιandea te
    otinda8andoronk.

12 aonιi sen esk8enhaon ondaie aat hondiιonr8annen χa te hat
    haienh8i ndaoten st' asaιotaseten n'on8e d'onn' ahonaiohe?

13 ndio sen tsichiennonnia iθondi ιaio, stihon ιaio ichien
    chi[e]ιannen tsondiιonr8annen, aonh8a ti ιaienh8i
    st'aιotase'tandik d'onn' aιonangate:

14 he aι8ataχen te ιatoιenk θo eιarih8tenk d'esk8erhon ondaie
    aιondiιont d' eienh8i on8e ιaio: ondaie aιondiιont d' eienh8i
    k8-aratati, atatase'ti,

15 eιihon ichien n'endi ιaio ichien otindiιonr8annens, stan te
    onι8andiιont de tion8e aιerhon ιaio onderati atistiaronk ιaio
    aat atienh8i d' atatase'ti.

16 8a ichien ennond aionι8andera8a chia aiaι8erhon
    aιondiιonr8annen ndaoten, ondaie aat aiestindiιonrandera8a
    d'anniaten te sk8atonk d'onnee te sk8aιannra stan ind
    ihotindiιonr8ten d' hatitsihenstati stan ies8a te hontandik
    stan ies8a te hatinnondandik n'ondende ionties

17 ondaie aionι8andera8a de t'aesk8enhaon taotia8endi d' etsak
    aχiesati, onχinnonh8e ichien aιonti etsa'k aχieiachasenni
    ichien ta ti te onχisk8ahens:

18 aχi8end8tas n' endi ichien, aιaonh8a de etionχinnhek ondaie
    aiaι8achiennonnia te sk8atonk taot eχa iotieren hatisk8aιon
    d'hatitsihenstatsi te θatirak8a ιenheon, te hatindoronk8a sθ'
    ennonhe, taot asen henderhe de hondaties atendota
    ιandiaha8asti ιandak8a?

5   Do you call his mind great, he who kills humans and chews all their bones?

6   An animal has equal sense, for it also has the ability to eat humans.

7   Does a human run inside a forest continually hunting, frequently cutting through the fir forest, never getting lost?

8   Do you examine his great mind for faults?

9   An animal, then, has an extremely great mind, for it knows how to run continuously, crossing the forest many times without getting lost.

10 Do you think he has a great mind, he who can quickly cut across a river to the far side when he is ready to go there?

11 An animal surpasses him in mind. A smelt, all fish are fast. They cut across a river and never find the river difficult.

12 Will you say, "He has a great mind, for he has the ability to hide from people when they go to kill him?"

13 Come on, praise an animal's name also: say, "An animal has a very great mind, for it has the skill to hide when people go after it."

14 Hey, my brothers, it will not have been true that it will be as you think, "They have reason, the humans that have the abilities of animals. They have reason, those that have the ability to run and to hide."

15 I will say, "Animals have great minds. We humans have no sense because animals are extremely fast and animals have a great ability to hide."

16 Other different ones we would admire, thinking, "They have great minds," if sometimes you say when you look at it, "What are the minds of the Charcoal like? They don't fear anything, keep anything on earth to leave behind."

17 We would admire it if you would say, "Why have we frequently caused to be mistreated those left behind who love us, and why are we frequently angry at those who do not hate us and argue with those who defend us?"

18 We would praise it if you say, "What are the insides of the Charcoal made of? They do not worry about dying. They do not value living. What are they thinking when they leave behind possessions, good food, and marriage?

19 taot io'ti sθ' ontetiesaθa hennondechotras ondechraᴕeti
     haaιonrihᴕaienstondes sten-iesθa te honatinnhaθa?

20 chia aeskᴕarihorenha aeskᴕerhon tsaιon sen ιatoιen d'ihontonk
     sθ' aonιᴕarihᴕaienstandik ιaronhiaιe eonkᴕasθa d' aιoθarati-
     hatie,

Page 665

1 onne θo aeskᴕarihᴕandiθa aeskᴕenhaon ιatoιen atiaondi d'
    hatiriᴕenhᴕa ihontonk ιaronhiaιe etsonχierisen n'
    onιᴕatatiesatihatie st'aχirihᴕaiestandihes aιonᴕe

2 hotindiιonratoιendi echa etsaιonnhej ιaronhiaιe d'aιorihᴕiosti,
    ondaie aat echi is['] atirikentandik de ιaronhiaιe
    es[']ennonnhontie

3 ahontiesa't atichien sθ ennonnhe de onhᴕa, onta te
    orihᴕarenhᴕi nondaie de s[']ennonnhe ιaronhiaιe

4 stan te hatinnonkontandend de stan ionties eχ'ondechate, onta
    n' ondaie te hondatrendaen de ιaronhiaιe haonentandi
    haᴕendio,

5 stan te honti'taᴕatandihend d'hatieronιe de ιaro eθende'θa,
    stan te henderhondend onnianni θo d' eonχichien eonχiesa't
    eonχitsistorej,

6 stan nondaie [te] henderhondend onta te hatirihᴕateri
    st'iotieren n'onιᴕatonnhatake

7 χ'ondaie aιᴕataχen aeskᴕandiιonraᴕenk d'onne te
    skᴕaιannraties, chia aiaιᴕerhon χahachia hotindiιonrᴕannen
    ndaoten hatienhᴕi kaatoreti.

8 estenniaιon aιᴕataχen tsindiιonrᴕannha ti tsiatoret asken ti
    aιᴕaiendᴕten d'aιᴕatsihenstatsi:

9 ti tsirihoret asken d'etsiatendotondik sterhon, taot ichien
    ahondatrak ahonnondechontionk onta te ιatoιen n'ondaie
    de θondatendotonnon,

10 onhᴕati aιon aιᴕataχen onhᴕati ontaioniᴕa'teᴕa'tandik n'onᴕe
    aχirihᴕaienstandik onta te ιatoιen:

11 aioniᴕanderat asen-chien, n'ondaie aᴕentenhaon
    aiaιᴕarihontataj d' otrihondi te ιen

19 Why is it that they are mistreated throughout all countries when they go about teaching people, asking nothing of them?"

20 At the same time, you would find the matter such that you would think, "Have courage. Let it be true that which they say when they teach us that those who go about doing good will be happy in the sky."

Page 665

1 Then you would strengthen this, saying, "It is completely true, the matter that they bring, saying that in the sky they will make recompense for we who go about mistreating others, while we go about teaching humans.

2 Those who believe are sure in their minds that they will live again in the sky. They really like the idea that in the sky they will continue to live.

3 Would they neglect it while they live now if it were not a stable matter that they live again in the sky?

4 They would not have scorned leaving this country if they did not pray to the sky, offering it to the Great Voice.

5 They would not have given up on their bodies coming here. They would not have thought, 'It is good that they will kill us, they will mistreat us and cover us with fire.'

6 They would not have thought that if they were not familiar with the matter of how it is done at the end of our lives."

7 This is the thought, my brothers, that should occur to you when you go about looking at it, when you would think, "They greatly have the skill to examine people with."

8 Have courage, my brothers. Have a great mind in examining the abilities of we who are called Charcoal.

9 Consider that which we tell you. Think, "Why would they have come a long way and abandoned their country if it weren't true that which they came to tell as a story?"

10 A long time ago, my brothers, a long time ago we would have been tired of teaching humans if it were not true.

11 We would certainly be mistaken. Continually, we would shake the matter if it were a made-up story.

12 tsakak8a ti aι8aat8ten a8eti ionι8atia8enre de stan haoten
ontentoiata'k8a n'on8e, onι8atiatra8an de ιandak8a, te
onι8ateχaska8an d' aι8atatennonhonk daat
onχinnonh8ennen aχiatontion de chiate aι8ask8a daat
onχichiendaentak,

13 onι8atonnhon ιannondihatiend de ιaro etionι8e'ti onι8eri stan
iθochien eonι8aata8enk de θo eaι8aon, stan iθochien eo'tik
eonχindaskonnia chi'eonχiesa't eonχio;

14 oιont ichien te onι8a'kerondi, chi aι8aronχa aι8ataχen ti
tsondech8ten, on8e etsitsistorech, on8e etsiataιaiach chi
aι8arihh8ateri n'ondaie,

15 oιont i chien ontaaι8arask8a, θo iθochien ontaaι8atita8aten
st'aιionnhe aaι8erhon onnianni θo d' eonιiatateιat, θo de
[e]onιiataιaia ondaie ichien ora8an d'aondechenhaon
eskonnhontie ιaronhiaιe,

16 θo atichien aionι8aerennen d' i8aia ta te onι8andιιonrhatandik,
ιannionιenhak[e] o'rast aontaiaι8entrontaj;

17 te oιenron n'ondaie ιaronhiaιe esonι8aerisen de
saι8a8ennenh8a;

18 estenniaιon ati aι8ataχen taι8atrihotat d'onn' aetsirih8aiensten;

19 ennonchien esk8erhon te onχiendιιonr8tas;

20 taot-ichien aia8enk aietsiendιιonr88as onιionh8a ichien
aιandera't aiaι8atatendιιonr8tas onta orih8atoιeti te ιen d'
aι8arih8andot, 8ade endi aat ondera'ti aι8arih8andoronk8a ti
ιarih8ten;

21 esk8arih8iosti a de sten-ies8a te sk8a'tonθa, stan ta te
sk8aatonties de sk8atatennonhonk, te sk8atiatra8as de
ιandak8a te sk8aties atendota, stan anniaten ies8a te
sk8[a]atat

Page 666

1 io'ti ichien sk8a8eιi d'esk8atatennonhonk, io'ti
etsironhiaentonk de sk8a . . .

2 ondaie atichien aiaιenhaon onχiendιιonr8tandik d'onn'
[e]etsirih8aiensten: onek inde stan-ies8a te etsin'dahatandik,

3 endi aat asonι8andιιonr8tas de sonι8annhandi iha8en
tsirih8aienstandiha n'ondechra8eti 8ade ιarih8a8eti
onι8atatiesati d'onne saι8a8ennrak8i,

12 Look at our nature: we are forbidden many things that humans
    fool around with. We separated ourselves from marriage; we
    disconnect ourselves from those whom we are related to and
    who loved us very much; we left them behind, those of
    equal worth to us, those who praised us very much.

13 We went around making a resolution to come here. We
    thought, "Perhaps it will happen to us when we arrive there.
    Perhaps they will make us prisoners, mistreat us and kill
    us."

14 Nevertheless, we do not fear it when we hear, when we know,
    my brothers, that your country is such that you cover
    humans with fire, eat them.

15 Nevertheless, when we departed we gave up on our living. We
    thought, "It is good that we will be burned there, and eaten
    there. It is good that forever life will continue again in the
    sky."

16 Would we not doubt it, even a little, while still we lived in
    France?

17 Is it of unimportance that he will make recompense in the sky
    for we who bring his word?

18 Have courage, then, my brothers. Listen to us when we teach
    you.

19 Do not think, "They will trick us."

20 Why would we trick you? We would greatly trick ourselves if
    the story we tell were not true, as we greatly value the
    matter.

21 Forever you are a believer if you lose all kinds of things, if you
    leave behind your relatives, separate from marriage, if you
    leave behind your possessions so you have nothing.

Page 666

1   It is as if you are together, forever related. We treat you
    well . . .[19]

2   Would they say, "They are tricking us," when we will teach
    you, because we don't cause you to lose anything?

3   Did he greatly trick us when he asked us, "Go teach them in all
    countries," because we were mistreated when we followed
    his word?

De Religione

4   onι8eri aiaι8arask8a θo aiaχirih8aiensten n'on8e, onek inde te
    aι8aataδeιihatie de ιaro etiaι8eθa,
5   a8aton ati aontaiaι8aha8it daat ιannonchia8asti d'aιiondaonk,
    daak ιandat8annen st' aι8andarek, din onι8atarochientonk
    onχinditonroiahak
6   stan te 8atondend te aι8erhe ondaie aiaι8aha8it ιatoιen aat
    esonι8enditonr88θ[as] de te oskenheati d'onne ιaro te
    sonι8atsarandi ha8endio,
7   ιatoιen aak arih8a8eti asonι8aesa't, onta te ιatoιen de
    sonι8astak8andi, iha8en ondaie tendendi d' aondechrenhaon
    esk8ak8as8a d'in n' ondaie [e]sk8ati n' ondende
8   ionties esk8erhon aiaχirih8aienstandiha stan ichien aι8ataχen
    stan i8aia te aι8erhe [e]tsaιon sen asonι8endionr88θas
    ha8endio
9   stan ichien te 8atondende te sonι8ak8endoiatandik:
10 aιerhon eha8endaιont d'onne stan asaιostak8as aιon8e stan te
    s'ak8endaron8as:
11 sterhon iθondi de tson8[e] d'onn'aetsiastak8as aaι8enhaon
    ιaronhiaιe esk8ak8as8a d'esk8arih8iost
12 sterhon, sterhon ιatoιen θo ea8enk, sterhon stan atiaondi te
    onχienditonr8tandik
13 taot aiaι8atondrak8at te etsienditonr8tandik?
14 taot aionι8araha te etsiata'tonθa
15 sten-ies8a ondi te sk8annha8a d'aiaι8erhon ondaie
    eonι8atendaha'ten ta te aχirih8aienstandihe ti ιarih8ten stan
    ta chi te aι8arachend, te sk8erhe aiaχinnha
    n'onχirih8aienstandik
16 te aι8erhe i8aia onι8e aat aonsaionχierisen d'aχirih8aiens8a
    itsaιondiask8i n' on8e,
17 seh8en aat esonι8aerisen ha8endio daat hon8esen aat, seh8en
    ehatones ha8endio de ιaronhiaιe eaι8et eaι8enhej
18 taot ichien t'aiaι8ennont[h]a aiaι8erhon; onh8a θo, onh8a isen
    θo etsonχierisen;
19 stan te onιionnhis atiaondi ιaronhiaιe esonι8aιondaten
    ιarih8a8eti ha8endio de [e]sonι8aerisen haondechrenhaon,
20 te haiennentache d' esonι8aronhiaentonhonj e8atanditenr

4   We thought, "We should depart for there to teach humans, because we do not go about here where we have come to."

5   It would appear that we would bring the very beautiful house we have as our place to a large village while we lived there, following our friends who amused us.

6   It would not have been possible for us to think, "We should bring it," if it were true that the Great Voice will very much trick us, when he caused us to fall.

7   It is true that the whole matter would be his mistreating us if it weren't true, his promise to us, when he said, "They will be worth each other, your being happy forever and your leaving earth behind."

8   "They leave it behind," you will think concerning our going to teach them: my brothers, not a little do we think, "Have courage. Let it be that the Great Voice has deceived us."

9   It would not have been possible for him to move us with his words.

10   Because he is a man of his word, when he promised humans, he will not take back his word.

11   Believe, also, you humans, when we promise you saying, "You will be happy in the sky when you will be a believer."

12   Believe it is true that it will happen. Completely believe, "They do not trick us."

13   How would we gain if we tricked you?

14   Why would we visit if we caused you to lose something?

15   If you asked all kinds of things of us, we would think, "It will cause loss for us if we will not go to teach them, if we would not have come to visit when you wished, 'We should ask of them that they teach us.'"

16   We do not think even a little, "Humans will pay us back for our teaching them," because they are too stingy.

17   Wait, greatly the Great Voice will repay us, for he is very generous. Wait, the Great Voice will be thankful in the sky where we will go when we die.

18   Why would we be in a hurry, thinking, "Soon now they will pay us back"?

19   We do not completely ignore that in the sky the Great Voice will give us in good measure, will pay us back forever.

20   He will not conclude with treating us well, with pity.

21 a de esk8atrihotat ek8a8eιik esa esonι8aataeriθon ha8endio de stan ek8atonk8andihon v/ ek8askannen.

22 esk8atrihotat iaon [taιendiιonraen aionderatik t'ask8atahonchiosten,

23 d' eonniannik eetsirh8aiensten onι8atonnhonιannondi d' a,8atsihenstatsi, stan te onι8ate8a'tandihe d' eetsiatendoton de di8 horih8a8an;

24 anniaten haonιe iθochien esk8atrihotat ιarihondi iθochien d'esk8andise8a ta te sk8a8endrak8ande,

25 esk8erhon ahonka aθo n' onχiatendotondik

26 ts[at]ita8[a']ten aι8ataχen stan ta te aι8ak8endiaχa v/ te onι8arihiaιi d'eetsiatendotondihi

27 e8a etsorhenha eaι8atatia ichien eaι8enhaon χ'ondaie iha8end8ten ha8endio ti tionnhe

Page 667

1 θo iθochien eonι8arih8entas de hesk8a8endaen chia θo θo esk8atatiat8tenst ti aι8aat8ten

2 θo haonιe iθochien askennonia eaι8atien d' eerih8iost ondecha8eti, θo haonιe eonι8andiιonk8astik d'aιotiok8a8eti n'on8e ehonachiendaen d'aat ha8endio, θo haonιe eaι8atronhiaenton d' a te ondeche θo eaιondiιonr8tenk ti [i]onι8andiιonr8ten

3 stan ichien te onι8andiιonhierihase d' ason skat aontaiaondecha8enrentenk te onχiatrihotaθe onek iθochien t'ask8a8endask8ahenk onek iθochien t'ask8achien

4 stan oιont te hesk8a8enda'tontande ha8endio; stan te sk8arih8iaχe d' horih8a8an stan te sk8arih8ate8ahe ιarih8iosti;

5 haesk8achiaιi d'okontak8i, ιaro eθondeti d'hatitsihenstatsi stan te ho8enda'ton d'ha8endio, io'ti saι8a8endandot din d' esk8achien deχ'ia[ι]8es, stan orast te hesk8a8enda'tonti,

6 8a ichien te sendatenst hatitsihenstatsi eθaonι8arhonatandihe /v te θaonι8endihendiha,[20]

7 ondaie ichien chia-ιat ehontendoton n'endi aι8arih8andot,

8 sahatsichien θo n'ondaie de [e]haonι8ennontren tatichien! ehesk8a8enda'tont ha8endio?

21 If you will listen to us, we will be together. The Great Voice will supply all that we need, all the things that we desire.

22 You will listen to us. I think it would have been a mistake if you would have turned a deaf ear to us.

23 We will teach you a long time. We who are called Charcoal have made a resolution: we will not tire of telling you the story of God's message.

24 In time you will listen to us. It is without reason you will delay, if you will not follow our word.

25 You will wish, "Let them quit telling us stories."

26 Give it up, my brothers. We will not cut our words in two. We will continue to tell you our stories.

27 And day will again come, when we will talk, saying, "This is the nature of the word of the Great Voice of our lives."

Page 667

1 We will conclude the matter of his words for you when you will be made to be such as we are.

2 At that moment, we will be peacefully placed among the believers all over the earth. At that moment our minds will be happy with all the group of humans who will praise the name of the Great Voice. At that moment we will be happy when in every country they will be of such a mind as we are.

3 Our minds will not be right while still one country would be missing, would not listen to us, if only you would hate our words, if only you would kill us.

4 You will not cause the words of the Great Voice to be lost. You will not break his matter. You will not flee from believing.

5 You killed at the beginning the Charcoal who came here. The Great Voice's word was not lost. When we tell of his word and you kill we who walk about here, still you have not caused his word to be lost.

6 Others . . . called Charcoal, when they come to deliver or save us.

7 It is equal: they will tell a story, and we tell the story of such a matter.

8 Kill again them, those who follow us; would you cause the Great Voice's words to be lost?

9 a8aton atichien te hesk8a8enda'tont esk8andi8at iθochien
sonatientenha8i 8a hatiatennond d' hatitsihenstatsi,

10 ondaie onsahatirih8annen vel onsahatirih8annhontren
d'hatirih8enha8ak di8 [h]orih8a8an;

11 esk8arih8iost echa a8ata χen esk8arih8iost
onı8andiıonratoıendi,

12 te handichi8annen ha8endio d'iha8en ondecha8eti eerih8iost
eondechontie, θo ati ea8enk ti ha8end8ten._

13 ondaie ichien eaıoatannonnen d'eostorenk eerih8iost ondaie
eontiatonta8a n'ondechon aiaıotetsiratinnen,

14 ondaie n'onh8a sk8andise8atandik d8a d'isk8erhe k8e de
t'aiaı8ate χaska d'on χinnonhonk ıehen

15 te sandııont ondaie ichierhe chieskechien aıotio'k8as χ8i de
sannonhonk ıehen te aıorih8iostinnen,

16 ondaie etsaıotiok8annenk de ıenhatie eerih8iost de
chie[h]8atsirata ti te chierhe aiaı8a8eıik n' ondaie
aiaı8ak8as8a ıaronhiaıe,

17 ondaie atichien achitiok8aıenten n' ondechon
eaıokaochonnenti,

18 te chierhe sen n'endi aıehent de ıeh8atsira, te chierhe sen
aırih8iost asen n'endi daat etiokontak8i, aiondaıeren sken de
χeena a8eti de χeatrea din de eondechontie eontonnia d'
aı8ah8atsira

19 he aıiata χen, aıiata χen chrihonniannonk d' ichiatonk, ondaie
io'ti te ırih8iosθa d' iıerhe aiaı8ariskon n'onnonhonk ıehen,

20 ndaoten te chiatehens ichierhe aionıiatatironten θo ıahachaıon
n' ondaie de ondechon onh8ati chi aıotetsirati,

21 te chierhe sen de sonh8a endi sken aıitiok8atironten ıaronhiaıe
de χennonhonk, te chierhe sen endi sken andiare a[ı]rih8iost
a χeahahak8en sken de χennonhonk de ıaronhiaıe eent
eaihej.

Page 668

1 θo sen te a8endi aıiata χen!

2 a8anskran aiesachiennonnia de cheena de cheatrea de
cheenh8aten, de cheıena a8eti d'onne ıaronhiaıe
aonsaiesaatorenha?

9 If you will lose his word, would you be surprised by other different ones again bringing the Charcoal?

10 They again publicize the news, pick up the story of those who brought God's message.

11 You will believe, my brothers. You will believe our minds are certain.

12 The Great Voice is not a liar, when he said, "All over the earth, they will believe, continuing throughout the land." It will happen according to his word.

13 They will have been taken care of; as quickly as they will believe, they will be released from suffering inside the earth.

14 You now cause to be delayed from others, thinking, "We would be separated from those who were related to us."

15 You have no sense, thinking that about a too small group that were related to you, who were not believers.

16 They will be a very large group, those who in the course of events are members of your lineage who will believe, if you think, "We would have been together, happy, in the sky."

17 Would you prefer a group whose badness will fall inside the earth?

18 Let it be that you wish, "I should be the first of my lineage." Let it be that you wish, "I should believe from the very beginning. Let all my children and grandchildren imitate me, continuing as long as the earth, with those born into our lineage."

19 Hey, my brother, you are making up stories when you say, "I don't believe," thinking "We would go together, me and those ancestors who are related to me."

20 You do not feel shame, thinking, "Those who are inside the earth would draw me inside the flame, where for a long time they have suffer."

21 Let it be that you wish, "I should become the first believer. I should seize the path for those I am related to so they will go into the sky when they die."

Page 668

1 Let it happen, my brother.

2 What would your children, your grandchildren, your nephews and nieces, your brothers, praise about you when they would find you in the sky?

3 aondechenhaon t'aiesannonronkȣannonhonj aiaɩenhaon oeri
   sen aat okontakȣi etisarihȣiosti de skȣahȣatsira isa atiaondi
   iseri st' onɩȣakȣasti n'onhȣa, stan iθochien aiotinnen te
   aɩȣarihȣiostandend onta desa okontakȣi te sarihȣiostinnen
4 χa ichien ahatier de skȣatatennonhonk de ɩaronhiaɩe
   t'aonseskȣatieraj.
5 onhȣa θo tsakonten aɩȣataχen onhȣa θo aat tsatrihaiensθa
   askȣahȣatsirenhaȣi't asken ɩaronhiaɩe
6 d'anniaten haonɩe eskȣatonnhaten aonsetsonnhontie sken
   aondechenhaon
7 onne ichien aɩatatia onn' aɩȣarihȣaiensten, tsatrihotat ati
   ennonchien eskȣatahonchoia.
8 aonɩi sen aɩȣataχen orihierihen d'a[ɩ]ȣatonk aɩȣatsihenstatsi
   ondaie-chon aionθa s n'ondechon aɩotetsirati? ondaie θo ara
   aiontonkȣandihi de ɩaronhiaɩe aɩokȣasti
9 tsinnen atichien aɩenhaon stan te ontondihend
   d'aondechenhaon aiaɩoatateɩannon te ontiataɩastan'dend?
10 tsinnen ati aȣatonhonj te ɩandoron d' aondechenhaon aionkȣasθa?
11 kȣaȣeti ichien ondi kȣaskȣahens ȣkaot, kȣaȣeti ichien
   kȣannonhȣe d'oraȣan
12 ondaie ati achia te kȣaskandend aondechrenhaon aionɩȣakȣastik
   ondaie atichien te kȣatandihend d' aot aionɩȣakaotaj?
13 ondaie ati iskȣerhe n'onhȣa a te skȣaataɩe stan ind eaɩȣatier
   eaɩȣatateɩarennien n'ondechon ɩandare d' ȣkaot,
14 iskȣerhe ichien eȣa stan ind aiaɩȣetchia aondechenhaon
   aiaɩȣakȣasθa ɩaronhiaɩe?
15 diȣ ichien haonhȣa hendiɩonraenk de ɩaronhiaɩe aionkȣasθa,
   diȣ ichien haonhȣa saɩoatannonstas de ondechon aieatenha
16 tsaten chiatandik ondechon, ichierhe ɩaronhiaɩe sen te
   ȣaɩakȣasti.
17 diȣ ichien haonhȣa ehiarihorenten st' echier chi'echiakȣasθa
   ɩaronhiaɩe

Baptism

18 θoia iθoichien ɩarihȣaɩe sonɩȣaterakatandik haȣendio
   d'aekȣarihȣaerit aekȣerhe ɩaronhiaɩe aiaɩȣet eaɩȣenhej.
19 ɩarihȣandoron i nonhȣa de sonɩȣatratsindik?

3 Forever they greet you with respect, saying, "Ah, at the very first you believed." Your entire lineage thinks, "We are happy now. We would not have been believers if you at first were not a believer."

4 This they would do, your relatives who in the sky would be mixed together with you.

5 Begin doing it soon, my brothers. Learn it very soon. Let it be that you will bring your lineage to the sky.

6 In time your life will stop. Your life would continue again forever.

7 I spoke when I taught you. Listen to it. Do not turn a deaf ear.

8 My brothers, is it correct that which we Charcoal say, "They should fear suffering inside the earth. They should only desire being happy in the sky"?

9 Who would say, "It would not be possible for people to burn forever in many places and not be consumed?"

10 Who would say, "It is not valuable that one would be happy forever"?

11 All of us together hate that which is bad; all of us love that which is good!

12 Would we not have desired to be happy forever, would we not have feared, ordinarily, that which would be bad?

13 You wonder, now, every one of you, "What will we do to get ourselves away from inside the earth?"

14 You wonder, also, "Where would we go to be forever happy in the sky?"

15 God alone thinks, "They should be happy in the sky." God alone keeps people from falling inside the earth.

16 You both fear inside the earth and wish, "Let me be happy in the sky."

17 God alone will suggest to you what to do to be happy in the sky.

BAPTISM

18 The Great Voice sets a few tests for us to accomplish if we would wish, "We should go into the sky when we die."

19 Is it a difficult matter that he now desires of us? Is it unimportant that one would be happy forever?

20 onek inde te oⱡenron d' aondechenhaon aionk8ast te oⱡenron d' aiontatiatorast n'ondechon 8teχa?

21 stan iθochien te ⱡarih8andoron ondaie sonⱡ8ateraka8indik okontak8i d'aiontatendek8aest ara θo ti 8atiesen n'ondaie te [ⱡ]aⱡenre aat a8en d'aieerat,

22 annen atichien aiondechentaj, ta te 8ache eⱡenk,

23 a8eti i8achonk8annion ⱡaronhiaⱡe ekangorens

Page 669

1 d'onn' aond8t etsak a te ondeche ⱡanda8atonnon ⱡaihonatonnon ⱡontaronk8annion, ⱡarhaⱡon nde etsak onda8t:

2 din d'anniaten esaihonaeh8aha sta8at aθo ara estekorenha n'ondechon a8eti atiaondi iⱡo,

3 ondaie io'ti st'iⱡatonk, ara iθo ti 8atiesen d' a8en stan i8aia te otendoronk8i.

4 andera8ach, aⱡ8ataχen, ti hondiⱡonra8asti d'ha8endio, stan i8aia te hondiⱡonrandoron,

5 chrih8iost aθo ti ha8end8ten,

6 chia aiesandek8aest χa iθochien a8eⱡaiaska aiesaeraten a8en, aⱡi8eⱡihatia d'atrendaen't

7 onne ichien achrih8aerit de skarih8at d'okontak8i sonⱡ8atratsistandik ha8endio.

8 θo haonⱡe iθochien aonsahiatochon8a d' 8kaot saatorinnen ondaie haoten d' aesaatonnentak8innen n'ondechon,

9 θo haonⱡe θo aonsahiataⱡenk ondaie d'esaatandoⱡaretinnen de ⱡaronhiaⱡe aⱡok8asti._

10 tsirih8ateha ati aⱡ8ataken, ti ⱡarih8andaⱡ8r d' atatendek8aesti,

11 chi-eaitak aondechenhaon eontetsirat n'ondaie de eennonkonten n'ondaie otrih8ichia[ⱡ]i atiaondi,

12 stan te sk8aⱡenhe de ⱡaronhiaⱡe aⱡok8asti onta te etsindek8aestande ondechon aat te sk8atonnhontaion8a a te sk8akonten,

13 din d'echiaaha aiaihej d' achia θo aiaⱡotondik ason te ontatendek8aestik aⱡenk stan ichien te eondend ⱡaronhiaⱡe, stan θo te onk8astandend,

20 Is it unimportant that one would be withdrawn from the fire that burns inside the earth?

21 It is not a difficult test he sets for us at the beginning. One would be struck with water [baptized] only. It is easy. There is nothing missing. One would use water.

22 Where would there be a country without water?

23 There is a great deal of water, including raindrops falling from the sky.

Page 669

1 When water flows in every country, there are many rivers, streams, lakes, and, inside the woods, several springs.

2 And sometimes you will need streams. Just dig and you will find water inside the earth.

3 Everywhere there is water. It is as I say. Water is easy. It is not even a little bit difficult.

4 I admire it, my brothers, for the Great Voice's thoughts are beautiful. His thoughts are not even a little difficult.

5 Believe, for his word is such.

6 As we strike you with the little water we would use on you, the striking and praying go together.

7 You have then accomplished at the beginning that which the Great Voice desires of us.

8 At that time he would cleanse you of the badness that covered you, that would have caused you to fall inside the earth.

9 At that moment he would have cleansed you of that which would have caused you to lose happiness in the sky.

10 Know, then, my brothers, that being struck with water is powerful.[21]

11 Forever they will be caused to suffer, those who deliberately scorn the whole matter.

12 You will not see the happiness in the sky if we do not baptize you. Inside the earth you will be tortured forever.

13 And children who would die as soon as they were born, still not baptized, they would not have as their country the sky. They would not have happiness there.

14 stan aondechenhaon te haɩonnonh8echend ha8endio, 8ade
    8kaot aɩoatorihatie:

15 isa ichien etsiendeoh8indik ti 8kaoch8ten d'onn' aetsiak8eton,

16 saɩosk8ahens ati n'ondaie d' a'son te tsaɩoataɩendi n'
    ontatrih8anderaɩindihatie d' echiaaha st' ontaontonnia,

17 k8a8eti onχiendeoh8indik ondaie haoten a[ɩ]okaoch8ten n'
    onχiak8etonk, k8a8eti onχiatachiaθa d' ason otonraɩon
    ik8annont;

18 chi sk8aatori d' 8kaot etsirih8anderaɩindi de sk8atatiena d'onn'
    esk8atonnhont

19 d'in n' endi chi 8aɩiatori iθondi d'8kaot onɩrih8anderaɩindi n'
    onɩiena st' ontaɩiatingenha ɩask8aɩon d' aɩak8eton;

20 θo iθochien aontahaɩesχ8ahendinnen ha8endio ara θo te
    8aɩiheonnen d'ason n'ondaie te tsotron8annen aɩennen;

21 atanditenr ichien ɩonnhon[tie] aɩatonnia, atanditenr aɩe'raha
    atatendek8aesti, θo ati aonsaonron8as d' 8kaot aɩiatorinnen,

22 a8entenhaon n'onh8a ɩatones t'[h]ennonronk8annionk
    ha8endio haɩentarestandi, ha8eri ahentandennia sen de
    honandek8aest,

23 ason te ɩrih8aterinnen ti 8atetsens ondek8atoɩeti
    n'ontatendek8aestak8a

Page 670

1 aioɩenronj ati aonɩatonesonnionk onne te ɩrih8aterinnen,

2 d'a8esk8ak ichien aɩatones ndaoten d'onne akendiɩonteɩra chia
   aonɩatendoton aaɩenhaon, χa ichien iesaeren st'ason
   satondia ɩehen esandek8aesti ache aaɩenhaon a8eti iθochien
   esarihondesenni de sk8atron8aθa ɩarih8anderaɩi,

3 onne ichien chi onde'k8aesti,

4 oten desa chi iθochien aesk8arih8ateha ason te etsindek8aesθa;

5 aesk8andoronk8at ichien andiare aesk8askand a8eti andiare,

6 d'a8esk8ak ati aietsindek8aest dinde aiaɩenhaon seh8en
   eetsindek8aest etsonniannika;

14 The Great Voice would not have loved them, as they go about being covered with badness.

15 You spread the badness to them when you gave birth to them.

16 He hates those children that are still not cleansed of going about being mistaken at the time they are born.

17 All of us have spread to us the badness of those who gave birth to us. All of us are killed by them while still we are inside someone's stomach.

18 You were covered with badness. Your parents involved you in their being mistaken at the time you received life.

19 And I, too, was covered with badness. My parents involved me in their being mistaken when I came outside the womb when she gave birth to me.

20 The Great Voice would have hated me, if I had died still with it not being effaced.

21 Mercifully, I continued living when I was born. Mercifully, I consented to being baptized. Then they effaced the badness I was covered with.

22 Continually, I give thanks, greeting with great respect the Great Voice for prolonging my days, wishing, "A day should arrived for him when they will baptize him."

23 Still I did not know that it cures, the true water that they baptize with.

Page 670

1 Would it be unimportant that they would have thanked me when I didn't know the matter?

2 Afterwards, I gave great thanks, when I opened my mind as they told me a story, saying, "This is what we did for you while still you were just born. We baptized you." They said, "We achieved all of it for you by effacing being mistaken."

3 That was when they baptized me.

4 But you are far from familiar with the matter, because we aren't baptizing you.

5 It should be valuable to you first. You should desire it first.

6 Afterwards, they would baptize you, saying, "Wait, we will baptize you in a very short time."

7   aesk8ennontaj ichien ndaoten aesk8enhaon, taot isen chien
      isk8erhe de sk8andise8atandik atiaondi oni8arih8iosti,

8   ndio sen tai8andek8aest ιaroιe k8e de onh8a θo t'aiaι8enhej
      d'ason te sk8andek8aesti, chi aioni8atandoιara de ιaronhiaιe
      aιok8asti:

9   χ'ondaie aesk8aer aι8ataχen te etsindise8a'tandik
      atatendek8aesti;

10   anniaten ichitron θora isak8eton

11   seennontandihi iθondi de cheena tiιarih8ten serhon onne sen te
      ontatendek8aesti de χeena, serhon areisaιen de χeena
      aiaιotendaha'ten iθochien de ιaronhiaιe onta te
      ontatendek8aestandend chi aiaihej.

12   te aιoatandiri d' echiaaha te aιonnonhonιaste; aιandi8ak
      iθochien onn' atiaιa8entiaθa

13   aioιenronj ati aietsire8ataj d'etsiena ιehen d'ason te
      ontatendek8aestik aιenk aiontonnhaten,

14   aiontonhonj ta sen te sk8ak8etonk esa, te sk8andoronk8i d'
      aionχindek8aestinnen

15   i8aia atichien aiaι8atoneska de sk8aenastinnen, onek inde te
      oni8atondrak8i de skionnhontinnen;

16   te sk8erinnen ehendihon ahontindek8aest ιaroιe, onne ichien
      n'onh8a aioni8ak8astinnen ιaronhiaιe;

17   χa ichien ehatier d'hatichiaaha ιehen te ontatendek8aestinnen.

18   tsindiιonratoιenk aι8ataχen stan di8 te saιoationθa ιaronhiaιe
      d' aιoatorihatie stan-ies8a d' onn' aaihej

19   areisaιen d'hatichiaa[ha] ιehen, ara θo t'eonskand
      deιaronhiaιe, chi ehenhaon d'ha8endio, stan desa te
      sk8aenteche ιaronhia 8atsek aθo stetaj,

20   chi ehendihon t8t eχ'io'ti sk8ate8aθa, te oni8arih8anderaι[i] aat
      en sten-iesθa itsaι8akeniesk8a ason st'ontaonιionrichenha,

21   θo ati ehenhaon ha8endio, ιatoιen d' isk8atonk, te
      on8arih8anderaιi, onek ichien etsiatachiatinnen d'
      etsiak8etonk, ondaie ichien etsiatach[i]atak8i
      d'etsirih8anderaιindi ehenhaon tati aιa8eri [e]ostorenk aθo
      aiontatiatochron8a d'aχirih8anderaιindi,

22   ondaie ehenhaon etsinda'ha'tandi de ιaronhiaιe
      aesk8endaιratinnen stan te esθitenri: te etsindek8aesti te
      tsetsiatingenh8i d' 8kaot etsiendeoh8indinnen;

7   You should be very impatient, saying, "Why do you think to delay us from believing completely?

8   Come on, baptize us quickly for fear that we would die still not baptized, bringing us the loss of the happiness in the sky."

9   This is what you should do if we delay for you the baptism.

10 Sometimes you live with several you gave birth to.

11 Hasten it also for your children. Wish, "Let my children be baptized." Think, "My children would lose the sky if they would not have been baptized when they die."

12 Children are not strong. Their lives are not strong. Suddenly, their days are cut in two.

13 Would it be unimportant that your children would speak against you if they were still not baptized when their lives stop?

14 They would say, "If only you hadn't give birth to us. It was not valuable to you that they would have baptized us.

15 Would we give thanks, even a little, for your making us your children?

16 We did not gain from your giving us life. You didn't wish," they will say, "'They should baptize them quickly,' so we would have been happy in the sky."

17 This is what those children not baptized will say.

18 Be sure, my brothers. God does not cause to enter the sky those who go about covered with many things when they die.

19 Children only desire the sky at the time when the Great Voice will say, "You will not get to know the sky. Go elsewhere."

20 At that time, they will say, "Why did you cause us to flee? We didn't make mistakes. We were much too small when our breath fell."

21 Then the Great Voice will say, "What you say is true when you say, 'We did not make mistakes.' They only killed you by involving you in their mistakes," he will say, "unless they wish, 'Let it be that quickly they would be cleansed of the mistakes that we involved them with.'"

22 He will say, "They caused you to lose the sky as you came into existence. They did not have pity on you. They did not baptize you. They did not again put you outside the badness they spread to you."

Page 671

1 θo ehaer ha8endio

2 oeri aι8ataχen, oeri! a8enskran ehaesk8eiachas de sk8atatiena
ιehen,

3 a8anskran ehaesk8a8end8taha ehendihon, ndioharon
d'haonι8ak8eton ihatiataesen! ondaie sen θo te
haaιotiataesatandihik n'ontriosk8a, ondaie ichien
askennonha endi iθondi d'haonι8aena haonι8atiataesatandi,
ti hondatendiιonratontandi:

4 ιatoιen aι8ataken ondaie ahendihon d'hatichiaaha ιehen stan ta
te ontatendek8aestinnen ahontonnhaten:

5 stan θo aat te s'annhatenhend atendota d'hokiι8annen,
d'anniaten eontahona'chiaten ahontendotaχ8a,

6 ondaie aat es'atinnhaten atatendek8aesti de sk8atatiena ιehen
8ade ahotionnen ιaronhiaιe te sk8erinnen st'ason
hennonnhek ahonatindek8aest te ostorendinnen sen te
sk8ennen hatsatrendaenhas endi ask8entak

7 onne ichien ahondak8astinnen ιaronhiaιe a8eti
atahotierindinnen d'ora8an stan iesθa te hotieh8achend,

8 oιenron ati d' eaχiak8endiha'ten n' onχiak8[e]nrask8a
d'etsaχiιen e8atondechaten etsaι8atonnhont,

9 oιenron d' aiaχiatronhi8a'ten d' aionχinnonchiateιat
d'atendota aιannonchik

10 isa aι8ataχen eιanderat eetsiatronhionnien etsiena ιehen te
tsisk8atateιen

11 ehendihon χa te hat d'oki haataesen, te sonι8entenri, te ha8eri
aionk8asθa ιaronhiaιe de χeena[!]

12 d'in d'onnhetien eskonaιen ehendihon χa i8e d'otiatatontandi
te aιoteiachi8tandi d'aιoena, te a8erh[on] aiontatiationt t'
etiaιok8asti,

13 nda[o]ten sk8aesati, ehendihon, sk8asa8endatindi / v
sk8annonstatindi d' aionχiatrendaentandinnen
aiondek8aestinnen.

14 isa, ehendihon isk8eri d'aondechenhaon eaι8aesaha, stan te
aι8aιenhe de ιaronhiaιe aιok8asti:

15 oιenron d' endask8a tsennhatenk st'aιonnhe d'
onn'aontatetsistorej, ondaie aat echi eskanderat
es[h]aatinnhaten sk8atatiena ιehen d'ahennonhontie
ιaronhiaιe te honatindek8aestinnen d' achia θo ahontonnia

Page 671

1 The Great Voice will do it.
2 Alas, my brothers, nevertheless, your children will be angry at you.
3 They will argue with you, saying, "Go away! Those who gave birth to us are cruel. If only they were mistreating their enemies. Those who have us as their children are peacefully mistreating us. They have frightening minds."
4 It is true, my brothers, what the children would say concerning not being baptized when their lives stopped.
5 Not long would he who is "rich" in possessions regret it when people act against him by seizing his possessions.
6 Your children would greatly regret not being baptized, for they would have arrived in the sky if you had so wished while still they lived, "They should baptize them." If only, quickly, you had said, "Pray for them" to us.
7 They would have been happy in the sky. Everything good would have been supplied to them. They would have needed nothing.
8 It is unimportant that we will reproach those who stole from us, when we see them again at the time when the earth ends and we are brought back to life.
9 It is unimportant, our anger at those who would burn our houses full of possessions.
10 Your children's muttering against you will be extreme, when you see each other again.
11 They will say, "Here he stands, the cruel spirit who doesn't wish, 'My children should be happy in the sky.'"
12 And a woman, when they see her again they will say, "Here she walks, the frightening one who does not trouble herself for her children. She doesn't wish, 'They should arrive where they are happy.'"
13 "Greatly you mistreated us," they will say. "You acted secretly against us, kept us from those who would have prayed for us and would have baptized us."
14 They will say, "You wished that forever we will be in a poor state, not leaving it for the sky, where people are happy."
15 Your children's regret will be extreme concerning their continued life in the sky, that they had not been baptized as soon as they were born.

16 stan-iesθa de ιαιaȣi aχeenhas cheena, chia ιanniennon aiaιoȣas
/ v aioιo′χȣa,

17 te ȣatonk ti chieiachasennik, chiengate, standichonkȣannionk
ιaentachientannonk chierontoiak

18 aȣeti ichierhe te ιakaochriaχonk asen,

19 harihonniannon (/ v chrihonniannonk) d′ aιiataχen stan iesθa
θo saιonnhatensennik saιoena, stan te saιonnhatensennik
d′aondechenhaon aiaιokȣastinnen!

20 Diȣ ιaronhiaιe esaιoentandi de cheena daat echi eskaιaȣi daat
echi eskaȣasti, daat echi eskandoron

Page 672

1 isa ati cheatiaȣenratindik d′ aiontatendekȣaest,

2 taot ati ichierhe? taoten n′ ondaie chras, d′ ihatonk haȣendio
aiontatiataιenk echiaaha st′achia t′aontonnia kȣe de stan
t′aaιoataȣenk chia ondechon aieesaha;

3 oeri te sandiιont chea′tontandik e cheena, ondaie d′haȣendio
saιoentandinnen ιaronhiaιe atiaondi ιarihȣaȣeti acheesat e
cheena, sachiensennik ati de ιanniennon aaιoȣas stan-iesθa
θo aontatienhas e cheena;

4 ta[o]t-ichien aιenk te chiatateiachasennihend d′ ehendihon de
skȣatatiena ιehen isa ichiatiha skȣaιȣandi aionιȣakȣastinnen,
isa skȣannhotondi de ιaronhiaιe, isa skȣaatannonenχȣati
n′ondechon, isa o′ndi te sarandi d′herhonhonk haȣendio
aiontatiataιenk ȣkaot echiaaha, chi eχeationt ιaronhiaιe de
stan eaιoataȣenk;

5 isa ichien, ehendihon, satreȣati d′aionχindekȣaestinnen, isa
sarihȣaskȣahendi d′ aonsaionχironȣandinnen d′ȣkaot
onιȣaatorinnen, isa sarihȣateȣati d′aionȣaatannondandinnen
ιaronhiaιe aionιȣe′tinnen

6 χ′ondaie ehatier ehesatehat hachiena ιehen.

7 taoten sen chien esandiιonraȣenk a[ι]iataχen de
[e]hachieȣendaronj hachiena ehesarihȣiosten d′
hotiatandoιaron de ιaronhiaιe aιokȣasti?

8 esandiιonrachen ichien aondechenhaon, stan iesθa te satsenθe,
echierhon iθochien taihen te oskenheati χeata′tonti de χeena
ιehen

16 I offered to your children all kinds of things that taste good. At the same time, a dog would take that from them.

17 Is it not possible that you would be angry at it, go after it, insult it, disapprove of its conduct and throw a stone at it?

18 All you wish is, "Let me many times break the badness."

19 He mocks it, my brother. He feels regret for his many children but does not feel regret for those who would have been forever happy.

20 God will put your children in the sky, where things taste very good, are very beautiful and are very valuable.

Page 672

1 You forbid their getting baptized.

2 Why do you wish it so? Why would you not approve of what the Great Voice says, that children would be cleansed at the moment they are born, so that it would not happen that at the same time they would be in a poor state inside the earth.

3 You have no sense. You lose for your children what the Great Voice offered them in the sky. You completely mistreated your children. The dog that took many things offered to your children hates you.

4 Would you not have been angry when your children say, "You alone took from us that we would have been happy. You closed the door to the sky for us. You caused us to sink into the earth. You didn't consent to the Great Voice's wish, 'The children would be cleansed of badness when I will cause them to enter the sky.'"

5 They will say, "You spoke against their baptizing us. You hated the matter that they would have effaced the badness with which we are covered. You caused to flee that which would have taken care of us and would have had us go to the sky."

6 This is what your children will do to cause you to feel shame.

7 What will happen to your mind, my brother, when you hear your children's words, when they attribute to you their loss of being happy in the sky?

8 You will be unhappy forever. Nothing will cure you. You will think, "What I caused my children to lose is astonishing."

9   esennhaten echierhon te 8aιrandinnen sen n'ontonhonk
ha[ti]tsihenstatsi aiaχindek8aest de cheena, onne ichien n'
onh8a aiaιok8astinnen ιaronhiaιe.

10 oeri ondi te 8aιendiιontak, echierhon, aionιiatatirontak
ιaronhiaιe de χeena ιehen te 8aιerinnen aiontatendek8aest;

11 echihon; ιatoιen endi ι8ak8aeron atiaondi; endi ι8aesati, endi
ι8aatontion n'ondechon; taot aιier ondi, te 8aιendiιontak;

12 chi'ehendihon d' hachiena ιehen, oeri ichien n'ondaie
d'ask8ak8aeronk aθo ara n' ondaie ichien askennonha de
sk8andahatandi d' aion8ak8astinnen ιaronhiaιe,

13 aioιenronj ati st' ehotindiιonra8enk hachiena ιehen d'
ehonkak8a etsak ιaronhiaιe aθondak8asti d'haιonatontak de
sonι8ak8eton,

14 oten d'honnonh8a ondechon ehatiataιontaj a8anskran
ehonendaskand hatindask8a ιehen de ιaronhiaιe ehonde'ti
ehendihon ati te chieskenhea θa de sk8aena!

15 o ichien hondak8asti d'hachietsistoresk8a hachiask8aentak,
8ade stan te hastonstatindi atatendek8aesti, endi ichien
n'ondaie sk8annonstatindi, ondaie ati io'ti st'onι8atetsirati
n'onh8a de sk8aenastinnen, ondaie ichien hondak8asti
d'hachietsistorinnen;

16 endi sen, ehendihon, te sk8atsistorinnen de sk8aena, te
sk8askok asen ondi, te sk8aataιaiennen sen, endi sen de
sk8aena te sk8annearitinnen

Page 673

1 skarih8a't aθo ara ask8entenratinnen, ondaie ichien
d'aesk8erinnen te 8asta8o ea χinda8erhaen d'
aiontatendek8aest,

2 onh8a de aionι8atonesonk ndaoten n'ondaie te sk8erinnen
aionι8enk oerisen aat aι8atatiena te haesk8atori d'
hatitsihenstatsi haonι8andesk8aesθak,

3 ara iθo ti ιandeia d' isk8eri ιaronhiaιe sken ahonk8asθa
aionι8ennen

4 ehendihon oeri ichien n'ondaie de sk8aio te onι8achiensennik
θo aat ιatsistaιe sk8aatontion, te onι8andiιonrota'k8ach i8aia
de sk8a[tsi]hen[st]a8i de sk8annearinnen, eo8endiati decha

9   You will greatly regret it, wishing, "If only I had approved, when the Charcoal said, 'We should baptize your children.' Now they would be happy in the sky.

10 Alas, I had no sense." You would think, "My children would have drawn me to the sky if I had wished they would be baptized."

11 You will say, "It is true, I killed you. I mistreated you. I abandoned you inside the earth. Why did I do it? I had no sense."

12 At the same time your children will say, "You killed us by causing use to lose happiness in the sky."

13 Would it be unimportant that the minds of your children, when they look to the sky where everyone is happy, will think, "He who gave birth to us tied them up."

14 However, those who will begin to be inside the earth forever will desire for those who were prisoners that they go into the sky. They will say, "You are astonishing, you who have us as children.

15 Oh, they are happy, those you covered with fire and put on the scaffold, for you didn't keep them from being baptized as you did us. We are suffering now because you made us your children, and those you covered with fire are happy."

16 They will say, "If only you had covered us with fire, we who are your children. If only you had boiled and eaten us. If only you had cooked the bones of we who are your children."

Page 673

1   "It is a single matter only, if you would have had pity on us, you would have wished, 'Let it not be that we will hinder them from being baptized.'"

2   Then we would have given great thanks. If you had wished it, we would have said, 'Hurrah for our parents. You didn't chase away the Charcoal from baptizing us.

3   It is only good that you wished, 'In the sky let it be that they would be happy.'"

4   They will say, "Oh, you are killing us. We don't hate it when you abandon us in a fire. We don't worry about it, even a little, that you burned us, cooked our bones . . .

5 ondaie ichien ora8an d'isk8eri ahonatindek8aest ondaie ichien
   8toιeti d'eonι8ak8astik aondechenhaon
6 χa ichien, aι8ataken ahatier d'haesk8aena ιehen
   d'ea8atondechaten te tsisk8atateιen onta ha8endio
   haιonrih8asetandik de haesk8andaha'tandi st' sk8eri ennon
   ehonatindek8aest
7 a'son n'onh8a te sk8arih8ateri ti aιoata8aens d'echiaaha ιehen,
   de eiaiheatande θo st' aontonnia,
8 stan te aιorih8andennion atatendek8aest, a'son iθondi te
   sk8andiιonratoιendi ti aιoata8ens n'ondaie d' ason θo te
   aιondiιontandi onn' aaihej tati te ontatendek8aesti
9 areisaιen aι8ataken, stan n'ondaie ιaronhiaιe te eonde,
   ondechon areisaιen eaιoatonnent,
10 stan θo t'eιen etioteχa stan θo te eatenche etiaιotetsirat, onek
   ati aιaonh8a chi-aιa8entak8i te aιorih8anderaιi d'aherhonk
   ha8endio aiontetsirat a8o aιoi iθochien honennendeoh8indi
   d'hondakaochorihatie, orih8anderatande
11 ondaie io'ti te hotiatateχa: hatiesas ichien onek, 8ade
   aondechenhaon te hotichoniese de stan iotieren ιaronhiaιe
   daat onniannihaton;
12 aioιenron atichien ehotindiιonrachenk te hatienteri n'ondaie de
   ιaronhiaιe aιok8asti?
13 atiaondi te ondaen d' aonsahatinnhatenhaj.
14 chi-hentak8a ati ha8endio te haιonrih8 taska8andik
   hatichiaaha, ιehen, ti aonesk8at de ιaronhiaιe aιok8asti,
15 iherhe k8e de t'ahotindiιonrachenk iherhe ondaie es'otiataj, d'
   ehenderhon ndaoten eonι8atendaha'ten, d'aonh8a ιarihien
   aionι8ak8astinnen;
16 stan θo te saιoerandik ha8endio n'ondaie d'etiaιa8entondinnen
   onn' aaihej ason te ontatendek8aestinnen
17 esaιorih8ataten n'ondaie sti aonesk8at de ιaronhiaιe aiontien,
   ondaie iθochien eetoj chi'eaιondiιonrachenk ate8akonten
   stan te tsaιoerihase

Page 674
1 ondaie etsaιoioθaj d'eaιenrhon chi 8aιitak8i aιiatandoιaron de
   ιaronhiaιe aonιak8astinnen, 8ade aιrih8anderaιi

5   It is good that you wished, 'They would baptize them.' It is
    fortunate that we will be happy forever."

6   This, my brothers, is what your children would do when the
    earth ends and you again see each other, if the Great Voice
    hides from them that you caused them to lose something
    when you wished, "Do not let them baptize them."

7   You still don't know what happens to those children who die
    when they are born.

8   Being baptized does not happen for them. You are also still
    uncertain what happens to those whose minds have not yet
    come to them, when they died not being baptized.

9   Alas, my brothers, the sky will not be their home. Inside the
    earth they will descend.

10 It is not where it burns. They do not suffer there because they
    didn't deliberately make mistakes themselves. The Great
    Voice would wish, "Others should suffer, who spread the
    badness of their mistake-making to them."

11 They do not burn. They are in a poor state only in that they will
    never experience what is done in the sky, which is very good.

12 Would it be unimportant that they'll be unhappy about not
    experiencing happiness in the sky?

13 It is not a place in which they would feel great regret.

14 The Great Voice deliberately doesn't show to the children the
    pleasure of happiness in the sky.

15 He wishes it in order that they would not be sad, that he would
    end their thinking, "It will cause us to lose the matter that
    we would have been happy."

16 The Great Voice does not do that to those who have grown up
    and die still not baptized.

17 He will make them aware of what is pleasing in the sky where
    they would have been placed. They will know that they will
    be unhappy, having entered forever a state of not being
    cured, healed.

Page 674

1   They will be "killed" again, devastated, when they think, "I
    deliberately lost being happy in the sky because I made
    mistakes."

2　ondaie etsaιoioθaj d'eaιenrhon aιonhȣa aιatanditahekenhȣi
　　d'aιatetsirati n'ondechon ȣade te ȣaιrandi n' ontonhonk
　　hatitsihenstatsi aiesandekȣaest.

3　chrihȣateha sken ti ochiatore d'aiontatendaha'ten de ιaronhiaιe
　　aiaιokȣastinnen,

4　ondaie ti chrihȣaχa't ontonιenhatie:

5　anniaten ihentron daat echi es[h]okiιȣannen n'onȣe, ιannonchi
　　atiaondi sθondaon akȣatendotȣen. θora iιaahe [aιarae]
　　d'onnonkȣarȣta, θora iιaase ιaachio d' onnenha, oιaresa,
　　ιannenhentaȣi ιaachichon iθondi ιennondi, ιenonhara daak
　　andeiaιstan t'etio'ton stan-iesθa:

6　onsahaon iθochien de ιaenχȣake ehaȣe'tinnen stan te
　　skannonchiaen,

7　onnonchia teιen ichien, ara iθo ti tsotsikȣeniarindi,

8　anniaten iaon d' onnonkȣarȣta χa iocharaȣante?

9　otentondi d' onnenha ιehen, oιenra onek isken de ιennonhara
　　ιehen ιennondi aȣeti, staniesθa te aιoaιenhȣi aonιi te
　　hondiιonrachenche?

10　aioιenronj? ennon n'ondaie e[he]chiechiennonniati
　　hondiιonraȣens d' honnonchiateιen

11　stan θo [a]at te hondiιonrachen stan θo aat s'annhatenk
　　hokȣateιasenni, ȣade chi ahotionnen d'onn' ahotonnhatak,

12　ondaie eιanderat ehondiιonrachenk de hotatiatandoιare'ti de
　　ιaronhiaιe ahokȣastinnen, eherhon, onιa'ton onne de te
　　oskenheati, d'aondechrenhaon aonιakȣastinnen, staniesθa te
　　ȣaιiehȣachende

13　onȣe θora ihokȣeton aȣeti ichien ieakȣastis, aȣeti iaιaȣentondi
　　de saιoenasti, stan iθochien te hehie'ra chia onta-onsat
　　aontatechien de saιoena ιehen, stan skat te aιotatenri,

14　areisaιen de haιotsindachia! aȣanskran ehondiιonraȣenk d'
　　ehatoj? aȣanskran esaιoatannhaten de de saιoena ιehen?

15　anniaten ichitron te chrihȣiostande aȣeti iθochien te
　　esandekȣaestande isa chien eιanderat eseatannhaten
　　ιaronhiaιeronnon de chi'eskȣaatat aiotonnon

16　oιenron ti tsontatiatichiach ontatiena ιehen, ȣade chia
　　t'aiaιoteχaskaȣannen θo aιotonnha[ta]ke,

17　ondaie aat eseatichiaj ιaronhiaιeronnon d' aondechenhaon
　　aeskȣaȣeιinnen ιarihȣaȣeti aiesaronhiaentatieskȣa

2   They will be killed again when they think, "I am treated as I
      deserve when I suffer inside the earth, because I didn't consent
      to it when the Charcoal said, 'We should baptize you.'"
3   Know that it is painful to those who would have caused their
      own loss of being happy in the sky.
4   Compare that with what I am going to say.
5   Sometimes a human lives who has a very large spirit [is "rich"].
      His house is full of all kinds of possessions: many bags of
      wampum, many large containers of corn, beans, corn seeds,
      and also many robes of fine fabric. Nothing is missing.
6   He returned from being in a field to there being no longer a
      house.
7   The house is burned to blackened embers.
8   How long would this [string of] wampum be?
9   The corn perishes. Only ashes remain of the fabric and all the
      new robes. Will he not be sad?
10 Would it not be unimportant? Do not praise him as it happens
      to his mind that his house has burned.
11 His mind is not very sad, regretting very much his burning,
      because he would have left it behind when his life ended.
12 His mind will be extremely sad regarding the loss he created of
      being happy in the sky. He will think, "I have lost it. It is
      astonishing that forever I would have been happy, not
      needing anything."
13 A person has several children. They are beautiful and have
      grown. He is not on his guard, and they have gone away,
      been killed. Not one remains.
14 Alas, for the old person he is. What will happen to the
      thoughts he will think. Will he feel regret for his children?
15 Some time you live, you will not believe. They will not baptize
      you. You will feel extreme regret that it would have been
      possible for you to be the same as the sky-dwellers.
16 Is it unimportant that those who were parents and children
      seek each other again, after being separated at the end of
      their lives?
17 You will search for the sky-dwellers again. You would have
      been together with them forever. They would have flattered
      you.

18 ιιone ichien te ochiatore d' aiaιotendota'ton
d'aiaιoh8atsira'ton; ondaie haonh8a ochiatore d'
aiaιaondechaton de ιaronhiaιe aiaιotondechentak

19 ti tsiatoret ati n'onh8a ti sk8atieronnonskon, ti sk8aataesen
d'esk8ak8eton d'onn' aetsinnonstasen d' etsiena
d'aiontatendek8aest, 8ade etsiaton'tandik ondaie d'
aondechenhaon aiaιotientak ιaronhiaιe

Page 675

1 θo ati a8eti aiontatiataeriθonk de stan aiaιotratsistinnen

2 stan θo aat te etsiatiataesatandihend aιokiι8annen te
etsinnonchiateιaθa d'aιondaonk, stan θo aat te
hesk8atonnheskandanden[d] haιotsindachia θora
s[aι]ok8eton de sk8entat ahesk8ah8atsiraιasten d'
ha[h]8atsira ιehen,

3 ondaie aat atatiesati ιaatsi d' etsiesaθa sk8atatiena d'onne
aetsiondaχ8a de ιaronhiaιe etsiondaχ8aθa te sk8aras iherhe
daat ha8endio ahonatindek8aest

4 taot isen chien ahontonhonj d' hatichiaaha ιehen de t'ahatitoj
ιandoron d'haesk8a'tontandi,

5 ahendihon ache: te oskenheati chiataesen de sk8ak8aton
skendaha'tandi de ιaronhiaιe aonιak8astinnen stan te
8aιatonesen i8aia d'aonda8andiha skonnhonti, ondaie aa
skennhatenk d' aondechenhaon ιaronhiaιe aιonnhontiend,

6 oeri ichien ahendihon, n' ondende skitrontak etiaιotetsiraties
aonι8e, ondaie aat askieron d'askondecha'χ8a de ιaronhiaιe
ondechen st' onι8ak8astinnen;

7 stan te ιatronhiaentonk ahendihon de skiatonti chiondaon,
ondaie aa i8aιech d' askennhoton de ιaronhiaιe
aonιiontak8innen

8 θo chien ondi skienastinnen [!] ahendihon, aionniannistinnen
te stask8entak te skiatontak, te sketsistorinnen, te skeskok, te
skiataιaiennen:

9 etsak achetsistorej, etsak achenneoιan[nen]d endask8a ιehen, ta
tie te n'ondaie te cheahaha8eιindi de ιaronhiaιe
eohahontie'ti, θo ichien eaιoon, θo ichien eaιok8astik
eιaontaj

18 It is evident that it isn't painful that people lose their possessions, lose their lineage. It alone is painful that they would lose the country in the sky they would have had.

19 Examine now, as you frequently caused damage, as you are cruel, you who will give birth, when you keep being baptized from your children. You caused them to lose forever that they would have been placed in the sky.

Page 675

1 There they would have been furnished with everything they would have desired.

2 You would hardly have mistreated the large spirits ["rich"] if you had burned their houses. An old man would hardly have borne you ill will if one day you consumed the several children he gave birth to in his lineage.

3 It is called great cruelty, mistreating your children, when you kept them from the sky by not consenting to the Great Voice's wish, "They should baptize them."

4 What would children say when they would know it is valuable, that which you caused them to lose?

5 They would say, "Truly, you are astonishingly cruel, you who gave birth to me. You caused me to lose being happy in the sky. I do not give thanks even a little that the time is going to be taken away that I would have lived in the sky."

6 Alas, they would say, "On earth you had put me where humans go about suffering. You did something destructive to me when you lost me the country in the sky and our happiness.

7 I am not in the sky." They would say, "When you caused me to enter your place, you closed the door to me to the sky. We would have been in such a state.

8 You made me your child." They would say, "It would have been better if you had taken me prisoner, tied me up, covered me with fire, boiled me, and eaten me.

9 Frequently you would cover prisoners with fire and render their bones into liquid. However, you didn't close the path to the sky to them. They will arrive there, where happiness will begin.

10 oten n'endi de skiena, daa askensesk8a, 8ade skatiataesatandi
    d'onh8a ιarihien, skahaha8eιindi de ιaronhiaιe etiohahontie'ti,

11 stan, areisaιen, θo te[aι] ionde aondechenhaon; oeri, oeri!,
    ahendihon ara θo ti 8aιatanditenstandi stan te ιronhiaιenhe,
    stan te ιienteche de sten iotieren de θo, ara θo n' endi
    t'[ι]ennonaχon,

12 ara θo t' eιaskand de θo aιok8asti, te aιoeh8as stan te
    8aιechonion.

13 ondaie io'ti χeaskannha n'endask8a ιehen, iιerhe endi sen te
    handaskondinnen d' aιiatatiena ιehen, endi sen te haιetsis-
    torinnen stan i8ochien aiotinnen te haιonda8erhandihend
    d'hatitsihenstatsi e8ondek8aestandend,

14 stan i8ochien aia8endinnen ιaronhiaιe aonιeiherak8innen
    aιatonnha[ta]ke,

15 oten n' onh8a akakonten ichien aιiesaha, stan te sk8aιendiaιendi

16 oten n' onh8a asa'skand ichien asa'skand a8entenhaon,

17 onek [i]8ochien ska'skannha onek i8ochien ιastaronk, onek
    i8ochien ιendienskratson8as skennhatenk aonsa8a'ton
    atichien?

18 satita8aten θo, e8aιatronhia8eιindik aondechenhaon; ondaie
    aat ochiatore n' onιendahatandi n' onιak8eton de ιaronhiaιe
    aonιetinnen,

Page 676

1 stan te8aιechiatorandend de tsa'ten n'ondaie te
   8aιendaha'tandinnen de stan aιiatennonhonk te ιennen.

2 te 8atonk, ehendihon atiaondi te 8atonk atonnhonιannonniak
   iιerhe ennonchien eskennhaten, aionteiataska te
   tsennhatenhend?

3 χa i8ochien a8eιaiosk8a, tendi θo t'aιangoraιennen
   aiongorendinnen ιieronιe, θoia i8ochien aio8endandeιennen
   aionιatrendaentinnen, chi'aonιiatochonι8annen
   n'aionιendeoh8indinnen d'8kaot;

4 a8eιaιon θo ara aiondek8aestinnen, θo i8ochien aιaa'kontatiend
   d' ahaιiatonesk8andinnen ha8endio, ahannonhonstinnen
   a8eti i8ochien ιaronhiaιe ahaιiatontinnen;

10 However, I who am your child, whom you greatly treasure,
   you treated me cruelly in closing the path to the sky to me.
11 Alas, it will never be my country." They would say, "Alas, alas,
   I am only pitiable. I will not see the sky. I will not know the
   many things done there, the only things I will desire.
12 I only will desire the happiness of those that don't need that
   which I haven't experienced.
13 I desire to be like those who were prisoners. I wish, 'Let it be
   that my parent took me prisoner. Let him cover me with fire,
   that he would not have hindered the Charcoal from
   baptizing me.'
14 I would have gone straight to the sky at the end of my life.
15 But I have entered a poor state forever. I haven't escaped.
16 But one desires it continually, greatly.
17 I desire it very much, in vain. In vain, I cry in mourning. In
   vain, I cry loudly my great regret. Would it be lost again?
18 Give up hope. I will have the sky closed to me forever. It is
   very painful that those who gave birth to me caused me to
   lose that I would have gone into the sky."

Page 676

1 "As someone else I would not have felt pain. I would not have
   lost it if we were not related.
2 It is not possible," they will say. "It is not possible to decide to
   think, 'Do not regret it.' Would one continue to be brave?
   Would one not regret it very much?
3 This water was equal to two raindrops that would have fallen
   on my body. A few words would have been joined, praying
   for me, at the same time purifying me of the badness spread
   to me.
4 It is pure water only they would have struck me with. I would
   then have gone about beginning to have the Great Voice
   pleased with me. He would have made me part of his
   family. He would have caused me to enter the sky.

5　te ιandoron d'aȣen, te ιandoron d'aȣeιoskon
　　aiontatendekochon askennon ati onnonstatindi,

6　ondaie ati io'ti st'onιiatach[i]endia d'ahaιienastinnen haȣendio,
　　aondechenhaon ahaιakaratatinnen.

7　chrihonniannonk, ahendihon, chrihonniannonk tiatatiena,
　　astonstasen atatendekȣaesti!

8　tsinnen ati esatiaȣenrasen, tsinnen esa'keronkȣen iaȣen eιonio
　　d'eontatendekȣaest e cheena?

9　stan n'ondaie te aιaȣen: din n'ondaie te aιaȣennen stan ichien
　　oιont te cheatrihotaθend aiontrihotat atichien ti aιonȣeha?

10　ondaie aat ahechieȣendrakȣinnen haȣendio d' ihaȣen, aȣeti
　　eontatendekȣaest n'onȣe eonton, d'eaιenrhon aionkȣasθa
　　ιaronhiaιe eaihej.

11　χondaie ahatiȣendȣtenk skȣatatiena ιehen d' oιone te hontatiak
　　θo ichien ahatier ahaeskȣareȣa't skȣarihȣandoιaron d'
　　ahonatindekȣaestinnen

12　estenniaιon ati de skȣakȣeton tsaronj asken d'aιȣahetsaron,
　　sθitenr asken d' etsiena :

13　te ιatoιen te etsinnonhȣe, θo θo aat eontonnia atsiatenhaȣi't
　　onnonchiatoιeti[ι]e dind' aιotiachenta eιenk ataιȣannhacha
　　n'onιȣatrihont, aiostorenk aiaχindekȣaest,

14　ennonchien eskȣandiseȣa te aιonnhonιaste d' echiaaha
　　aιaȣentandoronk ichien dȣa skȣentat aθo ti aιonnh[at]en
　　n'ondaie,

15　eskȣerhon ati de sten eaιoataȣenk ta[o]t ichien aia[ι]ȣaer,
　　onn'aonχiatonti de χeenastinnen,

16　areisaιen θo ara θo iθochien iond[ȣa]k etiaιaondarandinnen,

17　θo ichien chi aȣendi aiendaιȣraska de chi ona'ti
　　aiontatonnharest,

18　ondaie ichien ȣtoιeti, eskȣerhon, de ιaronhiaιe etsaιonnhontie
　　de χeena ιehen te aιoehȣache steniesθa;

Page 677

1　oten de [e]skandiseȣa stan iθochien te ontatendekȣaestande,
　　chi eaihej isa atiaondi eskȣatrihonθas d'eaιotendaha'ten de
　　ιaronhiaιe aiaιokȣastinnen

5   It is not difficult to get water. It is not difficult to get the pure
     water they would have used that was peacefully kept from me.
6   It is as if I was rejected for the Great Voice making me his child.
     Forever, he would have taken care of me.
7   You make up stories," they would say. "You who are my
     parent kept being baptized from me.
8   Who will forbid it to you? Who will cause you to fear, saying, 'I
     will kill all your children that have been baptized'?
9   One has not said it, and if one had said it, you would not have
     gone to listen to that person. Who would listen to mere
     humans?
10 You would have listened to the Great Voice's word, when he
     said, 'All humans will be baptized when they wish to be
     happy in the sky when they die.'"
11 The words of your children would have been such, if they
     spoke publicly. They would speak against your losing their
     being baptized.
12 "Have courage, you who gave birth to us." Hear our
     exhortation. Have pity on your children.
13 It is not true that we don't love you. As soon as they are born,
     bring them and those who are sickly to the true house. Come
     ask about our message. We would baptize them quickly.
14 Do not delay us from children not strong in life. A day is
     difficult for them. In one more day their lives will end.
15 You will think of many things that will happen to them. "What
     would we do when those I had made my children leave us
     behind?"
16 Alas, it is only a short period of time that is designated for
     them.
17 Then it happened that they would come to have power on the
     far side as they would have their lives prolonged.
18 "It is fortunate," you will think. "In the sky my children will
     continue to live again. They will not need anything."

Page 677
1   But if you delay it, they will not be baptized when they die.
     You will have the responsibility of the loss of being happy in
     the sky.

2   stan te χerasennihend iȣaia d' aiaɩenhaon te ȣastaθo
      ehinnonchia d' hatsihenstatsi ehendaȣaerhaen ara, te
      haoneskȣandik aat de aȣentenhaon honahonchoies;

3   o[ɩo]n[ɩ]e chrihonniak aɩiataχen

4   ondaie ichien aɩoneskȣandik d' aionɩennhaha aiaɩenhaon
      seatrendaentandiha deχeena,

5   ondaie aɩiatenhaȣi de ɩannionɩenhake ekȣaɩeti ondaie
      ekȣaɩeiheration, ondaie aɩen'dinnonk io'ti a te ȣentaɩe iɩerhe
      tsaten sen te ɩitenri d'xxxx anniaten-iesθa sen te haɩoneɩe
      eaihej.

6   ndio tsatrihotat ɩiatȣten de ɩetsihenstatsi, stan te
      ɩatonnharandend d'a te ȣentaɩe θora te onɩakonchiȣtandik,
      te ɩatonesend d' a te ȣentaɩe θora te onɩecharaȣha χa
      iocharaȣente, stan te ɩatronhiaentonden d'a te ɩandataɩe te
      onɩendaɩerati d'a te ondeche [te] onɩechiendaenk;

7   ondaie ichien aɩatronhiotak d'a te ȣentaɩe θora te onɩennhas, te
      ontonk sendekȣaestanda de χeena onhȣa θo aat aontonnia

8   dinde [ts]aten echihon taoten isenchien chiatrondrakȣa de
      chietsihenstatsi d'onn' achendekȣaest? taoten esannhaθa?

9   he aɩiataχen te chienteri sen ti saɩoatoneskȣandik haȣendio
      n'ontatiatachonniak onɩȣe d'onn' aontatendekȣaest,

10   te chieɩenk asen ti ȣatiatȣtensθa n'onɩȣennonkȣa't onn'
      aonχiatrendaenhas atatendekȣ[a]estiɩe, te chietoχa sen ti
      ɩandiangonchȣten,

11   achiaskand atiaondi achierhon te ɩrihȣanienhȣi sen ti
      ontatierha n'ontatendekȣaesθa, aȣentenhaon acheatichiaj,
      achierhon, anniaten iesθa sen te χeatorendi d' aχendekȣaest,

12   sehȣen echion ɩaronhiaɩe chi echrihȣateha ti onnianni d'
      aχindekȣaesθa;

13   tsinnen atichien, sendiɩonraen, daat eɩonachiendaen ɩaronhiaɩe
      d'aɩoatatoɩeti n'onɩȣe ɩehen? tsinnen aat aȣentenhaon te
      ɩonnonronkȣannionhonj

14   ondaie ichien te honannonronkȣannion ondaie ichien
      ehonachiennonnia d'hatsihenstatsi de saɩondekȣaesti;

15   eɩentakȣi ontatenderaȣach ɩaronhiaɩeronnon, eɩentakȣi
      ontatechiennonniak d'onn' ationtateɩen

16   θo de te chitron te ondaen d'acheatanderaȣa
      d'achechiennonnia echihon, χa hachia ɩandeia ti eatȣtens
      ɩaronhiaɩeronnon:

2   I would not have approved, even a little, of that which one
     would say, "Do not call for he who is called Charcoal. I will
     hinder him only. It does not please him to continually
     disturb his ears."

3   It is evident that you make up stories, my brother.

4   It pleases me that one would ask of me, "Go pray for my children."

5   This is what brings me from France. I came straight here
     desiring that it be such. Every day I wish, "Let it be that I
     have pity on someone every day when they die."

6   Come on, listen. I am such, I who am called Charcoal. I would
     not rejoice if every day one invited me [to a ceremony]. I
     would not have given thanks if every one gave me a wam-
     pum necklace. I would not have been flattered if every
     village chose me as leader, if every country praised my name.

7   I would be flattered if every day, frequently, they ask of me,
     "Strike my children with water as soon as they are born."

8   And sometime you will say, "What do you again, you who are
     called Charcoal, when you baptize them? For what reason
     did you ask for it?"

9   Ah, my brother, let it be that you know that the Great Voice is
     pleased by humans being prepared when they are baptized.

10 Let it be that you know the Great Voice is pleased by those
     humans who are prepared when they are baptized. Let it be
     that you know of its good nature.

11 You would desire it completely, wishing, "Let me know about
     what they have done for those who are baptized."
     Continually, you would search for those I would baptize,
     wishing, "Let it be that at some time I find them."

12 Wait, you will arrive in the sky at the same time as you know
     that it is good that we baptize them.

13 Who would it be, think of someone, that those who are true
     ones who were human will greatly praise in the sky?

14 They greet with great respect, praise the name of he who is
     called Charcoal who baptized them.

15 Continually sky-dwellers admire each other. Continually they
     praise each other's names when they see each other.

16 If you lived in such a place you would admire them, you would
     praise their names. You would say, "Here sky-dwellers are of
     good nature!"

Page 678

1 θo de [te] chitron te ondaen d' achearontonnion echihon,
   tsinnen sannonten d'ara θo ti ιaծichiaen satiatachronniati?

2 [h]atsihenstatsi ihen aiontonhonȷ dind' achihon taot eχ'iaծendi
   satatiatochonծan d'ծkaot [ι]ehen saatorihatiend, stan iծaia te
   skծahente?

3 hatsihenstatsi haιiatochonծan d' handekծaesti aonsaiontonhonȷ
   taot isaeren ateιon tsisatatreծati d'orihծanderatande?

4 hatsihenstatsi haծeri d'aծentenhaon haιe[he]tsaronhonk,

5 tsinnen aat esaatannonstat n'ondechon aesatetsiratinnen?
   hatsihenstatsi ihen, ondaie-chon ahonachiennondik d'ind'
   atatennonhծ[e]ndi ιaatsi,

6 tsinnen aak [ι]onannonhծe? tsinnen aak [ι]onaronhiaentonk
   [ι]aronhiaιeronnon? hatsihenstatsi ichien oιont

7 aծatanditenr tsa'ten achrihծiosti, endi ati aιondekծaest,

8 stan ichien ιaronhiaιe te sennonhծeche de sakծeton endi
   estonhծeha d'eιondekծaestik:

9 echierhon te ծaιatondrakծi n' onnonten de onιakծeton, ondaie
   ichien [ιentakծi] d' hatsihenstatsi haιechonnianni sθ'
   [h]aιatrendaentandi,

10 hatsihenstatsi, echierhon haιaθaratandi, te onιaθaratandi n'
   onιakծeton

11 hatsihenstatsi haծeri d' aondechenhaon eιonnhontie, χa
   iθochien iondetsiha n' onιonnhontinnen n' onιiena ιehen;

12 hatsihenstatsi, echihon, daak [ι]ato[ι]en aat haιienasti, ondaie
   atiaondi aιisten echihon.

13 tsinderaծa, aιծataχen, st' ehatihծatsiraska d' hatitsihenstatsi
   ιaronhiaιe,

14 θo iθochien ehaaιoenstik ιaronhiaιe st'eaιotiokծaska
   d'ehaaιondekծaestik

15 aioιenron atichien aιatonnharen d' enniot iծasen aχendekծaest
   aծeti atiaieon ιaronhiaιe d'onne aiaihej, ծade θo iθochien
   aiaιonk d' aχeenasθa

16 aιonhծa ichien aιakծatsirichien aιonhծa atiaondi ιehծatsirio
   aιenk

17 stan te oιenron ti aoneskծat n'ontatendare daat echi
   etseakծastis ontatiena

Page 678

1   If you lived in such a place you would inquire of them, asking, "Who gave to you the cincture [i.e., 'it girds'] that adorns you?"

2   "He is called Charcoal," they would say, and you would way, "What happened to purify you of that badness, not now even a little bit visible, that used to cover your body?"

3   "Charcoal purified me when he baptized me," they would say again. "Who spoke to you, every time speaking against your making mistakes?"

4   "Charcoal wished it and continually exhorted me."

5   "Who will keep you from suffering inside the earth?" "Charcoal is the one." They would have praised his name in what is called mutual loving.

6   Who do they love very much? Who do the sky-dwellers greatly praise? Charcoal, again.

7   Receiving pity, sometime you would believe, and I, then, would baptize you.

8   In the sky you will not love the one who gave birth to you. You will love me who will have baptized you.

9   You will think, "I didn't gain from that which they gave me, those who gave birth to me. Continually, he who is called Charcoal prepares something for me by praying for me."

10   "He who is called Charcoal," you will think, "he has done good for me. Those who gave birth to me haven't done good for me.

11   Charcoal wished that I would live forever. It is a short time that those who had me as their child gave me life."

12   You will say, "It is very true that Charcoal made me his child. He is completely my father."

13   Admire, my brothers, that the Charcoal will be a lineage in the sky.

14   They will have made them their children in the sky. They will form a lineage of those they will have baptized.

15   Would it be unimportant that I would rejoice that one hundred I would baptize all would arrive in the sky when they die, as those I made my children would have formed a lineage?

16   I, by myself, would make a lineage. I, by myself, would have a large lineage.

17   It is not unimportant that it is pleasing that the very beautiful parents and children exist with each other.

18 ara iθo ti onnianni st' aonkak8a ιah8atsira8asti ndaoten
   d'aιak8eton, a8eti iaιonnonk8ahioten, stan te eatra
   d'aιotiachenta,

19 ιaro ichien oιont iaonesk8a't de θora aiaιok8etonk daat
   aieak8astiska,

20 endi aat aonιonesk8en de θora at a8endia8ek aχendek8aestik,
   8ade θo iθochien eχeatorenha ιaronhiaιe d'aχeenasθa sti 8a
   d' aχendek8aestik

21 θo iθochien aiaιonk de t'aionιak8atsiraton

Page 679

1 stan te onιiatiatara8andihend, stan ta te onk8endiaχend
  d'aionιechiennonnia

2 aιonh8a ichien aιitrontaj d'aιeh8atsira[8ast]ik aιonh8a ichien
  aonιonesk8en aiaι8atatronhiaenton d' aι8atatiena
  aondechenhaon,

3 te aι8atatiatontiesend ta te aι8ateχaska8achend, stan te
  aι8atate8ennontiesand.

4 onh8a achia, aι8ataken, esk8arih8atehast' io'ti
  d'aι8annondandik atatendek8aesti,

5 aι8ak8atsirondiak io'ti d'aondechenhaon eaι8andiιonraen
  ιaronhiaιe, aχiatannonstas aιon8e d'aiaιotetsiratinnen
  n'ondechon ondaie ichien aχichronniannik d' aionk8asθa
  ιaronhiaιe,

6 endi ichien aι8erhe de saιonnonhonsθa n'on8e daat ha8endio
  d'onn'aχindek8aesθa, stan te saιonnonh8echend onta te
  ontatiatochon8ahend d'8kaot atatendek8aestiιe:

7 ondaie atistirihonti d'isk8erhonhonkte 8astaθo esaι8annhacha
  d'hat[s]ihenstatsi d'eontonnia d' echiaaha;

8 tsa'ka d' isk8atonhonk; te onnianni d' a8entenhaon as'ennhaha
  d'hat[s]ihenstatsi aiaιenrhon asaιondek8aest;

9 [a]ιrih8entaha sen de sk8atre8aθak isk8atonhonk ti
  hontieronnonnionk hatitsihenstatsi haaιondek8aesθa

10 ennonchien etsisk8enhaon stan ies8a te 8atondrak8i
   atatendek8aesti; sten ies8a te 8atetsens;

18 The beautiful lineage that I gave birth to is only good to look at. All are good-natured. The sickly are not among them.

19 Here, it is pleasing when one gives birth to several that are beautiful.

20 They would be very pleasing to me, the several hundreds I would have baptized, as I find those in the sky that I made my children by baptism.

21 There my lineage would form a group, surrounding me.

Page 679

1 They would not have been taken away from me. They would not have broken their word concerning praising my name.

2 I, alone, would dwell with my beautiful lineage. It would be pleasing to me, having we who are parents and children forever flattering each other.

3 We would not have left each other behind. We would not have separated from each other. We would not have left behind our promises to each other.

4 Right now, my brothers, you will know the matter of what we take care of with baptism. We make a family forever.

5 We will think in the sky, "We keep humans from suffering inside the earth. We prepare them for being happy in the sky."

6 We think, "The Great Voice adopts humans into his family when we baptize them. He would not have loved them if they would not have been cleansed of badness in being baptized."

7 Leave behind your thought, "Let us not go to ask Charcoal at a time when those who are children are born."

8 Abandon what you used to say, "It is not good that continually they would ask of Charcoal that he would baptize them."

9 Let the matter end of your speaking against us, saying, "The Charcoal do many damaging things in their baptizing."

10 Do not say again, "One gains nothing from being baptized. It doesn't cure anything."

11 andoronsk8annen, aι8ataken, andoronsk8annen
   atatendek8aesti, ondaie isen-chien [e]onι8aationt ιaronhiaιe
   ondaie [e]onιionnhont aondechenhaon, ondaie eonι8aenhas
   a8eti d'ora8an, ondaie onι8aatorak eonι8entron ιaronhiaιe d'
   etsik8atonnhont e8atondec'haten:
12 aiontita8aten θo ara n'on8e, te onde ιaronhiaιe, d'eaihej, onta te
   tsotron8ank eιenk d' 8kaot aιoatori,
13 atatendek8a[e]sti ati skaron8as n' onι8aatachaθa ιarih8anderaιi
14 taot ichien aia8enk te k8annondandihend? taot ichien aιenk te
   aχiennontandihend echiaaha atatendek8aesti;
15 ondaie iθochien areisaιen aontaiorih8atonk eeronιe d' echiaaha
   ιehen, onne ichien aiaιoatandoιara de ιaronhiaιe onne ichien
   aiontetsirat ondechon.
16 sk8arih8ichiach ichien nonh8a, aι8ataχen, isk8erhe taot eχa
   iondiak ontatendeoh8indik ontatiena d'onn' aontonnia,
17 onne ichien aι8atendoton hotirih8anderaιi daat okontak8i
   n'on8e ιehen te hiataιennen skat onnhetien, skat
   handiahaon;

Page 680

1 stan θo aat te onniannindi on8e eθondaton, chi'ahirih8anderaj
  θo haonιe ache 8kaot ahiatatiatoka st' ahirih8anderaj
2 θo io'ti d' aiontatetaroka d'anniaten aieskoha ιataι8annen
  ekataro;
3 onne ichien ahiak8eton, tat ichien ahaaιondeohas echiaaha d'
  [h]atiton,
4 ondaie d' honnonh8a eθotiatorinnen, aonniannik ahonnentoha
  d'hatichiaaha,
5 onn' ahotindiaχa ahonk8eton ichien onne hare
  onsahonennendeohas, hon[ta]tiena t'ontahontondia ondaie
  ichien ahaaιondeohas d'hatiton
6 chi hotiatorihatiend θo iθochien aa8enche aondechontie;
7 8a onsaontonnia n'on8e tsontatendeoh8indihatie d'8kaot
  etiaιoatorinnen daat okontak8i n'on8e ιehen

11 It is of great value to me, my brothers, being baptized. It certainly will cause us to enter the sky. It will give us love forever. It will offer us all that is good. It has made us intact for when we will dwell in the sky, when we will again be given life when the earth will stop.

12 Those humans who will not enter the sky when they die would give up hope if the badness they are covered with would not have been effaced.

13 Baptism effaces the mistake-making that corrupts us.

14 What would happen if we had not taken care of it? What would be if we had not hastened baptism for the children?

15 The children would lose the sky. They would be made to suffer inside the earth.

16 You search through the matter now, my brother. You wonder, "How is it done, this spreading from parents to children when they are born?"

17 We tell that humans made mistakes at the very beginning. Two had a dispute, one a woman and one a man.

Page 680

1 It was hardly any time from when they became humans, and the two made mistakes. At that moment, truly, they spread badness to each other as they made mistakes.

2 It is as if they would spread mud on each other when they would fall into the water of a swamp where there is a great amount of mud.

3 They two give birth, and they would spread it to their children . . .

4 The children themselves were covered with it for a long time until they were grown.

5 When they got married, they gave birth, again having parents spreading it to children. They were born again, spreading it to them . . .

6 At the same time, as they went about being covered with it, it was going to happen that the earth was going to continue.

7 Other humans were born. They again went about spreading the badness to each other that they were covered with from the very beginning.

8 onne ichien n'onhȣa eskȣarihȣateha aιȣataχen, ondaie iondiak
   te ontatiatonθa ιaronhiaιe echiaaha ιehen te
   ontatendekȣaesti st'ason aιoatori d'ȣkaot
   n'ontatendeohȣindihatie t'ontaontonnia
9 ondaie etiorihontie'ti n'ontatendeohȣindi d'etiaιorihȣanderaιi
   daat okontakȣi n'onȣe ιehen
10 staniesθa aesaatorik ȣkaot chia acheendeten echiaaha
   acheatoka ichien n'ondaie
11 θo atiaondi iaȣendi st'ontatendeohȣindi daat okontakȣi
   ontatakȣeton n'onȣe etiaιoatorinnen d'eton onn'
   aontatennontrasen d' echiaaha,
12 taot ichien aiaȣenk te ontatendeohȣindihend ȣade ȣkaochaιon
   onȣe etiontonk [eiatatakȣa] ȣkaochaιe iθondi etieatingens
   onn' aontonnia
13 eιanderat ichien eskȣatoj ti ιarihȣten d'eιȣatendoton daa st'
   etiotrihontaȣa'ti, onne ichien aιrihȣtaska daat
   ekarihȣaιenchaθa.

CREATION

14 tsatrihotat, chi hentron daat haȣendio st'ason staniesθa te
   ιandarek haatataιe chi hahȣa aȣeti d'oraȣan;
15 stan t'etio'ton ti hentron: haȣendio ιehen te haȣerinnen te
   ȣastaθo eιonhȣentsonnia din de steniesθa akȣten: haȣendio
   ιehen te haȣerinnen te ȣastaθo stan eιier onek inde te
   hendiθa stan haoten d' aherhon aιierat:
16 haonhȣa chi ahentak ahendiιonraenton aherhon aonniannisθa
   iιerhe stan iesθa aιatierannon, aȣahentenk asken t'indaιȣr ti
   ȣaιendiιonrannen ti ιonȣesen.
17 ιaronhia ontahakontak chia n'ondecha, ondaie aherhon θo θo
   agontien [aιontien] de stan akȣatiatȣten egontonnhonθon
   d'eιenhatie;
18 stan te hoerati steniesθa st'oteiendi chiaιi ιaronhia din
   n'ondecha, ahatatia θo ara onn' aȣatronhiatat
   aȣatondechatat o'rakȣannentaιi d'

8   Now you know the matter, my brother. Children who have not been baptized and are still covered with the badness spread to them when they were born, they will not be introduced to the sky.

9   Their spreading to each other when they make mistakes has continued from the very beginning of humans.

10 You spread to them all kinds of badness you are covered with as you enveloped them, held them against your breast.

11 It has happened that humans have communicated it to each other from the very beginning when they give birth to each other while covered with it, when children are put inside [the womb].

12 How would it happen that they would not have spread the badness inside to each other when they become humans, when they go out, when they are born?

13 It will be to an extreme that you will know the nature of the matter that I will recount to you when the matter is disposed. I declared the matter to you to the very top of it.

CREATION

14 Listen. The Great Voice existed when many things did not exist. At that time he brought all that is good.

15 Nothing is missing while the Great Voice existed, if he had wished, "Let it not be that I will make the earth and all kinds of things by asking for something to do it with."

16 He himself consciously thought, "My wishing to do all kinds of things would be better. I would appear powerful, wise, and generous."

17 He began the sky and the earth at the same time. He wished, "Soon they are placed. All kinds of living beings will be given life in the process."

18 He did not make the sky and the earth with anything. He spoke, only, and the sky and the earth appeared.

Page 681

1 a8esk8ak aharak8ichien aherhon t'aiorhaθej sken, stan
n'ondaieθo ara te on[ι]8endi deχ' ιιar d'ation8arhaθeten;

2 a8eti iθochien on[ι]8enditi, n' onιiondechatandik aontaιandiok
atichienstaniesθa deχ' ondechate onta andiare te
ondechatarihatandend orak8ennentaιi

3 onne θo ahateiennonnia ιandichar de 8asonteιe i8es a8eti d'
[h]atironnon, ondaie d'aherhon t'ahatirhaθeθaj de 8asonteιe

4 oten de ιaro aιaronhiati ahachonnia d' iok8as ondaie
k8atonieθa ondaie iθochien aionι8aeh8aha,
aek8atonrisk8eten ichien de stan te k8atoniesend

5 ondende aat hoteiendaιate ha8endio de sten hochonniannon;

6 te 8arati atiaondi ti ιaιe de steniesθa ak8ten hoteiendichiahon
8ade aιonnhe d' hoteiendichiaιi oten d8a te aιonnhe:

7 8hista ιarih8ta, ιandek, oιenra, ιata te 8ennonnhe;

8 ιaronta i8aia θo onek ionnhe, aιerhon a8entos aonnon'restache
oιennhaιe, onek ichien te 8es ιaronta, te ιatoχa a8eti;

9 ιaio de skat ahaatonniannon, ιatoχa ichien n' ondaie, arask8as,
ochiatorha, ondaie θo ara, etio'ton d' aiondiιontaj

10 chi aherhon de di8 tsinnen aat te 8annonronk8annion de
steniesθa aιateiendichiahon

11 stan ιaronta te ιaienh8i k8atatennonronk8annion, steniesθa te
8atienh8i, iθondi d' otironties ιaio ιah8enta a8eti, te
otindiιont aat n'ondaie;

12 onek iθochien t'ahoteindichiannen ha8endio deχ' ondechate,
din deχa ιaronhiate stan tsaten te ιachiennonniandend stan
anniaten te aιondera8ahend ti haiendandaι8r

13 d' honnonh8a θo ara te haιonatichia[ι]innen ιaio onek iθochien
t'ahaιondatinnen de stan-iesθa ak8ten n'ondende hotieson,
stan ichien orast te ιontonesend ιaio.

14 ason te ιandarek [d]e tion8e, chi8atindare ιaio ιah8enta,
otironties a8eti ichien n'ondaie haιonatesk8andik ha8endio

15 ondaie θo ara 8a io'ti d' otirihonnhis ιaio d'ahonachiendaen de
haιonatichiaιi

Page 681

1 Afterwards, he made the sun, wishing, "Let it become light." It didn't happen only for us, this rising of the sun.

2 All we need is that which warms our earth. Would there be sprouting of all kinds of things on this earth if the earth had not been warmed by the sun?

3 He skillfully made the sky-body that rises and goes at night, and all the stars. He wished, "They should brighten up the night."

4 On this side of the sky, he prepared that which blows as wind. We breathe by means of it. We would be missing something, out of breath. We would not have breathed.

5 The Great Voice has an abundance of skill in preparing many things on earth.

6 It is innumerable, the many things he skillfully made, for he made those that live and others that do not live.

7 Metal, stone, sand, dust, and mud do not live.

8 A tree lives only a little, because it grows, its scalp becomes longer in summer. A tree does not walk. It does not know all.

9 An animal is one of the many things he made. It knows how to run away and to feel pain. It is only missing that it would have sense.

10 At that time, God wondered, "Who greets me with great respect for the many things I made?"

11 A tree does not have the ability to greet someone with respect. Many things do not have the ability. Birds, animals, and fish do not have rationality.

12 If the Great Voice had made only this earth and this sky, no one would have praised his name. Nothing would have admired his powerful ability.

13 If he had made only animals, if he had only caused to grow all kinds of things on earth that are light-hearted, then still animals would not have given thanks.

14 Still we humans did not exist at the time that there existed animals, fish, birds, all those that the Great Voice made light-hearted.

15 They are only other. Animals cannot conceive of praising the name of he who made them.

16 θo ati aherhon de diȣ χeatonnia sen n'onhȣa anniaten iesθa
     aieatȣtenk de aiaιondiιontaj, chi aherhon onȣe sen
     aiondaιrat aionιechiendaen;
17 onne ichien asaιoatonnia n'onȣe chi[e]ιannen
     asaιondiιonrondat st' asaιoat ichien,

Page 682
1   aherhon t'aieatoret asken ti ιateiennonniak aȣeti
      ιechonniannonk aionιechiennonnia d'eaιonderaȣa
2   stan-iesθa aiaχichonnien n' onȣe onιioneskȣandik
      onn'aontonnharen d'onn' aontronhiaenton,
      onn'ationχinnonronkȣannion, aionιȣandiιonrȣtakȣa

16 Then God wished, "Let it be that I will make those who would possess reason." At that time he wished, "Let humans be made so they praise my name."

17 He made humans. Greatly he augmented their minds as he made them.

Page 682

1 He wished, "Let it be that they would examine that which I made, all I prepared, so they would praise my name in admiring it."

2 Many things we would prepare for humans. We are pleased when they rejoice, when they are happy. When they greet us with respect, our minds stand.

Notes

Introduction

1. *Wendat* is a term for which no good translation exists (see Steckley 1992b). It is the term that the Huron, and probably their neighbors the Petun, used to refer to themselves. I have chosen to use *Huron* to refer to the people and *Wendat* to refer to the language. I made the latter choice because I believe the Petun and Huron spoke dialects of a common language. My main reason for believing this is that some dialects spoken by member nations of the Huron alliance (i.e., the Southern Bear and the Cord) were closer to Petun (as evidenced in the language of the Wyandot) than they were to the dialects spoken by other members (notably the Rock nation).

2. Hereafter, references to *De Religione* include simply the page and line numbers.

3. The name Hechon is derived from the French *Jean*, with the *he* adding a masculine pronominal prefix to the word. Following Brébeuf, this name was passed on to Father Joseph-Marie Chaumonot, and after him to Father Daniel Richer. It is my honor to bear the name today.

4. One of these biases is that of patriarchy. This can be seen in the fact that of 301 Wendat names that appear in the Jesuit Relations, only 34 are female names.

5. The verb root for the paternal relationship is -*ndichia*- (FH1697:254), which is different from -*chiot*- 'to be a maternal grandparent' (*De Religione* 650:15) and *atre* 'to have a maternal grandchild' (*De Religione* 650:13, 15, 667:18, 668:2).

6. Michelson and Doxtator 2002:936 and *De Religione* 653:5, Oneida and Wendat, respectively.

7. Michelson and Doxtator 2002:1038 and *De Religione* 632:17.

8. Michelson and Doxtator 2002:1182 and *De Religione* 633:17.

9. Michelson and Doxtator 2002:1179 and *De Religione* 679:17.

10. This name is written *atinnia8enten* in *De Religione* 660:17.

11. The existence of the Ataronchronnon nation is debatable; only two references to it appear in the Jesuit Relations.

12. The Petun were so named because they supplied much of the *petun* ('tobacco') for the trade. It is often mistakenly assumed that they grew tobacco, but their territory was too far north for that. They obtained their tobacco in trade from members of the Neutral nation, which lived in southwestern Ontario, where tobacco was and still is grown.

13. In Dennis Meadows's terms, the Jansenists believed in "the impossibility of salvation for the majority of mankind. Further, whole categories of men and women were essentially corrupt. Marriage was little better than whoredom; buying and selling as a means of livelihood were sinful occupations; the sacraments were the reward of virtue, not an aide and a solace for sinners [as the Jesuits believed]. Above all, the frequent reception by ordinary, mediocre Christians was plain sacrilege" (Meadows 1958:25).

14. Jesuit practices in Asia can best be seen in the work of Matthew Ricci (1552–1610) in China and of Robert de Nobili (1577–1656) in India (see Hollis 1969:55–65).

15. Probably the main person on whose work Sagard drew was Father Joseph Le Caron, who had traveled with Samuel de Champlain in his trip to Huronia some years earlier.

16. Caution concerning the concept of the Eucharist would continue. The word the Jesuits used later was *8karistia* (Potier 1920:448), a Wendat noun based on the French *Eucharistie*. It was one of a very small number of words borrowed from French into Wendat.

17. *Sa . . . passion* refers to the killing of Jesus. Contrast the translation given here with the following more grammatical and more literal translation, which is given with *honaio* (lit. 'they killed him') (Potier 1920:489): "La passion de N[otre]. S[eigneur]. J[esus]. C[hrist]. ti honaeren d'ies8s honaio."

18. Brébeuf 1830:4

19. Brébeuf 1830:4

20. Brébeuf 1830:5

21. Brébeuf 1830:6. See the discussion of this verb later in this chapter, in the passage about *oki* spirits. If this verb had taken the instrumental root suffix here, then it would have had an *a* rather than an *i* between the *t* and the *k*.

22. Brébeuf 1830:7. This verb takes no root suffixes.

23. Of the fifteen noun stems formed from verb roots in *De Religione*, thirteen were created by means of the nominalizer, which the Jesuits represented as -*ch(r)*- (the -*r*- appears only in some Wendat dialects, such as Petun and Southern Bear). The remaining two noun stems were created

through the addition of the instrumental verb root suffix -*k8*-. In these two instances, however, a noun was created. One of the two involves the verb root -*ɩentio*- 'to be a maternal clan' (Potier 1920:391: "ɩentio . . . etre de band ou de parenté differente"), which produces a noun meaning 'band, group' (Potier 1920:455). The noun thus created was often used to make reference to clans, as can be seen in the following examples (FH1697:74): "famille . . . de quelle famille as tu? [family . . . of what family are you?]; ndia8eron esentio'k8ten [What is the nature of your group (maternal clan)?]; andia8ich [turtle] de la tortue [of the turtle], ɩannionɩen [it is a bear] l'ours [bear]." This noun has cognates in other Northern Iroquoian languages: Onondaga "-*ityohkw*- . . . crowd" (Woodbury, Henry, and Webster 1992: 342), Mohawk "-*tyohkw*- band, group" (Michelson 1973:64), Oneida "-*ityohkw*- . . . group, crowd" (Michelson and Doxtator 2002:439), and Tuscarora "-*i?nyuhkw*- 'company, army, troup, group' (Rudes 1987:190, no. 684). None of these cognates seems to refer to clans. Perhaps this is because none has maintained the verb root from which the noun is derived, possibly the effects of long-term contact.

The other of the two noun stems in *De Religione* created by the addition of the instrumental verb root suffix -*k8*- involves the verb root -*r*- 'sun to rise' (Potier 1920:324). The instrumental creates a noun stem meaning 'sunray, sun or moon' (Potier 1920:452). See *De Religione* 632:2, *orak8ennentaɩi* 'a sunray is attached', and 648:2, *eɩarakontie* 'sun will continue to rise, run its course'.

24. Although it is difficult to assign a precise date to the Great Law, most writers estimate its year of origin as either 1451 or 1536, both years in which there was an eclipse of the sun, as is mentioned in the story.

25. The name *Iroquois* came from Europeans. It is now generally thought to be derived from a Basque word meaning 'to kill' (Bakker 1990).

26. The Haudenosaunee became six nations early in the eighteenth century, when the linguistically and culturally related Tuscarora were driven off their land by white settlers in Virginia and North Carolina and were invited by the Oneida to share their land.

27. The two are usually said to have been living somewhere around the eastern end of Lake Ontario. It is also generally interpreted that they were Huron, who then lived in the area.

28. The word *Gandaouague* is written in Wendat, which can be discerned primarily through the presence of the *d* in the word.

29. A *jongleur* was a medieval magician or minstrel, one who entertained and sometimes tricked the audience.

30. In this prayer, Brébeuf referred to the Father of the Trinity as *d'[h]oistan* (lit. 'he who is father to him'), followed by *ichiatsi* (lit. 'you are called'), similarly calling the Son *Hoen ichiatsi* (lit. 'he has him as child, you are called').

31. FH1697:28, "Buffet ou l'on met les utensiles. Endicha." FH1697:13, "Andichon lieu élevé ou l'on met q[uelque]. c[hose] table, buffet. Endicha."

32. The stative aspect is a suffix that usually gives the connotation of being in a state of doing or being something. The Jesuits typically used it in their dictionary entries as if it were the base or root form. Likewise, the pronominal prefix given as the lead-in to the entry is the feminine-zoic, or she/it, form.

33. The optative prefix often takes the meaning 'should.'

34. Typically, when there is a mixed gender collectivity, the male plural form is used. For example, this was true of the names for the Cord and Bear nations.

35. See Sagard 1866:21, 25, 31, 46, 87, 126, 143.

36. That the phrase was written in the Northern Bear dialect can be seen in the absence of the *w* in the "our" pronoun, *-one-* (as opposed to *-onιℲe-*).

37. The original translation gives the word *limbs* where I have substituted *fingers,* which I think represents a more accurate translation of the Italian word *membri* in the original.

38. The word *endionrra* employs the noun root *-ndiιonr-,* which can be translated as 'mind, spirit of thoughts, or thoughts' (Potier 1920:449).

39. This verb was used by the Jesuits to express the concept of grace.

40. Although the pronominal form of the verb taken here appears to be the feminine plural, with the French capacity at this time to miss or fail to represent an initial *h* in Wendat words it is equally likely that the form is *hondaki* 'they (masculine) are spirits.'

41. In the same prayer he referred to *aki* spirits as killing by using poison.

42. Joseph Onasakenrat was a nineteenth-century Mohawk chief at Kanehsatake, or Oka.

De Religione

1. (629:4) Here, in the word *d'[h]oki,* and elsewhere throughout the Wendat text, when an *h* at the beginning of a word is preceded by the *d* of the definite article, the Jesuits delete the initial *h.*

2. (629:1) The expression "Great Voice in our lives" is translated in the ethnohistorical documents as "Master of Our Lives" (see the discussion of *-Ⅎend-* 'word, voice' and *-io-* 'to be great, large' in the introduction). This expression became a common feature in the translation of Native speeches in the seventeenth and eighteenth centuries. A classic example appeared in a speech by the Odawa leader Pontiac in 1763 (see Parkman 1894: 204–5).

3. (629:1) Whenever the word *God* is given in English, it is a translation of *diℲ* (i.e., the French *dieu*).

4. (629:5) See discussion of the concept of the life-provider in the introduction. The noun root -*ndiᴜonr*- (Potier 1920:449) is the third most frequent in *De Religione*, appearing with twenty-nine different verb roots, after -*at*- 'body' (Potier 1920:446) with eighty-six and -*rih8*- 'news, matter, affair, message' (Potier 1920:453) with sixty.

5. (629:6) The noun stem -*ondech(r)*-, derived from -*onde*- 'to have as one's country' (Potier 1920:408) meant 'country, earth.' It did not just refer to the physical entity 'country, earth' but also to Huron religious beliefs and practices, as was reported in the Jesuit Relations: "Moreover, the body of the Hurons being only an assemblage of various families [clans] and petty Nations, which are associated together for the purpose of maintaining themselves against their common enemies, each one has brought its special dances, customs and ceremonies, all emanating from the same source, which are communicated to the whole country, which are then observed according to the dream or ondinonc [*ondinnonk* 'wish'] of each one, when he is sick or by the order of the native Physician. . . . And such observances are called among them "Onderha" [*ondecha*], that is to say 'the ground' [*la terre* in the original French; JR10:196], as one might say the prop and maintenance of their whole State" (JR17:195–97).

Potier recorded that -*ondech*- was used with the verb root -*inde*- 'to drag, crawl' to mean something like 'since the beginning of time' when referring to the practice of carrying a corpse in a traditional burial ceremony: "Onᴜ8atondechinde onᴜ8ahoarinnenha8i [we drag, draw it from the country, we carry a corpse]; nous avons cette sorte de danse depuis le commencement, la naissance, l'origine de notre pais [we have had this kind of dance since the commencement, the birth, the origin of our country]" (Potier 1920:323). *Ondecha* also meant 'country' in the political sense. In the Jesuit Relation of 1636 we learn that "formerly only worthy men were Captains, and so they were called [*H*]*Ennondecha* [they country]. The same name by which they call the Country, Nation, district, as if a good Chief and the Country were one and the same thing" (JR10:231).

6. (630:3) Other than copper for jewelry, metal was not present in Huron culture prior to contact with Europeans. Therefore, a word for metal had to be developed. The noun root -*8hist*-, used to refer to metal and glass in *De Religione*, traditionally referred to hard objects that were not rock. These included fish scales, as was indicated in virtually every Wendat dictionary from Sagard to Potier (Sagard 1866:116; FH1697:59; HF59:128; HF62; HF65:140; FH67; Potier 1920:452), and the hard skin covering the kernels of flint corn, which was less often referred to in the dictionaries (FH1697:23; Potier 1920:452). After contact, -*8hist*- was used to refer to "toute sorte de metaux [all kinds of metals]" (FH1697:15, cf. FHO; HF59; HF65; FH1697; Potier 1920:452), particularly iron, the main metal that the

French traded in and used (FH1697:75; FHO; FH62; FH67:97). The verb root -ɩenrat- 'to be white' was added for 'silver' (FH1697:123), and -ndoron- 'to be valuable' for 'gold' (FH1697:123; see *De Religione* 638:14; see also Michelson and Doxtator 2002:636 for the same combination meaning 'gold or silver').

Although the Hurons referred to a number of metal objects as -ȣhist- (see Potier 1920:187 and FH1697:117 for 'medal'), the object most often found in the Wendat dictionaries is "bell" (Potier 1920:307, 423, 432; FH1697:37). It was said to have voice, as can be seen in the following: "a te ȣaɩek asken skȣaȣeti atsatrendaendeska d'oȣhistatoɩetoɩeti eȣatatiahaj [I wish that all of you will pray every time the true -ȣhist- talks]; je vous prie tous prier toutes les fois que la cloche sonnera [Come, I ask of you, all pray every time the bell will ring]" (Potier 1920:242).

7. (630:4) The noun root -hȣatsir-, which I have translated as 'lineage', was the term the Jesuits most often translated as 'famille' (JR21:255, 257; FHO; HF59:78; HF62:40; HF65:93; FH1693:141; FH1697:74; FH67:95; Potier 1920:447). It referred to the matrilineally determined lineage, as opposed to the clan, which was represented by the verb root -ɩentio- (Potier 1920: 391). For cognates, see Michelson and Doxtator 2002:413–14 (Oneida) and Michelson 1973:58 (Mohawk).

8. (630:14) The word for 'ax', -ach- (Potier 1920:445), was a prolific source of imagery in the Wendat language. In *De Religione* it was used with eleven different verbs (630:14, 643:4–5, 663:2, 11, 664:2). Potier recorded the following war expressions using the noun *ax*, as translated into French: "La hache . . . est Le simbole de La guerre [the ax is the symbol of war]. Lier La hache de guerre . . . ces faire suspension d'armes [to tie up the ax of war means to suspend arms]; affiler La hache . . . c'est vouloir commencer la guerre [to sharpen the ax . . . it is to wish to commence war]; jetter la hache dans le plus profond de la terre . . . ce ne plus entendre parler de guerre [to throw the ax into the deepest depths of the earth . . . is to no longer listen to talk of war]. Repecher la hache d'un riviere . . . c'est recommencer la guerre [to fish the ax out of the river . . . it is to recommence war]; oter la hache . . . c'est faire cesser les attaques e les hostilités de guerre [to take away the ax . . . it is to cause a cessation in the attacks and hostilities of war]; jetter la hache au ciel . . . c'est faire une guerre ouverte [to throw the ax to the sky . . . it is to cause an open war]. Baisser la haeche . . . faire cessation d'armes [to drop the ax . . . to cause a cessation of arms]. Reprendre la hache . . . recommencer la guerre [to regain, retake the ax . . . to recommence war]; attacher la hache a la porte . . . faire un defi [to attach the ax to the door . . . to issue a challenge]" (Toupin 1996:284).

9. (634:8) The Huron did not call the Jesuits "Blackrobes" but referred to them as *hatitsihenstatsi* 'they are called charcoal', from the Wendat term for the color black.

10. (639:3) The term for 'greeting with respect' combines the noun root -*nnonr*- 'scalp' (Potier 1920:451) with a verb root, -*onk8*-, that means 'to oil, anoint' (Potier 1920:311), with a meaning of 'oiling the scalp many times' (see 639:3, 5, 640:7, 653:6, 668:3, 669:22, 677:13–14, 681:10–11, 682:2).

11. (644:25) The verb root -*nnionıen*- means 'to be French' (Potier 1920:451). To the best of my knowledge, there is no reliable etymology of this verb root.

12. (653:7) This passage is one of the few in *De Religione* in which the name *Jesus* is invoked. Generally in Wendat Christian prayers, God (*di8*) is referred to much more frequently than Jesus.

13. (657:3) The line here represents a name to be filled in.

14. (661:1) *Ataratiri* means 'it is supported on clay, swamp' (see Potier 1920:191, 453, for the noun root -*tar*- and the verb root -*atiri*-). For a discussion of the name Hechon, see the introduction. *Hatironta* means 'He draws, attracts' (Potier 1920:192).

15. (661:2) I have yet to translate the name Te assaosteiaj, although with the dualic prefix *te*- and what I suspect is the verb root -*iaı*- 'to cut' (Potier 1920:263), I think the meaning 'cut in two' is part of the name. *Arontoıennen* means 'under a tree' (with the noun root -*ront*- 'tree, log' [Potier 1920: 453] and the verb root -*oıennen*- 'to be under' [Potier 1920:405]). I suspect this name originated in Father Daniel's first name, Antoine.

16. (661:3) I have yet to translate the name of the Petun community Etharita. It begins with the cislocative prefix -*et*- 'where'. The noun root for the name 8racha means 'cloud' (Potier 1920:445). The name Ok8entondıte means 'at the place of the (little) fish' (with -*h8ent*- 'fish' [Potier 1920:448] and -*ondi*- 'to make' [Potier 1920:405]). The name Te otiaıı (an *h* that does not belong in this word is added in *De Religione*), for Montreal, means 'it is split in two' (Potier 1920:263), referring to the way the St. Lawrence River splits in the Montreal area. The name Chihoatenhwa is constructed from the noun root -*at*- 'body' (Potier 1920:446) and the verb root -*enh(8/o)*- 'to bring, take' (Potier 1920:35). The name Ondechrase is constructed from the noun stem -*ondech(r)*- 'country' (Potier 1920:455) and the verb root -*ase*- 'to be new' (Potier 1920:174).

17. (661:4) The noun root for Onnontsira is -*tsinnonr*- 'head' (Potier 1920:451). The word θentenha8iθa is constructed with the noun root -*ent*- 'field' (Potier 1920:454) and the verb root -*enh(8/o)*- 'to take, bring' (Potier 1920:35).

18. (662:16) The Wendat names for these groups in the corresponding line of *De Religione* have the following derivations. The word 8endake, for the Huron, means 'at the Wendat'; *etionnontate*, for the Petun, means 'where there is a hill' (i.e., Blue Mountain); *ıeraıenrek*, for the Neutral, means 'they roll over'; *Trak8ae*, or Trakwae, means 'at the sunrise'; *Rie*, for Erie, is short for an Iroquoian term meaning 'long tail', referring to the cougar; *askik8annhe*

is the as-yet-untranslated Iroquoian term for *Nipissing;* and *ehonke* is the as-yet-untranslated Iroquoian term for a group of the Algonquin. The first five terms refer to nations that spoke Iroquoian languages, and the last two, to nations that spoke Algonquian languages.

19. (666:1) It is unclear what the letters are in the original Wendat.

20. (667:6) I have as yet been unable to translate the word *sendatenst.*

21. (669:10) From this point forward, I shift from the literal 'struck with water' to 'baptize' and 'baptism'.

References

Unpublished Sources

Barbeau, Marius
n.d.   "Huron-Wyandot Dictionary." Manuscript.

FHO
ca. 1656   "Dictionnaire Huron et hiroquois onontaheronon." Manuscript,
            Archive Seminaire de Quebec.

FH62
ca. 1656   French-Wendat section of manuscript 62 (as cited in Victor Hanzeli,
            Missionary Linguistics in New France, 1969, The Hague, Mouton),
            Archive Seminaire de Quebec.

FH67
n.d.   French-Wendat dictionary, manuscript 67 (as cited in Hanzeli
            1969), Archive Seminaire de Quebec.

FH1693
ca. 1693   French-Wendat dictionary. Manuscript, Archive Seminaire de
            Quebec.

FH1697
ca. 1697   French-Wendat dictionary. Manuscript, John Carter Brown
            Library, Brown University, Providence, Rhode Island.

HF59
n.d.   Wendat-French dictionary, manuscript 59 (as cited in Hanzeli
            1969), Archive Seminaire de Quebec.

HF62
n.d.   Wendat-French section of manuscript 62 (as cited in Hanzeli
            1969), Archive Seminaire de Quebec.

HF65
n.d.   Wendat-French dictionary, manuscript 65 (as cited in Hanzeli
            1969), Archive Seminaire de Quebec.

Published Works

Bakker, Peter
1990   "A Basque Etymology for the Word *Iroquois.*" *Man in the Northeast* 40:89–93.

Barbeau, Marius
1915   *Huron and Wyandot Mythology.* Memoir 80, no. 11. Geological Survey, Canadian Department of Mines, Ottawa.

Brébeuf, Jean de
1830   "Doctrine Chrestienne, dv R.P. Ledesme de la Compagne de Iesvs." In *Voyages: Ou journal des descouvertes de la Nouvelle France,* vol. 3, by Samuel de Champlain. Paris.

Bruyas, Jacques
1970   *Radices Verborum Iroquaeorum.* (Written in the seventeenth century; first published in 1860.) Edited by J. G. Shea. AMS Press, New York.

Chafe, Wallace
1961   *Seneca Thanksgiving Rituals.* Bulletin of the Bureau of American Ethnology, no. 83. Smithsonian Institution, Washington, D.C.
1963   *Handbook of the Seneca Language.* State University of New York, Albany.
1967   *Seneca Morphology and Dictionary.* Smithsonian Contributions to Anthropology 4. Washington, D.C.
1970   *A Semantically Based Sketch of Onondaga.* International Journal of American Linguistics, Memoir 25.

Champlain, Samuel de
1929   *The Works of Samuel de Champlain,* vol. 3, Edited by H. P. Biggar. Champlain Society, Toronto.

Fenton, William, ed.
1968   *The Code of Handsome Lake, the Seneca Prophet,* by Arthur C. Parker. In *Parker on the Iroquois,* Book 2. Syracuse University Press, Syracuse, New York.

Foster, Michael
1974   *From the Earth to beyond the Sky: An Ethnographic Approach to Four Longhouse Iroquois Speech Events.* Paper no. 20, Canadian Ethnology Service, National Museum of Canada. Ottawa.

Hewitt, J. N. B.
1895   "The Iroquoian Concept of the Soul." *Journal of American Folklore* 8:107–16.

1928   *Iroquoian Cosmology*, part 2. Forty-third Annual Report of the Bureau of American Ethnology. Smithsonian Institution, Washington, D.C. Reprint, 1974, AMS Press, New York.

Hollis, Christopher
1969   *The History of the Jesuits*. Weidenfeld and Nicholson, London.

Jesuit Relations (JR)
1959   *The Jesuit Relations and Allied Documents*. 73 vols. Edited by Reuben Gold Thwaites. Pageant Book Company, New York.

Kick, Shirley, Marge Henry, Evelyn Jacobs, and Geraldine Sandy
1988   *Cayuga Thematic Dictionary*. Woodland Publishing, Brantford, Ontario.

Lounsbury, Floyd
1953   *Oneida Verb Morphology*. Yale University Publications in Anthropology no. 48. New Haven, Connecticut.

Meadows, Denis
1958   *A Popular History of the Jesuits*. Macmillan, New York.

Michelson, Gunther
1973   *A Thousand Words of Mohawk*. Mercury Series no. 5. Ethnology Division, National Museum of Man, Ottawa.

Michelson, Karin, and Mercy Doxtator
2002   *Oneida-English/English Oneida Dictionary*. University of Toronto Press, Toronto.

Monture-Angus, Patricia
1995   *Thunder in My Soul: A Mohawk Woman Speaks*. Fernwood Publishing, Halifax.

Parkman, Francis,
1894   *The Conspiracy of Pontiac and the Indian War after the Conquest of Canada*, vol. 1. Little, Brown, Boston.

Potier, Pierre
1920   *Fifteenth Report of the Bureau of Archives for the Province of Ontario*. C. W. James, Toronto.

Richter, Daniel K.
1992   *The Ordeal of the Longhouse: The Peoples of the Iroquois League in the Era of European Colonization*. University of North Carolina Press, Chapel Hill.

Rudes, Blair
1987   *Tuscarora Roots, Stems, and Particles: Towards a Dictionary of Tuscarora*. Algonquian and Iroquoian Linguistics, Memoir no. 3. Winnipeg.

Sagard, Gabriel
1866   *Histoire du Canada . . . avec un dictionnaire de la language huronne.*
         Edwin Tross, Paris.
1939   *The Long Journey to the Country of the Hurons.* Edited by G. M
         Wrong. Champlain Society, Toronto.

Steckley, John L.
1978   "Brébeuf's Presentation of Catholicism in the Huron Language:
         A Descriptive Overview." *University of Ottawa Quarterly*
         48:93–115.
1982   "The Cord Tribe of the Huron." *Arch Notes* (Ontario Archaeolog-
         ical Society) 3:15.
1985   "A Tale of Two Peoples." *Arch Notes* 4:9–15.
1987   "An Ethnolinguistic Look at the Huron Longhouse." *Ontario
         Archaeology* (Ontario Archaeological Society) 47:19–32.
1991   "The First Huron-French Dictionary?" *Arch Notes* 3:17–23.
1992a   "The Warrior and the Lineage: Jesuit Use of Iroquoian Images to
         Communicate Christianity." *Ethnohistory* 39(4):478–509.
1992b   "The Wendat: Were They Islanders?" *Arch Notes* 5:23–26.
1993   "Huron Kinship Terminology." *Ontario Archaeology* 55:35–59.
1997   "Wendat Dialects and the Development of the Huron Alliance."
         Northeast Anthropology 54:23–36.

Toupin, Robert, S.J.
1996   *Les Ecrits de Pierre Potier.* Collection Amérique Française no. 3.
         University of Ottawa Press, Ottawa.

Woodbury, Hanni, Reg Henry, and Harry Webster
1992   *Concerning the League: The Iroquois League Tradition as Dictated in
         Onondaga by John Arthur Gibson.* Algonquian and Iroquoian Lin-
         guistics, Memoir no. 9. Winnipeg.

Index of Remaining Roots in De Religione
(in Conjugations and with Primary Source)

A- CONJUGATION

-a- vr 'to be such a number, magnitude' (Potier 1920:161)

-acha- vr 'to double, be double' (Potier 1920:162)

-achahaton- vr 'to move' (Potier 1920:162)

-ache- vr 'to be water' (Potier 1920:162)

-achie- vr 'to be an ash tree' (Potier 1920:445)

-achit- nr 'foot' (Potier 1920:445)

-ae- vr 'to hit, strike, run into' (Potier 1920:163)

-ahah- nr 'path' (Potier 1920:445)

-ahente- vr 'to be evident, visible' (Potier 1920:163)

-ahi- nr 'fruit' (Potier 1920:445)

-ahia8ir- nr 'toe' (Potier 1920:445)

-ahont- nr 'ear' (Potier 1920:445)

-a ˌon- vr 'to be pure, empty' (Potier 1920:163)

-a ˌon- vr 'to be inside' (Potier 1920:

-a'ka- vr 'to quit, abandon' (Potier 1920:164)

-akaen- vr 'to be slow' (Potier 1920:164)

-akak8- vr 'to look at' (Potier 1920:164)

-akaot- vr 'to be bad' (Potier 1920:164)

-akaratat- vr 'to take care of' (Potier 1920:165)

-akarot- vr 'to be obscured' (Potier 1920:165)

-akense- vr 'to consider' (Potier 1920:166)

-akeron- vr 'to be afraid' (Potier 1920:166)

-aki'8a- vr 'to go to war' (Potier 1920:167)

-ak8aeron- vr 'to kill' (Potier 1920:168)

-a'k8as- vr 'to cover, be covered' (Potier 1920:169)

-ak8at- vr 'to be windy' (Potier 1920:169)

-ak8endiha- vr 'to reproach, blame' (Potier 1920:173)

-ak8enra- vr 'to steal' (Potier 1920:168)

-ak8eton- vr 'to give birth' (Potier 1920:170)

-a8- vr 'to give' (Potier 1920:170)

-a8a- vr 'to be short' (Potier 1920:162)

-arase- vr 'to be cousins' (Potier 1920:171)

-arask8a- vr 'to leave, depart' (Potier 1920:171)

-arat- vr 'to count' (Potier 1920:172)

-aratat- vr 'to run' (Potier 1920:171)

-a'rent- vr 'to cry' (Potier 1920:173)

-arhon- vr 'to rest, be at rest' (Potier 1920:173)

-ariskon- vr 'to go, venture together' (Potier 1920:173)

-arist- vr 'to retain, detain' (Potier 1920:173)

-aron ˌ- vr 'to listen' (Potier 1920:173)

-aronton- vr 'to inquire, ask' (Potier 1920:174)

-asa ˌann- vr 'to talk strangely' (Potier 1920:174)

-asaonk8- nr 'medicine' (Potier 1920:445)

-ase- vr 'to be new' (Potier 1920:174)

-asen- vr 'to be ten' (Potier 1920:175)

-asenχ8- vr 'to cry out' (Potier 1920:176)

-ase't- vr 'to hide, be hidden' (Potier 1920:176)

-askand- vr 'to desire' (Potier 1920: 177)

-ask8- nr 'scaffold' (Potier 1920:445)

-asχ8- vr 'to extinguish' (Potier 1920: 177)

E- CONJUGATION

-ent- nr 'field' (Potier 1920:454)
-enta- vr 'to conclude' (Potier 1920:381)
-ento- vr 'to grow' (Potier 1920:382)
-enton- vr 'to hang, be suspended' (Potier 1920:381)
-er- vr 'to wish, think, hope' (Potier 1920:382)
-erochi- nr 'hair' (Potier 1920:454)
-es- vr 'to be long' (Potier 1920:385)
-et- nr 'field' (Potier 1920:454)

EN-/-I- CONJUGATION

- ˌen- vr 'to be' (Potier 1920:54)
- ˌend- nr 'robe' (Potier 1920:455)
- ˌende- vr 'to trick' (Potier 1920:386)
- ˌenhaon- vr 'to say' (Potier 1920:38)
- ˌenonhar- nr 'fabric' (Potier 1920:455)
- ˌenhe- vr 'to die' (Potier 1920:387)
- ˌenh8aten- vr 'to have as sister's child (man speaking)' (Potier 1920:108)
- ˌenk8ar- nr 'cloth' (Potier 1920:455)
- ˌennon- vr 'to call for' (Potier 1920:388)
- ˌennon ˌ- vr 'to make peace' (Potier 1920:388)
- ˌenron- vr 'to be opposite sex siblings' (Potier 1920:388)
- ˌent- vr 'to talk about' (Potier 1920:388)
- ˌent- nr 'excrement' (Potier 1920:455)
- ˌenta- vr 'to sleep' (Potier 1920:389)
- ˌentaheken- vr 'to treat appropriately' (Potier 1920:388)
- ˌentak8- vr 'to do deliberately' (Potier 1920:388)
- ˌentonr- nr 'stomach' (Potier 1920:455)
- ˌentsonr- nr 'bowels' (Potier 1920:455)
- ˌeroh8- vr 'to be an oak' (FH1697:233)
- ˌi- nr 'canoe' (Potier 1920:455)
-i- vr 'to be full' (Potier 1920:393); 'to be unique'; 'to be two'
-ia8ist- vr 'to extend, stretch' (Potier 1920:394)
-ichia ˌ- vr 'to search for' (Potier 1920:386)
-inde- vr 'to drag, crawl' (Potier 1920:323)
-innion- vr 'to arrive, penetrate' (Potier 1920:396)
-io- vr 'to be great, large' (Potier 1920:396)
-isk8- vr 'to contest' (?) (Potier 1920:649)
-i'ti- vr 'to be like' (Potier 1920:400)

O- CONJUGATION

-o- vr 'to be in water' (Potier 1920:401)
-och- nr 'winter' (Potier 1920:455)
-ochon- vr 'to put over, cover' (Potier 1920:404)
-o ˌannen- vr 'to make flow, render into liquid' (Potier 1920:404)
-o ˌat- vr 'to molest' (Potier 1920:404)
-o ˌennen- vr 'to be under' (Potier 1920:405)
-ohie- vr 'to mix' (Potier 1920:406)
-o ˌon ˌe- vr 'to be visible, public' (Potier 1920:405)
-oka- vr 'to spread, communicate' (Potier 1920:406)
-ok8- vr 'to divide, separate' (Potier 1920:407)
-on- vr 'to be together' (Potier 1920:408)
-ond- nr 'space' (Potier 1920:455)
-ondaon- vr 'to have as one's place' (Potier 1920:408)
-onde- vr 'to have as one's country' (Potier 1920:408)
-onde- vr 'to achieve' (Potier 1920:411)
-onni- vr 'to make' (Potier 1920:408)
-ondiast- vr 'to torment' (Potier 1920:411)
-onesk8- vr 'to please' (Potier 1920:412)
-onh8- nr 'self, alone' (Potier 1920:455)
-onh8ents- nr 'earth, world' (Potier 1920:455)
-on ˌo- vr 'to penetrate' (Potier 1920:413)
-on ˌ8e- vr 'to be a human being' (Potier 1920:417)
-onk8- vr 'to be water' (Potier 1920:647)
-onk8a- vr 'to oil, grease' (Potier 1920:311)
-onnent- vr 'to descend, fall' (Potier 1920:414)
-onnh- nr 'life' (Potier 1920:455)
-onnhe- vr 'to live' (Potier 1920:415)
-onnhi- vr 'to ignore, be unaware, ignorant of' (Potier 1920:415)
-onnhon ˌannonni- vr 'to make a decision' (Potier 1920:416)
-onnhonsk8aen- vr 'to be a toad' (FH1697:231)
-on8esen- vr 'to be generous' (Potier 1920:417)
-on8e't- vr 'to be discouraged' (Potier 1920:418)

General Index

CPSIA information can be obtained
at www.ICGtesting.com
Printed in the USA
LVHW032134170221
679356LV00003B/537

9 780806 168814